Advance Praise for *Progressive & Religious*

"Robert P. Jones understands that progressive faith is not simply a 'left' alternative to the religious right, but a bringing together of religious belief and practice with progressive politics. The common ground of social justice, peacemaking, protecting the environment, and promoting the common good is forging new paths to the future. *Progressive & Religious* convincingly shows how people of many different faiths are creating an authentic social vision for a pluralistic America. I commend this book to all who are seeking to join their faith and politics in working for a better world." —**Rev. Jim Wallis**, Sojourners, author of *The Great Awakening*

"This important book is a compelling rebuttal to the widespread bias in our society that the more fundamentalist religious people are, the more authentic they are. *Progressive & Religious* powerfully reminds us that working as God's partners to heal the world is a profoundly religious task that stands in the mainstream of our religious ethical traditions." —**Rabbi David Saperstein**, Religious Action Center for Reform Judaism

"This is an exceptional book. It is both a window into a post-religious right America and an invitation to people from all faith backgrounds and none at all to build what Robert P. Jones calls 'a land of new possibilities.'" —**Eboo Patel**, Interfaith Youth Core, author of *Acts of Faith*

"In a world plagued by religiously motivated violence, anyone who wishes to become part of the solution and not part of the problem must read Robert P. Jones's book. Wonderfully written and an enjoyable read, this is a timely, insightful, and critically important book. It should be read and carefully pondered, not only by every Jew, Christian, and Muslim, but by every person who cares about the fate of humanity." —**Khaled Abou el Fadl**, UCLA School of Law, author of *The Great Theft*

"Through his work with Third Way, Robert P. Jones has been working hard to heal religious fractures, bringing together political progressives and conservative Christians so they stop culture warfare and start behaving more Christianly toward one another, collaborating for the common good. In *Progressive & Religious*, he engenders hope for a new day by identifying the growing chorus of voices seeking—in the words of the Hebrew prophets—to beat swords into plowshares and spears into pruning hooks." —**Rev. Brian McLaren**, author of *Everything Must Change*

"*Progressive & Religious* tells the story of a shared journey toward social holiness. These progressive faith leaders demonstrate a kind of militant tolerance and a passion for healing the world. We religious progressives are finding our voices and testifying to this truth: God loves this world and all that is within it. And we are asking you to do the same." —**Rev. Dr. Susan Brooks Thistlethwaite**, Chicago Theological Seminary

"No one who reads this book will end up doubting the breadth and depth of commitment to progressive visions that are deeply rooted in the wisdoms of the whole spectrum of American religious life, and everyone who reads it will end up knowing a great deal more about both progressive thought and religious life. Hallelujah!" —**Rabbi Arthur Waskow**, Shalom Center, author of *Down-to-Earth Judaism*

"By seeking out and presenting American opinion leaders who are committed to human rights and social justice from their respective religious perspectives, *Progressive & Religious* is particularly timely in these perilous times of polarization and social regression among religious communities. A pioneering initiative for social change." —**Ahmed Abdullahi An-Na'im**, Emory University School of Law, author of *Islam and the Secular State*

"Let's face it: Jesus was a rabble-rouser. The Hebrew prophets castigated the rich. Muhammad challenged Arabian elites. The Buddha opposed the status quo. By insisting that social injustices and not just personal moral infractions are matters of concern for any religiously grounded ethics, the people and organizations profiled in Robert P. Jones's *Progressive & Religious* are challenging dominant visions of religious activism as inherently conservative. It's about time." —**Kecia Ali**, Boston University

"Robert P. Jones has made a significant contribution to the fields of contemporary religious and political studies. In sharing the stories of progressive faith leaders from several different traditions he has helped all of us better understand our commonalities and differences and the possibility of working together for the common good."—**Rabbi Or N. Rose**, Rabbinical School of Hebrew College, author of *Righteous Indignation*

"*Progressive & Religious* finally puts to rest the myth that one cannot be both religious and politically progressive. This book makes a major contribution to our understanding of religion in public life by highlighting the deep, authentic connections that exist between progressive religious belief and practice on the one hand and a commitment to a politics of the common good on the other." —**Rev. Jennifer Butler**, Faith and Public Life, author of *Born Again*

"This book is long overdue. *Progressive & Religious* tells the inspiring story of leaders who are declaring that religion is not simply about personal holiness, but also about public holiness. My hope is that the many religious Americans who recognize their own religious convictions in these pages become part of this new face of public religion that brings people together and calls for justice for all." —**Rev. Leah Daughtry**, Democratic National Committee

Progressive & Religious

How Christian, Jewish, Muslim, and Buddhist Leaders Are Moving beyond the Culture Wars and Transforming American Life

Robert P. Jones

ROWMAN & LITTLEFIELD PUBLISHERS, INC.
Lanham • Boulder • New York • Toronto • Plymouth, UK

ROWMAN & LITTLEFIELD PUBLISHERS, INC.

Published in the United States of America
by Rowman & Littlefield Publishers, Inc.
A wholly owned subsidary of The Rowman & Littlefield Publishing Group, Inc.
4501 Forbes Boulevard, Suite 200, Lanham, Maryland 20706
www.rowmanlittlefield.com

Estover Road
Plymouth PL6 7PY
United Kingdom

Distributed by National Book Network

British Library Cataloguing in Publication Information Available

Library of Congress Cataloging-in-Publication Data

Jones, Robert P. (Robert Patrick)
    Progressive & religious : how Christian, Jewish, Muslim, and Buddhist
leaders are moving beyond the culture wars and transforming American life /
Robert P. Jones.
        p. cm.
    Includes bibliographical references and index.
    ISBN-13: 978-0-7425-6230-1 (cloth : alk. paper)
    ISBN-10: 0-7425-6230-1 (cloth : alk. paper)
    eISBN-13: 978-0-7425-6550-0
    eISBN-10: 0-7425-6550-5
    1. United States—Religion. 2. Religion and culture—United States. I. Title.
II. Title: Progressive and religious.
    BL2525.J66 2008
    201'.70973—dc22   2008015952

Printed in the United States of America

⊚™ The paper used in this publication meets the minimum requirements of
American National Standard for Information Sciences—Permanence of Paper
for Printed Library Materials, ANSI/NISO Z39.48-1992.

To my teachers:
Jeff B. Pool, who opened the door,
and
Jon P. Gunnemann, who helped me walk through it

Contents

Acknowledgments

This book is in many ways a record of a personal and professional journey to find "the other religious America."

I owe the first words of thanks to my wife, Jodi Kanter, and my daughter, Riley, who provided encouragement and patience throughout the process of completing this book. I especially want to say thank you to Jodi for graciously agreeing to marry both me and the book. Along the way, she was the first and last reader of every chapter. Her considerable gifts for writing and clarity have made the book much more readable and lively. And her deep concerns about the impact of loss on individuals and communities illustrated the beautiful concept of *tikkun olam*, the task of healing the world, long before I heard it explained by a rabbi. My seven-year-old daughter, Riley, has been learning to read as I've been writing and has increasingly been my teacher not only in yoga but also in learning to see the world with fresh eyes. The inspiring people I have encountered over the last three years have buoyed my hope that the world she is growing into will be a world where religion works for justice, equality, and inclusion for all, and unites rather than divides.

I've had an institutionally nomadic existence over the last three years, and I have been fortunate that each of the institutions of which I've been a part have supported this work directly or indirectly. Missouri State University provided me with my first full-time faculty position out of graduate school and a summer faculty research grant to begin the journey. My colleagues in the Religious Studies Department at Missouri State University, especially John Schmalzbauer, Martha Finch, and Steve Berkwitz, helped me think through my earliest lists of potential interviewees.

I owe a large debt to Eli Segal—longtime friend of my in-laws, Arnie and Carol Kanter—entrepreneur, former assistant to President Clinton, and founding director of the Corporation for National and Community Service and its flagship Americorps program. Based only on a few phone conversations with me (and decades of friendship with the Kanters, who stuck their necks out vouching for their not-yet son-in-law), Eli generously helped set up many introductions that eventually led to contacts for the book and my work in Washington. I will always regret that I had only one memorable dinner with which to thank him before his untimely death. I like to think that this book would seem to him a good outcome of his investment.

In 2005, I accepted a position as the founding director and senior fellow at the Center for American Values in Public Life at People for the American Way Foundation (PFAWF) in Washington, D.C., which supported my pursuit of this project alongside those duties. PFAWF also provided a generous one-year grant after I left that position, which supported the bulk of the interviews in 2007. Peter Montgomery and Rev. Steve Baines were indispensable conversation partners, advisors, and allies during that period of the research.

Beginning in 2007, I began working as an independent consultant in progressive circles in Washington, D.C., a position that allowed me to be the beneficiary of considerable insights and advice from a number of quarters. Rev. Jennifer Butler and Rev. Ron Stief of Faith in Public Life granted both insights and interviews, and Katie Barge generously helped open doors to key leaders and to many new colleagues. I also want to thank Melody Barnes for the opportunity to serve as an affiliated scholar at the Center for American Progress in 2007 and Sally Steenland and John Halpin for early advice and encouragement about the project.

As I completed the book, I began work as a visiting fellow in religion at Third Way, a progressive organization that has understood the benefits of bringing religious voices, even unlikely ones, to the table for a true two-way conversation. Matt Bennett, Jim Kessler, and Jon Cowan were some of the first people I talked with during my initial research trip to Washington, D.C., in 2005, and I count myself lucky to have been able to work with the forward-thinking Third Way team ever since in various capacities. I want to thank especially Rachel Laser, director of the Culture Program, who has modeled how original thinking, coalition building, and faith in what's possible even amidst real differences can really change the landscape.

Most directly, I am grateful to the nearly one hundred progressive religious leaders from all over America who talked with me in their synagogues, churches, mosques, meditation halls, and homes. Without them and the amazing work they are doing across the country, there would be neither subject nor book. Several additional people provided particular guidance in vetting my interview list and providing introductions. For this critical task, I would like to thank Rabbi David Saperstein, Rabbi Jennie Rosenn, Rabbi Doug Heifetz, Alexia Kelley, Vince Miller, Kevin Jacques, Abdullahi An-Na'im, Eboo Patel, and Alan Senauke. Rabbi Or Rose and Omid Safi gave critical feedback to the final drafts of the chapters on Judaism and Islam respectively.

Various others have contributed significantly to the project as well. I want to thank John Loudon, Sarah Stanton, and Chris Anzalone from Rowman & Littlefield, and Alan Wolfe, the series editor, for seeing the value of the project and helping me polish it to be the best it could be. Dan Cox and Bob Francis were both superb research associates, synthesizing information, analyzing interviews, and helping the writing communicate clearly. Karen Myers professionally transcribed over one hundred hours of audio into fifteen hundred pages of transcripts. Several generous friends lent me a bed or a couch during my considerable travel: Ted Freeman, Rebecca Taichman, Caitlin Dixon, Jim and Dorothy Hunt, Phyllis Segal, and Selma Freed. Sean Thibault provided cutting-edge web development for the website companion to the book, and Emily Hanford brought her considerable public radio expertise to professionally producing the compelling podcasts of the interviews. Many leaders in the book also talked about the importance of fellow travelers, and I have been blessed with many both old and new: my parents, Pat and Cherry Jones; Ted Smith; Chris Scharen; Brad Hadaway; Missi Stewart; Alan Wright; Ken Hester; and our spiritual community at the Interfaith Families Project (IFFP) of Washington, D.C.

Finally, I dedicate this book to two of my teachers. Interestingly, my own experience with the dark side of religion and power occurred during my days at seminary. Each of these mentors and friends helped me deal with the troubling aftermath of the ruthless fundamentalist takeover of Southwestern Baptist Theological Seminary during the last semester of my MDiv program. Jeff Pool, my systematic theology professor and an ordained Baptist minister, provided a window into a wider world of feminist and liberation theology; he also modeled enough integrity during this dark time to lose his job and gain the lifelong admiration of a group of otherwise disillusioned students. Jon Gunnemann, an ordained United Church of Christ (UCC) minister, taught the first graduate seminar I attended at Emory University and was my dissertation advisor. Over many years, he helped me see that the demands of justice and the demands of faith were not in fact in conflict.

Moving beyond the Culture Wars
Finding Progressive Religion in America

God Is Not a Republican:
The 2004 Elections in Missouri

Gwen was one of my brightest students. She was the rare student who often came to my office in the Religious Studies Department at Missouri State University to follow up on topics we had discussed in class, and in challenging herself, she often challenged me. Our conversations were typically lively, wide-ranging, and fun. But this day, in the fall of 2004, Gwen was obviously not enjoying the conversation. As she sat across my desk, the look on her face was part bewilderment and part dismay. "I don't understand," she told me. "How can you possibly have agreed to be the faculty advisor for the Students for John Kerry group?"

As we talked, it quickly became clear that Gwen was disturbed because she believed there was an inherent contradiction between her understanding of me as a religious person and my role organizing on behalf of a Democrat. In Gwen's mind that day, the connections were clear and straightforward:

1

Truly religious people care about life, and only Republicans are "pro-life." What made this encounter even more unusual was that this student who could not connect the dots between my respect for religion and my support of a Catholic Democratic candidate was also "Sister Gwen," a novice in the last stages of becoming a Catholic nun.

I was not alone in this experience. Brett, a colleague of mine who taught communications at a nearby Southern Baptist university, lamented regularly that fall that his students had difficulty understanding how Christians could support anything other than the current Republican version of political conservatism. He also found to his dismay that few of his fellow faculty were willing to push students to question these deeply ingrained assumptions. He finally felt so consistently embattled in the fall of 2004 that he emblazoned a Sojourners "GOD IS NOT A REPUBLICAN—or a Democrat" bumper sticker on his car and arrived early for classes in order to park it prominently in the faculty lot.

As I knocked on doors in Springfield, Missouri, as a precinct organizer for the Kerry campaign, I found myself repeating variations of these encounters with my neighbors. These reactions were striking to me, but they weren't shocking; this problematic assumption that being religious necessarily meant being politically conservative was paradigmatic of my own cultural upbringing as a Baptist in the South. But what had become more palpable and more troubling was that for so many in 2004, the public relevance of their faith had been narrowed not just to conservative ideology but to a single political party and to a few litmus-test issues such as abortion and same-sex marriage.

These accounts of my experience during the 2004 presidential election capture a localized snapshot of a remarkable national moment, where a single political party exclusively, and for a time fairly successfully, claimed the mantle of faith. This overreaching by the Christian right in the 2004 elections, along with fears about religiously motivated terrorism in the wake of September 11, 2001, also birthed a new backlash by angry atheists. In many ways, these two extreme groups are mirror images of one another: a self-righteous religious right who are certain they have God on their side and an angry anti-religious left who are certain that religion itself is one of the greatest threats to society. The prominence of these two groups also left the great majority of Americans—two-thirds of whom say religion is very important to them[1]—somewhat bewildered.

Like many of my friends, I did some real soul-searching in the aftermath of the 2004 elections about the role of religion in American public life. For me, it was also the beginning of a three-year journey to find "the other religious America," authentic voices that are deeply rooted in religious traditions; voices that unite rather than divide; and voices that demand attention to a broader agenda of peace, social justice, care for the environment, respect for pluralism, and the common good.

How Did We Get Here? The Republican Branding of Religion and "Moral Values" in the 2004 Presidential Elections

The perceptions I experienced on the ground in Missouri reflected not only short-term political strategy but long-term religious trends. Following a long period in which conservative religious voices were largely absent from national public debates, the 1980s witnessed the emergence of a number of politicized conservative evangelical groups that became known as the Christian right. These groups—especially Rev. Jerry Falwell's Moral Majority, Rev. Pat Robertson's Christian Coalition, and James Dobson's Focus on the Family (FOF)—developed major media infrastructure and began to have unprecedented political access.

The Influence of Conservative Religious Voices

A full explanation of the rise of the Christian right is beyond my purposes here, but two factors that account for this rise are particularly relevant for understanding the quiescence of progressive religious voices over the last few decades: phenomenal infrastructure-building and a shift toward single-party affiliation among conservative religious Americans. First, conservative religious organizations have built institutions and media empires over the last few decades that have staggering resources. Note, for example, the resources and reach of just two of the central organizations behind the "I Vote Values" campaign in 2004, the Southern Baptist Convention (SBC) and FOF and affiliated organizations. The SBC is the largest Protestant denomination in the country, with more than sixteen million members in forty-two thousand churches who voted 80 percent for Bush in 2000. For 2003–2004, the SBC's annual budget was $182 million.

James Dobson's sprawling FOF organization has its own zip code in Colorado Springs. FOF's ten monthly magazines have 2.3 million subscribers, and Dobson's programming is carried each day by more than a thousand radio stations and eighty television stations in North America. Dobson also established the Family Research Council (FRC, now an administratively separate organization) with its half a million members, and Focus on the Family Action (FOFA) and Family Research Council Action (FRCA) as lobbying arms of FOF and FRC. Together, FOF, FOFA, FRC, and FRCA had combined revenues of $162 million in 2005.[2]

Although Dobson has until recently been less visible than Falwell or Robertson, as Dan Gilgoff noted in *The Jesus Machine*, Dobson has become "the new standard bearer of the Christian Right, with more influence than any organization the movement has ever known."[3] To put Dobson's reach in perspective, he is heard on more radio stations than National Public Radio (NPR) (one thousand radio stations compared to NPR's presence on eight hundred), and his magazine empire has more than twice the subscriber base of the *New York Times* (2.3 million readers compared to 1.1 million).[4] And Dobson's media empire is only one example of a full parallel sphere of conservative religious media that was built over the last half of the twentieth century.

The creation of this vast infrastructure was accompanied by increased affiliation of white evangelicals with the Republican Party. Despite the virtual marriage between the GOP and evangelicals in recent years, it is notable that as recently as 1988, evangelicals were evenly split between the two parties. During the 1990s, however, evangelicals were a critical part of what political scientists Merle Black and Earl Black called "the Great White Switch,"[5] when the Republican Party made strong gains among Southern whites.[6] By 2004, 56 percent of white evangelicals identified with or leaned Republican, with only 27 percent identifying with or leaning Democrat.[7] Moreover, the overwhelming majority of evangelical independents voted Republican, with George W. Bush commanding 78 percent of the white evangelical vote in 2004.[8]

The "I Vote Values" Campaign

These trends reached their climax during the nationally successful "I Vote Values" campaign run by the GOP and conservative religious groups.[9] The genius of this bold plan was to brazenly claim all of religion and morality for one party and to radically contract the scope of these terms to a few narrow wedge issues such as abortion, same-sex marriage, and embryonic stem cell research.[10] The leading conservative religious groups named above—the Southern Baptist Convention (SBC), Focus on the Family (FOF), and the Family Research Council (FRC)—jointly launched this strategy as the "I Vote Values" campaign on April 15, 2004. This coalition effort involved mirrored websites, with SBC hosting ivotevalues.com and FOF/FRC hosting ivotevalues.org. These sophisticated websites contained state-specific voter registration information, guidelines for churches about legal political activities developed by Pat Robertson affiliate Jay Sekulow of the American Center for Law and Justice, and an eight-page comparison of the Democratic and Republican Party platforms, in which, not surprisingly, the Republican Party emerged as the party of moral values.

At the SBC's annual meeting during the summer of 2004, key leaders were personally handing out buttons that declared, "I'm a values voter." The SBC also toured the South and battleground states with their "iVoteValues.com Mobile Voter Registration Rig and Information Center," a semitruck outfitted with seven interactive computer stations to register voters and introduce them to the SBC's particular brand of being a "values voter."[11] For his part, Dobson—for the first time in his career—personally endorsed a candidate, Republican George W. Bush, and organized six stadium-sized rallies to urge Christians in battleground states to "vote their values."[12] The campaign explicitly admonished conservative Christians to consider their "Bible-based values" and "not their pocketbook" when voting.[13]

"Moral Values" on the 2004 Exit Polls

These strategies were certainly influential, but the key to the creation of the enduring mythology of the "values voter" as a conservative religious voter animated by narrow wedge issues was the controversial inclusion of "moral values" on the official 2004 exit polls. The exit poll listed "moral values" alongside six other issues as possible answers to the question, "Which issue mattered most in deciding how you voted for president?" The results showed that more voters picked "moral values" from this list than any other issue and that these voters voted decidedly for Bush. The results of this exit poll question set off a firestorm of debate, with religious conservatives crowing that they had delivered the election to the president. For example, Southern Baptist leaders declared that "this election was a clear and resounding victory for moral values" and claimed that the deciding factor in the election was "the faith factor."[14]

Much of the television media ran with stories that offered "values voters" as the deciding voting block.[15] MSNBC announced that "Moral values . . . propelled Bush," and CBS news analysts offered "moral values" as one of two major explanations for "why Bush won."[16] Print media also carried this story line. The *Chicago Tribune* reported that "Faith, Values Fueled Win." Even the *New York Times* chimed in with the headline "Moral Values Cited as a Defining Issue of the Election;" the *Times* story concluded, "in the survey, a striking portrait of one influential group emerged—that of a traditional, church-going electorate that leans conservative on social issues and strongly backed Mr. Bush in his victory over Senator John Kerry."[17]

These hasty conclusions about "moral values," however, ignored serious problems with the survey question.[18] As CBS news editorial director Dick Meyer concluded, the "moral values" question "is like asking, 'What is most important to you—jobs, terrorism, health care, education, or the issue that is really the most important to you.' It's tautological."[19] Perhaps the most prominent public objection to the construction of the question came from Gary Langer, director of polling for ABC News and a member of the committee that crafted the exit poll questions. In a *New York Times* Op-Ed four days after the election, Langer lamented that the committee had rejected his argument that "this hot-button catch phrase had no place alongside defined political issues," and he cautioned that "its presence there created a deep distortion—one that threatens to misinform the political discourse for years to come."[20]

Evidence of the successful Republican–Christian right branding of "moral values" can be seen in the extreme partisan divides on the exit polls themselves: only 18 percent of Kerry supporters compared to 80 percent of Bush supporters were among those who chose "moral values" as the most important issue.[21] Significantly, a postelection poll by the Pew Research Center for the People and the Press found that a remarkable 8 percent of the public expressed a *negative* reaction to "moral values," noting explicitly that the idea was being used as a "wedge" against Democrats.[22] Langer's worries have unfortunately proven warranted. Four years later, the misperception that all religious voters are conservative Republicans who care mostly about abortion and same-sex marriage has hung on in much of the mainstream press.[23]

The Branding of Religion: Two Reactions

This overreaching attempt to claim all of religion and morality for a narrowly defined conservative politics has generated at least two major reactions. On the one hand, it has precipitated a strong backlash among angry atheists who argue that this narrow, divisive version of religion is one more piece of evidence that religion itself is a threat to society. On the other hand, the new generation of Americans who have grown up during the dominance of the Christian right are coming to the conclusion that Christianity has lost its moorings and has in fact become "un-Christian."

The Anti-Religious Left

The recent success of the Christian right has precipitated a strong backlash on the left. This movement has picked up an old thread within political liberalism that runs back to the beginnings of the Enlightenment in the seventeenth century—the idea that religion is the ultimate source of the most intractable divisions in society and that politics works best when separated from religion. In the West, this important insight led of course to the critical principle of separation of the institutions of church and state. It is important to note, however, that in most mainstream political theory, from John Locke and Immanuel Kant to John Rawls, the separation of church and state implied neither the full separation of religion from politics nor the secularization of society. Mainstream political liberalism had an agenda of religious disestablishment, or in its strongest form religious privatization, but not religious abolition.

A new spate of antireligious books has become wildly popular. At the time of this writing, for example, the top five books Amazon.com customers tagged under the category of "religion" were all by authors who are explicitly hostile to religion: Richard Dawkins, Christopher Hitchens, Sam Harris, and Daniel Dennett.[24] These authors pull few punches; they unapologetically declare that "God is not great"[25] and pronounce the urgency of shattering the "God delusion"[26] and "breaking the spell" of religious superstition for the good—in fact, for the salvation—of society.[27]

The popularity of this all-out assault on religion as a cancerous element of society that "poisons everything" is something new on the scene.[28] The central arguments of these books, of course, are not new. In fact, nearly all of them can be read directly (and in more sophisticated form) from the pages of Hume, Feuerbach, or Marx that were written more than a century ago. Three factors, however, have given these sentiments new life. First, the polarized political climate generated by the Christian right has justifiably opened up these religious expressions to harsh criticism. Second, worries about Islamic extremists in the post–September 11 environment raised new fears about the dangers of religious extremism. Finally, the proportion of nonreligious Americans nearly doubled from 7 percent in the early 1990s to between 10 percent and 14 percent of Americans today;[29] these books serve as something of a battle cry as nonreligious Americans find their voice.

Disillusioned Youth

One noteworthy indictment of the excesses of the Christian right is that the younger generation of sixteen- to twenty-nine-year-olds, who have grown up with the Christian right as the dominant expression of Christianity and of religion in America, have overwhelmingly negative views of Christianity. In his recent book, *Unchristian: What a New Generation Really Thinks about Christianity*, David Kinnaman, the young president of the Barna Group, a research firm that is known for public opinion research and that is run by and primarily for evangelicals, found that "Christianity has an image problem" among America's youth.

This image problem exists particularly for those Kinnaman defined as "outsiders" to Christianity, but it is also persistent even among those meeting Kinnaman's strict criteria as Christian churchgoers.[30] For young outsiders, "the three most common perceptions of present-day Christianity were antihomosexual [*sic*] (91 percent), judgmental (87 percent), and hypocritical (85 percent)."[31] Moreover, these three negative attributes were the only attributes from the entire list of ten positive and ten negative attributes that a majority agreed *strongly* describe present-day Christianity. Less than one in five young outsiders associated trustworthiness, hope, and love—key attributes Christians are commanded to embody in the New Testament (1 Corinthians 13)—with modern Christianity. Kinnaman concluded that younger Christian outsiders have come to think that "Christians no longer represent what Jesus had in mind"; in short, they believe that Christianity has become "un-Christian."[32] Moreover, even young "Christian churchgoers" shared many of these views. As Kinnaman noted with some dismay, "four out of five young churchgoers say that Christianity is antihomosexual [*sic*]; half describe it as judgmental, too involved in politics, hypocritical, and confusing."[33]

Where Have All the Liberals Gone?

Missing from these two reactions to the Christian right—the charge that "religion poisons everything" and the judgment that Christianity has become "un-Christian"—are the voices of liberal religion. Religious liberalism has a long tradition in American society. It was instrumental in the abolitionist movement in the nineteenth century, the social gospel movement that led to many of the New Deal reforms such as Social Security in the 1940s, and the civil rights and antiwar movements of the 1960s. But in the last few decades, these voices have been less discernable amidst the din created by the Christian right media machine.

The Size of the Religious Left

This public dominance by conservative religious voices has led to the false perception that they vastly outnumber all other religious voices, but survey research says otherwise. One of the more interesting analyses of the post-2004-election American religious landscape was "The Twelve Tribes of American Politics," by well-known political scientist John Green and Steve Waldman at beliefnet.com. Taking into account measures of religious affiliation, practice, and political affiliation, they found that "the religious left is just about the same size as the religious right."[34] Green and Waldman found that the religious right made up 15 percent of the electorate while the religious left made up 14 percent (up from 11 percent in 2000).

Taking into account measures of religious belief and practice, the 2006 American Values Survey (AVS), which I directed, also confirmed that the religious right only modestly outnumbers the religious left.[35] AVS found that "religious traditionalists," those who exhibit more conservative religious beliefs and practices, make up 22 percent of the general public, while "religious modernists," who exhibit less traditional beliefs and practices, made up 18 percent of Americans.[36] Moreover, analysis by the Pew Forum on Religion and Public Life found that conservative religious prominence is not due to any recent growth in this group's size as a percentage of the population; white evangelicals, the core of the GOP religious base, have made up a steady one-fourth of the general population since the early 1990s.[37]

So what then accounts for the quietude of liberal religious voices that were prominent just four decades ago? There are at least four reasons why liberal religious voices have not been heard despite their size. To put it succinctly, they are diverse, dispersed, and timid, and they have been overlooked.

Diverse Unlike the Christian right, which is a fairly homogeneous group dominated by white evangelical Protestants concentrated in the South and Midwest, the religious left is a broad inter-religious and inter-denominational coalition. The diversity of the religious left is partly a function of increasing religious pluralism in the United States as a whole. Fifty years ago, noted sociologist Will Herberg wrote an account of the American religious landscape that was more or less accurately entitled *Protestant, Catholic, Jew.*[38] To be accurate today, that title would have to be extended considerably to include Islam, Buddhism, and a myriad of other non-Judeo-Christian traditions that are flourishing in America. Dr. Diana Eck, director of the Pluralism Project at Harvard University, concluded her recent study of religious pluralism in America by declaring that the United States has now become "the world's most religiously diverse nation."[39] While the Christian right has remained somewhat insulated from these changes, the religious left reflects this increasing diversity.

Green and Waldman described the makeup of the Christian right as "theologically conservative white evangelical Protestants," compared to the religious left, which they described as "theologically liberal Catholics, mainline and evangelical Protestants."[40] Similarly, AVS found that a majority of religious traditionalists were white evangelical Protestants (with less than 3 percent non-Christian) while religious modernists were dominated by Catholics (36 percent), mainline Protestants (32 percent), and even a significant number of white evangelicals (15 percent). Additionally, fully 8 percent (4 percent Jewish and 4 percent other religions) of religious modernists are non-Christian.[41] This theological and demographic diversity presents unique challenges in coalition building and in speaking with a unified voice.

Dispersed   In addition to being spread across a number of religious traditions and denominations, many activists on the religious left are more dispersed in terms of the organizations in which they work. Rabbi David Saperstein, director of the Religious Action Center for Reform Judaism, explained:

> Back in the 1930s, '40s, and '50s, . . . many people did their social justice work through the churches and synagogues. Their rabbis and clergy were often the key spokespersons. The very success of the revolution that they wrought in the 1960s and '70s led to a splintering of that large cohort into an array of single-issue advocacy groups and service-delivery groups. Now, who are the people who are the leaders, the donors, the board members, the activists, and the professional staffs of those groups? They're the members of our churches and synagogues. They just don't need to do that work through our churches and synagogues. . . . But to dismiss as irrelevant the religious passion, idealism, and values that lead people into the serving professions and to be contributors to social justice and charitable causes—to ignore these acts as expressions of their religious values—is to distort the reality of America. So I actually think we're doing much better than we think.[42]

Moving into the 1960s, many liberal religious activists continued their activism through the growing number of nonprofit issue advocacy groups. In these settings, the norm was that religion often served as a private motivation for work, but it was not part of the public culture of the organizations. As Saperstein noted, the staffers and supporters of many of these organizations are members of the churches and synagogues—and, increasingly, mosques and meditation halls—that represent the religious left. The fact that these organizations do not have explicitly religious missions or ties, and the fact that these supporters and staffers function in their individual capacity rather than as members of specific religious groups, however, has made this presence difficult to measure and to see.

Timid Compounding the problem of diversity and dispersion is a tendency toward timidity in response to the "in-your-face" public religiosity of the Christian right. Because many on the religious left considered this abrasive, confrontational style not only worrisome in terms of blurring the lines separating church and state but also simply foreign to their own sense of decorum, many liberal religious activists reacted by toning down or even hiding their religious and moral claims. They offered instead a more cautious and constrained discourse focused on statistically based justifications and technical solutions—all head and no heart.

In his study of progressive grassroots religious activists in the 1990s, for example, Stephen Hart summarized progressive tiptoeing around religion and values this way:

> Progressives often fail to articulate, and sometimes even try to hide, the ethical values that ground their proposals. The right, meanwhile, engaging in discourse that is generally more passionate and transcendent, has seized the discursive high ground.[43]

Hart illustrated this point by noting that progressive religious groups often acted as if the following rules were in effect:

> "Don't talk about anything other than the practical steps of achieving the immediate goals the organization is trying for! Don't bring up any basic values (religious or political) that underlie your commitment to the organization! Don't ask anyone to articulate their reasons for participating in the group! Don't talk in terms that engage people's passion! Discuss issues in purely instrumental terms whenever possible!"[44]

Robert Wuthnow's recent study of the old mainline Protestant denominations also revealed a shift to a more subdued style of public engagement.[45] During the 1960s, these denominations had a robust public presence, especially around the issue of peace and civil rights. Since the 1970s, however, in part because of declining memberships and budgets, they have greatly reduced their national lobbying presence. By 2002, Wuthnow found, for example, that only one in five mainline Protestants knew that their denomination had a national office in Washington, D.C., at all.[46] Wuthnow and his colleagues characterized the current mainline Protestant engagement as "the quiet hand of God" to describe the "less showy, behind-the-scenes activities" that occur in places like congregations, faith-based service agencies, and clergy councils that address specific problems.[47]

Overlooked   Finally, liberal religious voices, in part because of the challenges listed above, have simply been overlooked. Contrary to the loud accusations of "liberal media bias" by many conservatives, when it comes to religion, the media coverage is actually skewed heavily to the right. In a recent report entitled "Left Behind: The Skewed Representation of Religion in Major News Media," Media Matters for America, a progressive media watchdog organization, demonstrated a clear conservative bias in coverage of religion since 2004.[48] Coverage of religion by the media increased significantly during this period, and Media Matters found that conservative religious leaders were quoted, mentioned, or interviewed in news stories nearly three times as often as liberal religious leaders in newspapers and television. The media matters study concluded that this "distorted picture allows a vocal minority to exercise an outsized influence on the issues and politicians that shape the direction of the country" and that this distortion is "particularly meaningful" in a country such as our own with relatively high rates of religious adherence.[49]

Looking for the Religious Left, Finding Progressive Religion

In the wake of the disappointing 2004 presidential elections, I set out to find the religious left, but I found something more important—progressive religion. At the beginning of this journey, I knew most clearly what I was *not* looking for: the religion of the self-assured culture warriors that proffered a politicized Christianity focused on banning same-sex marriage and abortion. I also knew I was looking for more than a liberal political platform with a thin coat of hastily applied religiosity, the kind of touch-up job one does when selling a used car.

In my interviews, I asked leaders to respond to a 2006 front-page *Washington Post* story that opened by trumpeting, "The Religious Left is back."[50] To my surprise, I realized very early on in the interview process that few of the people I had initially classified as the religious left strongly identified with that term, and many rejected it as too reactionary and narrow. The following are just a few representative examples from religious leaders across the religious spectrum.

> The current moment is not about taking back the faith—we've done that now; it's about how our faith could change the wind on the big issues: climate change, global poverty, HIV/AIDS. We don't need a religious left to balance a religious right. Left and right are political, not religious, categories; they don't fit us. I talk a lot in the new book about a moral center, which is different than a soulless centrism or a mushy middle. We say, "Don't go left, don't go right, go deeper."[51]
>
> —*Rev. Jim Wallis, Sojourners/Call to Renewal*

> I don't want to be part of anything anymore in my life that makes those boundaries barriers. I don't want to be defined as right or left. I want to be defined as a Christian with the world in mind. The people who are really leaders are trying to move us all without internecine warfare into a very spiritual world, a very new world.[52]
>
> —*Sr. Joan Chittister, OSB, Global Peace Initiative for Women;*
> *Network of Spiritual Progressives*

> If the progressive religious movement is going to be successful, it will be because it's been able to generate conversations across party and ideological lines. And honestly, if we're not having those conversations and just become the polar opposite of the Christian right,

then I will have failed as a person of faith who really believes that we should be creating the kingdom of God on earth.[53]

> —*Rev. Jennifer Kottler, Protestants for the Common Good*

I hope something other than the establishment of a religious left will happen: that we can effuse society with a sense of spiritual yearning and spiritual search. That's what King and Heschel and at his best, Malcolm, were doing. They brought Amos and Jesus and Isaiah and the Constitution and the Declaration of Independence and the Gettysburg Address all into relationship with each other, and they changed the whole atmosphere in the country.[54]

> —*Rabbi Arthur Waskow, The Shalom Center*

I'm not part of the religious left. I am part of a vision of a society where people from multiple religious and nonreligious viewpoints can live together in ways that serve the common good. I think it is a higher value to have people live together than it is to advance a progressive agenda. In a different moment, I think that the priorities could be changed.[55]

> —*Dr. Eboo Patel, Interfaith Youth Core*

Even among leaders who accepted the "religious left" label, virtually all were clear that they had something larger in mind than a mirror image of the religious right. For example, The Very Rev. Tracy Lind, dean of Trinity Episcopal Cathedral in Cleveland and a leader in the group We Believe Ohio, displays a bumper sticker on her car that reads, "Proud member of the Religious Left." But when she described what that means to her, it became clear that she also rejects a narrow, reactionary mirroring of the Christian right:

So I think this emerging religious left is about people of faith who want to help us reclaim a vision. We want not just to react over and against something, but to articulate something new. It's about dreaming the dream of God again. It's about proclaiming vision. It's about finding ways of living differently on this earth and with one another.[56]

Part of the issue, I discovered, is that the developments on the ground, which are broad and complex, have outrun the usual labels. Saleemah Abdul-Ghafur, for example, identified this difficulty in describing the emerging landscape. "I think the language is a problem. We don't have language to identify what is happening among Muslims in the West."[57] Throughout my interviews, I heard thoughtful leaders struggling with language to describe the new energy and coalitions they were seeing. They were clear that it was "a different voice on faith and politics" as John Cobb Jr. of Progressive Christians Uniting put it,[58] but many not only stumbled for a term but, as the quotations above indicate, actively resisted labels in an atmosphere where many were feeling "sloganed out."[59]

While I am sympathetic to the desire to avoid labels, especially in our current polarized political environment, I've chosen to use the word "progressive" in this book to describe this broad and complex movement. It has the advantage of being a term with some common coin among these leaders, even used in the official name of several organizations such as Progressive Christians Uniting, the Progressive Jewish Alliance, and the Progressive Muslim Union. It also has the advantage of being a fairly new term that has not been overly defined and a term for which many people have affinity.

Realizing an inductive approach was necessary to understand this emerging, complex movement, I began the research with a rough working definition of "progressive." I used it primarily to apply to a particular social and political outlook that includes broad commitments to social justice, democratic pluralism, and equality of all people. As I conducted and analyzed the interviews, I sharpened my understanding, eventually arriving at the five characteristics of progressive religion that I outline in the conclusion.

It is important to note that this use of the term "progressive" refers to a social and political outlook and not necessarily to a religiosity, a distinction many leaders took pains to make. That is, while some leaders here would consider themselves theologically liberal, a progressive religious leader might just as easily ground the political views described above in traditional or orthodox religious beliefs and practices.

Finally, the word "progressive" also has the advantage of capturing the sense of "progress" many leaders cited with regard to moving beyond the old left-right dichotomies of the culture wars. In fact, one mark of these emerging progressive religious voices is that they are building a strong coalition of left and center, liberals and moderates. For example, Omid Safi described a rapprochement between left and center leaders—a phenomenon I heard across all four religious traditions—that he saw as a healthy development.

> In their own hearts and in their own personal lives, Muslims are beginning the process of commingling these ideas, of taking some of the moral, ethical imperatives of progressives and combining them, mixing them, blending them with the mastery of the tradition that sometimes they have learned from more moderate leaders. I think that's happening, and that's tremendously encouraging.[60]

This combination of progressive moral, ethical, and political perspectives with a "mastery of the tradition" and commitment to religious practice often associated with more moderate or conservative voices provides a powerful amalgam that is creating a promising path forward.

This new path forward, a progressive coalition of left and center, is a mark of maturation in a new stage of development with regard to religion in American public life. Its emergence has certainly produced some growing pains over the past few decades. But it is being ushered in both by a maturing and broadening of the agenda among evangelical Christians and by the arrival of significant numbers of Muslim, Buddhist, and other non-Judeo-Christian voices in the public sphere.

About the Book

My hope is that this book will paint a compelling portrait of an emerging progressive religious movement in America. The foundation of the book is nearly one hundred interviews with progressive religious leaders in the four most prominent world religions in America: Christianity, Judaism, Islam, and Buddhism. This rising chorus of progressive religious leaders is moving from quieter to more public roles in the last few years to declare, as Rev. Jim Wallis of Sojourners often puts it, that "the monologue of the religious right is over."[61] The vast majority of these interviews were conducted in person, and together they comprised more than one hundred hours of audio and more than fifteen hundred pages of transcripts and field notes. I have employed ethnographic research techniques to identify clear patterns and tensions in the interviews in order to paint a coherent but complex picture of what it means to be progressive and religious in these traditions. These interviews were exceptionally rich, and although I have attempted to use direct quotes generously to allow these leaders to speak in their own voices here, there is much I wanted to include in the book that I could not because of space limitations. Longer excerpts of interviews, including audio podcasts, are available on the book's companion website at www.progressiveandreligious.org.

It is also worth clarifying briefly my own relationship to the religious traditions I write about here. I grew up Southern Baptist in Mississippi, and I have a master's degree in theology from a Southern Baptist seminary. My PhD work in religious ethics was done at Emory University, which afforded me the opportunity to broaden my study of the American religious landscape and to think more carefully about the relationship between politics and religion. Emory also afforded me the opportunity to teach introductory comparative courses in Buddhism and Christianity and to practice meditation and attend public teachings by Geshe Lobsang Tenzin in 1999 and 2000 at the Drepung Loseling Monastery, a center of Tibetan Buddhist studies. My own journey, precipitated by the fundamentalist takeover of my seminary during my last semester, has meant that my own religious identity has shifted over the years, from evangelical Christian to disillusioned Christian to progressive Christian. My wife, Jodi, is Jewish, and I have been a welcomed guest, *D'var Torah* leader, and speaker in Reconstructionist synagogues over the last few years. We are currently members of the Interfaith Families Project in Washington, D.C., a vibrant community who are struggling, celebrating, and learning together what it means to be interfaith families and an interfaith community.

Professionally, I have been a careful observer in the Jewish, Muslim, and other religious worlds I have traversed over the last few years. In addition to the interviews with religious leaders, my analysis draws on participant observation in synagogues, meditation halls, and religious conferences such as the Islamic Society of North America annual meeting. Moreover, as a consultant on religion and progressive politics in Washington, D.C., I have been an insider activist in formal and informal partnerships at the national level with many of the organizations I am describing. While this "front row" perspective has its advantages, such as intimate knowledge of social networks and a real-time sense of where the new energy is located, it also has its downside of potential bias, which I have endeavored to check both by careful attention to evidence and by seeking a variety of external feedback.

Although there have been a number of excellent edited volumes containing collections of essays by progressive religious leaders—*Progressive Christians Speak: A Different Voice on Faith and Politics,*[62] *Righteous Indignation: A Jewish Call for Social Justice,*[63] *Progressive Muslims on Justice, Gender, and Pluralism,*[64] and *Mindful Politics: A Buddhist Guide to Making the World a Better Place*[65]—this is the first book that has attempted to synthesize broad progressive themes not only within each tradition but across multiple traditions.[66]

What This Book Is Not

It is important at the outset of a book about religion and politics, the two topics that conventional wisdom suggests avoiding in polite conversation, to say what this book is *not*. First, this is not a book about how Democrats can win elections by appealing to people of faith. Almost all of the nearly one hundred religious leaders from Christianity, Judaism, Islam, and Buddhism that I interviewed for the book emphasized that religion should always transcend politics, and many had critical evaluations of both political parties. Nor is it a book touting the emergence of a politicized religious left to counter the politicized religious right. The last thing we need in this polarized political climate is an additional dose of narrowly politicized religion.

Further, it is not a book that claims that all authentically religious people must be politically progressive or that makes any claim that the progressive voices presented here represent "true Christianity" or "true Judaism" or "true Islam" or "true Buddhism" (whatever those things might be). Religious traditions that have flourished across multiple cultures for centuries are by their very nature exceedingly complex. They do not fit neatly into any given ideology. I am not arguing here that conservative religion ought to vanish from the American scene, although like many leaders I interviewed, I believe that much of the conservative religion that has dominated American public life has drunk too deeply at the well of power and at this moment in our history has lost its way.[67] The present is a crucial time for progressive religious leaders to find their voice and provide a new kind of leadership that connects faith to a different kind of politics. Finally, it is not a book that claims that one needs to be religious in order to have deep, admirable moral convictions. Perhaps the only thing that needs to be said for that proposition is that it is a view for which the empirical evidence has always been wanting.

What This Book Is

This book makes the much more modest claim that there is an authentic, growing movement that is both progressive and religious, and that this progressive religious movement has critical contributions to make in our current polarized environment that is characterized by a vocal Christian right and a reactionary antireligious left. I wrote this book because I believe that the success of the American experiment in pluralistic democracy is jeopardized when a single religious voice claims to speak for all or when religious voices are excluded from the public sphere. True democratic pluralism requires a healthy balance of religious and nonreligious voices. At this point in our nation's history, the voices that have been largely missing from the public debate are those highlighted in these pages: voices that are both deeply religious and politically progressive. These voices plumb the depths of religion for enduring truths; they call faithful religious people to work for a better society for all; they work for an America that is, in John Winthrop's memorable biblical allusion, "a city set on a hill," a beacon for the highest of democratic ideals rather than an empire set on military domination; and they unite rather than divide.

One reading of the Latin root of our English word "religion" means "to bind together."[68] In this sense, religion not only binds humans to the divine but, at its best, connects us with one another. A century ago, sociologist Émile Durkheim talked about religion as a powerful force for creating a sense of unity and meaning among people by means of common symbols and collective experience.[69] Throughout human history, religion has been a strong source of tribal and communal identity. The unique challenge of religion in modern pluralistic society, however, is whether particular religions can contribute to some sense of solidarity beyond their native sectarian communities. There have clearly been times in recent memory where religious leaders have used particular symbols to invoke universal causes; Rev. Martin Luther King Jr.'s evocation of "the beloved community" and Rabbi Abraham Joshua Heschel's "praying with his feet" during the civil rights movement were mentioned time and time again in my interviews as the kind of work for a common vision that the best of religion can offer.

Abraham Lincoln, who has been called one of our nation's greatest public theologians, famously offered another image of "binding up" that is relevant for our time, when our nation is so polarized over moral and religious issues. At his second inaugural, Lincoln addressed a nation divided over deeply held cultural beliefs and over a costly war where both sides had claimed that God was on their side:

> Both [parties to the war] read the same Bible and pray to the same God, and each invokes His aid against the other. . . . The prayers of both could not be answered. That of neither has been answered fully. The Almighty has His own purposes. . . . With malice toward none, with charity for all, with firmness in the right as God gives us to see the right, let us strive on to finish the work we are in, to bind up the nation's wounds, to care for him who shall have borne the battle and for his widow and his orphan, to do all which may achieve and cherish a just and lasting peace among ourselves and with all nations.[70]

Lincoln's words offer some relevant direction for our own time. First, Lincoln articulated a fundamental principle about the relationship between religion and politics, between divine purpose and human endeavors: Divine purposes always transcend human aims. No human political cause, however noble, can claim to be God's cause.[71] Second, Lincoln illustrates what rich and complex cultural resources religious traditions are. At a time of deep political division in which religion is often the tip of the spear, it is tempting to think that the solution to our divisions would be to sequester religion from the public sphere. Lincoln, however, evoked religious imagery effectively in mending a rift where the causes had been intertwined with religion.[72] The appeal to charity, healing wounds, caring for the orphan and the widow, and working for a just peace are all prominent biblical themes. These two insights—a humility about divine purposes and the hope that religion has much to contribute to the healing of the divides in our nation—are two hallmarks of the voices that are both progressive and religious that I highlight in these pages.

Whom This Book Is For

This book is for religious Americans who are wary of progressive politics but who have a deep sense that the full political implications of their faith are distorted when they are told that the only issues that matter are homosexuality and abortion. This book is also for political progressives who are wary of religion but who remember that the peace movement, the civil rights movement, the women's movement, the abolitionist movement—in fact virtually all major progressive political movements in American history—have had influential progressive religious voices helping to lead the way.

This book is for those who are worried about the growing divides over religion in our country. Dr. Eboo Patel, a young Muslim who founded the Interfaith Youth Core, an organization that is building the interfaith youth movement, articulated a helpful image for understanding these divides over religion. Adapting W. E. B. DuBois's concept of "the color line," Patel talked about the importance of grasping the significance of an emerging "faith line" in world politics:

> I think that we have a new line in the twenty-first century, and that new line is "the faith line." A lot of people thought "the color line" separated black and white and yellow and red, and it took a visionary like Martin Luther King Jr. to say, "No, no, no. What the color line separates is people who want to live together as brothers and people who would perish together as fools." I think of the faith line in the same way. The faith line does not separate Muslims and Christians or Jews and Hindus. The faith line separates those I call religious pluralists and religious totalitarians.[73]

Religious totalitarians, Patel explained, want "their way of being, believing and belonging to dominate everything and for everyone else to suffocate."[74] Patel also noted that the totalitarians and the neoatheists ironically stand on the same side of the faith line—each believe that religion is an inherently divisive force and that solutions must be binary winner-take-all battles. Religious pluralists, on the other hand, believe in their own traditions and might even think their own tradition is the only right one, but nevertheless believe "in a society where people from different backgrounds have the freedom and the right to live by their own traditions and where those different groups of people can live together in equal dignity and mutual loyalty."[75] The voices represented in this book stand squarely in the religious pluralist camp, inviting thick dialogue and engagement, confident that shared values and goals are attainable.

This book is also for members of the media who sense that the wind is shifting in the American religious landscape but who have been unsure of their footing on the new terrain. As Rev. Tim Ahrens, founder of We Believe Ohio noted, "In fairness to the press, we certainly defy many categories and present an interpretive challenge to the 'five hundred words or less' news bites."[76] The progressive and religious voices highlighted here will help them paint a more accurate portrait of religion in America. This portrait must encompass a broader religious agenda that goes beyond narrow, divisive issues to include the broader, more central questions of how our public institutions treat the least, the last, the lost, and the stranger among us and how America can regain its respected place as a force for peace and justice in the world. Finally, this book is for the growing movement of Americans who are both progressive and religious and who are increasingly finding their voice at this critical moment in our national life.

These voices show how progressive commitments shape religious life and how religious convictions strengthen progressive activism. In our present moment, where too many have been told that they need to choose between their religion and their politics, this message is hopeful news.

CHAPTER 1

Lifting the Line of History
How Progressive Jews
Are Healing the World

A Seder in the Streets of Washington

I met Rabbi Arthur Waskow on Capitol Hill in Washington, D.C., on a rainy May day. He had come to Washington from Philadelphia, where he founded the Shalom Center, to attend a major interfaith meeting of Jews, Christians, and Muslims to talk about the possibility of planning a national day of fasting and repentance for the war in Iraq. He has a memorable look: multi-colored *kippah*; long, wiry gray beard; animated eyes that dance behind oversized glasses; and sandal-clad sock-feet. He also has a particular gift for weaving ancient texts into contemporary life and for storytelling. In the middle of the interview, Rabbi Waskow told a powerful story about how the Exodus narrative erupted into his life on the streets of Washington four decades earlier, shortly after Martin Luther King Jr. had been murdered:

> The one piece of Jewish practice that I had kept as a grown-up was the Passover Seder, and only that. It was about freedom, and I treated it seri- ously, but it didn't seem to me it had much to do with the rest of my life. On April 4, 1968, Martin Luther King was murdered. On April 5,

25

the black community of Washington exploded like black communities everywhere in America, and by nightfall on April 5, President Lyndon Johnson sent the Army to occupy Washington—and I do mean occupy: the schools, the major streets, the traffic circles, et cetera—and he imposed a curfew.

The first night of Passover came ten days after Dr. King was killed. I walked home to get ready for the Seder, and that meant that year walking past the Army with a jeep with a machine gun pointed at the block I was in. And what began welling up from my guts much more than from my brain was, "This is Pharaoh's army. I'm going home to do the Seder, and this is Pharaoh's army."

Dr. King's last speech had been, "I'm standing on the mountaintop looking at the Promised Land," straight from Moses. Many of the freedom songs from the black South were straight out of the biblical Exodus. So it all exploded like a volcano—energy I had no idea was inside. So it all exploded in an enormous energy that night, and it felt as if the Seder was in the streets and the streets were in the Seder.[1]

For Rabbi Waskow, on a spring night forty years ago, the grief of the assassination of Dr. King, the social unrest in the African American community, the stark military presence, and the general struggle for civil rights became part of the Seder. Simultaneously, as Waskow put it, "Jewish religious tradition rose up unexpectedly in the context of the American upheaval of 1968."[2] The previously dormant power of the master narrative of the Exodus created an explosion of energy that ruptured time. Through this fissure, the occupied streets of Washington ran through the Seder, and the message of liberation of the Seder flowed into the torn city.

Judaism and Social Justice

Of the four religious traditions covered in this book, Judaism arguably has the strongest and most engaged progressive voice. As Rabbi David Saperstein, director of the Religious Action Center for Reform Judaism (RAC), put it, "Culturally, there's no group more progressive on the social issues—whether you're talking about separation of church and state, abortion rights, equal rights for gays and lesbians—that more strongly embraces those ideas than the Jewish community does."[3]

I heard this theme articulated consistently and with some pride during my interviews with twenty-one Jewish leaders who spanned the entire range of the American Jewish denominations: Reform, Reconstructionist, Conservative, and Orthodox. This identity is rooted in a strong history of social action in the twentieth century, especially the civil rights movement.[4] Al Vorspan, civil rights leader and former head of the RAC, talked passionately about traveling with a group of rabbis at Rev. Dr. Martin Luther King Jr.'s request to St. Augustine, Florida, where they were jailed with King and others for working to desegregate public places such as a restaurant and swimming pool.[5] Rabbi Saperstein pointed out that the Civil Rights Act of 1964 and the Voting Rights Act of 1965 were written by a group of African American and Jewish attorneys at the very table at which we conducted the interview at the RAC.[6] And Arthur Waskow spoke movingly of the impact of King's death on his own spiritual life.

Reconstructionist Rabbi Steve Gutow, director of the Jewish Council for Public Affairs, noted that across the Jewish spectrum, "social justice is part of the fabric of the tradition and the community and how it thinks and how it sees itself."[7] Conservative Rabbi Jill Jacobs, education director for Jewish Funds for Justice, talked about the centrality of social justice and noted the growing engagement with social justice issues among younger Conservative rabbis.[8] Even Dr. David Luchins, vice president of the Orthodox Union, in response to a question about how it was possible to be "an Orthodox liberal," quipped, "[Being an Orthodox social conservative] would be pretty lonely because you don't have too many sources, because the vast part of our religious tradition talks about . . . *tikkun olam*, helping others; it's the number one priority of faith."[9]

All of this is not to say, of course, that there are not still important and sometimes heated debates and divides within Judaism—especially with regard to the Israeli/Palestinian conflict and issues of sexuality—but a commitment to social justice provides strong connective tissue throughout American Judaism. A quick glimpse at voting patterns also provides a window into the strong progressive thrust of Jewish political engagement; in the 2006 midterm elections, nearly nine out of ten Jews (88 percent) voted for Democratic House candidates nationwide.[10] Moreover, of the forty-three members of Congress (thirteen senators and thirty House members) who are Jewish, all but three are Democrats.[11]

Despite this commitment to progressive policies and politics, however, many Jews have often felt that they had to leave their religious identities behind in order to participate in social justice work. Rabbi Michael Lerner, founder of *Tikkun* magazine and the Network of Spiritual Progressives and author of *The Left Hand of God: Taking Back Our Country from the Religious Right*, described clearly the bias against religious people he experienced as a leader in the antiwar movement in the 1960s:

> I was surrounded by people who were motivated by the same ethical and spiritual values that I held, but the vast majority held very antagonistic feelings toward anybody who was into religion or spirituality. So it was increasingly clear to me in the sixties that my spiritual and religious life had to be kept in the closet lest my national leadership role be undermined completely. . . .
>
> The left as a whole projected then and has projected ever since the notion that "we want you religious people to be part of our movement, but we want you to leave your religious and spiritual ideas at the door because our movement is fundamentally secular. We basically suspect that in order for you to be religious or particularly to believe in God, you must be at a lower level of intellectual or psychological development than the rest of us, but we hope that by hanging out with us in our movement you will eventually no longer need those intellectual or psychological crutches that are the only thing that we can imagine you must get from being a religious person."[12]

More recently, Conservative Rabbi David Rosenn, director of AVODAH, the Jewish Service Corps, cited the "gap" he experienced between the number of Jews working for social change and the number who personally and publicly identified as Jewish as one of the key motivations for starting AVODAH.

> There was this gap between the synagogue folks and the social change folks. A lot of my social change buddies just felt like I was foolish to be involved with a religion at all and had a lot of contempt for it, and

if anything, would just tolerate the fact that this was a part of who I was. And honestly, the members of my congregation, whom I loved, a lot of them in their professional lives were doing things that made a big difference, but what we did collectively as a congregation was not really very much.[13]

Dr. Leonard Fein, an older, well-known Reform Jewish writer and founder of a number of progressive Jewish organizations such as *Moment* magazine and the antihunger organization MAZON, also noted a similar impetus for his work with hunger organizations:

> When you go to the table where people who care about hunger assemble, what you find there represented are the Catholic charities, the Lutherans, the Methodists. You find Jews disproportionately on the staff of such organizations but not as Jews on the board. And I think that's bad news for the Jews. I think specifically that the disproportionate number of Jewish staff people is a resource that needs to be replenished, that it's only replenished if the community is seen as on the barricades on these issues.[14]

Dr. Fein's sentiments captured two key aspects of this dynamic. First, as many leaders I interviewed noted, the Jewish community has supplied a disproportionate number of people who staff progressive advocacy organizations. Second, while Fein notes that this presence has been a strong resource for the progressive movement generally, he worries that unless there is both a sense within Judaism and in the public that the Jewish community is "on the barricades" on social justice issues, this resource may dissipate. Being on the barricades includes both the presence of organizations that represent Jewish responses to social justice issues and opportunities for individual Jews working for social justice causes to connect this work directly to their Jewish cultural and religious identity.

Which World? Trends in Jewish Social Activism

In addition to the legacy of civil rights involvement, the Jewish leaders I interviewed cited a number of trends that have, over the last several decades, facilitated the continuation and even the expansion of the Jewish commitment to social justice. A majority of the progressive Jewish leaders I interviewed (and nearly all of the leaders under fifty) talked about the rise of Jews to a secure, established place in America as a significant factor in increasing Jewish engagement in broader social justice issues beyond the Jewish community.

Making It

Outside of the Christian denominations, Judaism is the second largest religious tradition in America. The recent massive U.S. Religious Landscape Survey by the Pew Forum on Religion and Public Life put the Jewish population at 1.7 percent of the adult (18 and over) population, or approximately 3.8 million Jewish adults.[15] The vast majority of Jews are affiliated with the four major groups: Reform, Conservative, Orthodox, and Reconstructionist. The Pew survey also found that Jews in America have one of the highest retention rates for keeping childhood members of any religion at 76 percent, second only to Hinduism (90 percent).[16]

As Daniel Sokatch, director of the Progressive Jewish Alliance (PJA), noted, "I think Jewish America is a fascinating experience, so that for the first time in the history of the Jewish people—in the long, long history of the Jewish people—there's a country where, although Jews are not in the majority, they've basically made it."[17] Certainly there are some clear signs of Jewish "making it" in American politics and society. The forty-three Jewish members of the 110th Congress (thirty in the House of Representatives and thirteen in the Senate) represent an all-time high and a remarkable achievement; although Jews make up only about 2 percent of the adult population, they now make up 13 percent of the U.S. Senate. Beyond politics, there are other signs of Jewish achievement. For example, 13 of *Time* magazine's 100 most influential Americans of the twentieth century, including the person of the century, Albert Einstein, were Jewish.[18]

This achievement is remarkable when seen against the backdrop of discrimination against Jews in the early twentieth century. To take just one example, as Jewish upward mobility was first taking hold and Jewish enrollment at elite universities was rising, Jews found themselves pushed out of Ivy League schools in the 1920s through notorious discriminatory policies.[19] The Jewish community responded by founding institutions like Brandeis University in 1948, which they conceived as "the Harvard for Jews." By Brandeis's fiftieth anniversary in 1998, however, the *New York Times* noted that "Harvard became the Harvard of the Jews as did Yale, Columbia, the University of Pennsylvania and the rest of elite American colleges."[20] Jewish undergraduate enrollment at Harvard University currently stands at about 30 percent, fifteen times the proportion of Jews in the national population.[21] Pew also found that one-third of Jews have attained a postgraduate education, compare to only one in ten in the general population.[22] And stemming from this educational attainment, Jews have the highest levels of household income of any major religious group, with nearly half (46 percent) having a household income over $100,000, compared to only 10 percent in the general population.[23]

Making it involves not just achievement but acceptance, and here too, there is solid evidence that Jews have become accepted as part of mainstream American society. In a recent poll by the Pew Forum on Religion and Public Life, Jews registered the highest favorability rating of *any* religious minority group; among the general public, 76 percent held favorable views of Jews—a favorability ranking equal to Catholics and significantly above Evangelicals (60 percent), Mormons (53 percent), and Muslim Americans (53 percent).[24] Noteworthy also was the recent selection of Senator Joseph Lieberman (D-CT) as running mate of Vice President Al Gore in the 2000 presidential elections. Lieberman himself reflected on the significance of his candidacy in a speech given after the race at the launch of the Pew Forum on Religion and Public Life:

> Most Americans . . . seemed totally accepting of my faith, not just the fact that I was Jewish, but my observance of Judaism. And by the end of the campaign, in which I say joyously I experienced not one whit of anti-Semitism, barely anyone was even mentioning my religion, which was exactly what we had hoped for. All of which I think is powerful evidence that I have experienced of just how tolerant and inclusive a nation we have become.[25]

Sokatch, however, also noted "the paradoxical threat of America, which is a golden land for Jews, is that Jews can just become Americans. . . . You can even create an identity that is whatever you want it to be; your Jewishness is part of that menu of who you are."[26] Here Sokatch identifies a key concern for the contemporary Jewish community. On the one hand, "making it" has ensured a solid standing and real influence beyond their numbers for Jews. On the other hand, "making it" has also weakened the external forces that served to demarcate sharp communal bounds and reinforce distinctive communal identity, a real concern for a relatively small religious minority.

New Priorities

Conservative rabbi Jill Jacobs identified three commonly recognized "core pieces" of traditional Jewish identity that arose out of the experience of World War II: anti-Semitism, the Holocaust, and Israel.[27] Not surprisingly, although I didn't ask about it explicitly, the vast majority of leaders I interviewed talked about the shifting of this basis of Jewish identity and the challenges this new terrain presents to Judaism. Although this sentiment was decidedly more pronounced in the younger leaders, it was clearly present across many of the older generation as well.

There was considerable tension around the issue of the centrality of Israel for progressive Judaism. Rabbi Eric Yoffie is the president of the Union of Reform Judaism. Acknowledging the developing new pillars of Jewish identity, such as renewed interest in integrating religious observance and social justice, Rabbi Yoffie also talked about the importance of retaining traditional Jewish support for Israel as part of "a balanced progressive Judaism:"

> We found ourselves in the midst of a religious revival as Reform Jews, and it didn't mean distancing ourselves from social justice or from Israel. But there was an awakening of interest in Jewish study and ritual observance, and ultimately in Judaism all those various strands are interrelated. You can't be strong in one unless you're strong in all.[28]

Rabbi Sharon Brous is founder of the vibrant IKAR (literally, "essence" or "root") Congregation in Los Angeles, a congregation named by the Slingshot Fund in 2007 as one of the fifty most inspiring and innovative organizations in the North American Jewish community.[29] Like the majority of younger leaders I interviewed, Rabbi Brous expressed a desire to de-emphasize what she called the "old Jewish modes of engagement," such as the "defense organizations" that have at their center an emphasis on support for Israel, and to move toward an emphasis on social justice and positive social engagement as the core of Jewish identity.[30] Thirty-something Rabbi Jacobs explained the problem this way:

> In the last fifteen years, the Jewish community in the United States realized that that [the traditional motivation for identification] wasn't really working for younger people who weren't around in '67 [the Six-Day War] and who didn't grow up with anti-Semitism, and who, if they knew any [Holocaust] survivors, were already a couple of generations removed from them. I think it's not actually healthy to form your entire identity around, "Everybody hates us, therefore you should be Jewish." I don't find that very compelling. I think younger Jews are looking for other ways to connect, sometimes through culture. . . . Like most of my peers, I grew up with all these big luxuries, and I think that that forces a search for identity. What does it mean when Jews are just as white as the next white person? I think [this realization] led many younger people back to thinking about social justice.[31]

Dr. Leonard Fein concurred. Fein argued that "the community is beginning to edge away from its obsession with Holocaust and Israel as the two motives for Jewish life—not abandoning them, but edging away, which is an altogether healthy thing."[32] Dr. David Luchins of the Orthodox Union echoed these concerns but made the even stronger argument that an overemphasis on support for Israel has inhibited the progressive impulse in traditional Judaism:

> I think you can make a case that the trauma of the Holocaust and the creation of the State of Israel has changed, has drained traditional Judaism of some of its progressive social justice aspects. Israel has become the moral equivalent of *tikkun olam*, and that's bad. And that's not good for Israel either.[33]

Especially among the younger leaders I interviewed, there was clarity that the present demanded a more balanced, critical approach to issues relating to Israel. Rabbi Or Rose, associate dean of the Rabbinical School at Hebrew College and editor of *Righteous Indignation*, summarized this position this way:

> American Jews must reflect carefully on our relationship to the state of Israel. Are we willing to celebrate its accomplishments and critique its shortcomings? Have we been sensitive enough to the suffering of the Palestinian people? Are we advocating for a peaceful and just solution to this tragic conflict for both parties? Progressive Jews have to push our community to engage in conversation about these thorny issues with honesty and respect.[34]

For most of the progressive leaders I interviewed, the shift in emphasis away from the older mode of engagement around the defense organizations to a broader mode of engagement that emphasized social justice was seen as a healthy thing. It was also seen as a necessary move, especially for engaging a new generation of Jews who have grown up as part of mainstream American society with considerable privilege and who are looking for ways to bring their Jewish identity and values into play in the broader world.

Healing the World: Town-Square Judaism

The combination of making it in America and the decentering of the triad of the Holocaust, Israel, and anti-Semitism as the core motivating factors for being Jewish in contemporary America have led to a shift in the focus of Jewish work for social justice. This shift in focus is symbolized by a shift in what the adjective "Jewish" modifies—away from modifying the object of concern in social action and toward modifying the subjects who act.[35] For example, Dr. Fein noted this tension—a debate he reported having with his own father—at the founding of MAZON twenty-one years ago:

> MAZON was a *Jewish response* to hunger, not a response to *Jewish hunger*. And that got some people's noses out of joint who said, "Jews

have enough problems of their own," and so on and so forth. My father used to say to me, "Why *Jews* against nukes? I mean, march with everybody." And I would say to him, "Look, Pop, if what you're saying is that in all the great issues of our time we march with the polyglot hoard, you are implying that when we come back to home territory, it's to debate such things as whether or not to re-pave the temple parking lot. And I've got to tell you, people are not going to come back for that." So it's quite apart from whether we have a particular take on nukes or on hunger. It has to do with the nature of America and group identity in America.[36]

Here, Fein identifies the tension that moving the adjective from the object of concern to the acting subject had within the Jewish community. This fault line was a strong theme in my interviews. Simon Greer, president of Jewish Funds for Justice, described this shift as a movement from what he called "cul-de-sac Judaism" to "town-square Judaism," which he described as "making a difference in the world, living Jewish values in non-Jewish settings as a way of being Jewishly identified."[37]

One important movement within progressive Judaism is that a burgeoning "town-square Judaism" is challenging what is properly a Jewish concern. Ruth Messinger, president of American Jewish World Service—a group that has experienced phenomenal growth over the past nine years and has played a major role in directing Jewish social concern toward universalistic causes such as the genocide in Darfur—put the question this way, "Which world are we trying to heal? Does this mean just the Jewish world or does it mean the broader world?" Messinger went on to explain that, especially after the experience of September 11, 2001, "I'm finding more and more Jews, Jewish communities, Jewish organizations who are thinking about [the broader world]."[38]

Daniel Sokatch also emphasized the importance of particular religious engagement with issues of universal concern and grounded this perspective in the widely cited biblical text of Isaiah 58:

Isaiah does not say, "Remove the stumbling block from in front of the Jewish blind." He does not say, "Clothe the Jewish naked" or "Feed the Jewish hungry" or "Let the oppressed Jews go free." That's not what

Isaiah says. And those are universalistic demands that are made of humanity and of the Jewish community. . . . It's Jewish to go to Ghana and do service. It's Jewish after Katrina to go down and not just rebuild the synagogue that was destroyed in Mississippi but to go serve the people of New Orleans Parish who suffered, the non-Jewish people as well. It's a Jewish thing in Los Angeles to stand with workers who are just struggling for the American dream. And it's Jewish for these reasons, because it's part of who we are as a Jewish community.[39]

For Sokatch, and for a majority of progressive Jewish leaders I interviewed, the adjective "Jewish" has clearly shifted from modifying the object of concern to a place of describing the identity of acting subjects. These progressive leaders tended to emphasize that the great truths of Judaism require the Jewish community to work for the healing of the world as a whole.

Tikkun Olam: Healing the World

Perhaps the clearest, most passionate expression of God's call for human engagement in the world is the central Jewish notion of *tikkun olam*, healing the world. Rabbi Or Rose gave a concise account of this term from the Jewish mystical tradition:

Our mystical masters teach us that in the beginning God attempted to create the cosmos by fashioning a series of vessels filled with divine light. Unfortunately, God's light was too powerful for these vessels, and they shattered into countless pieces. As a result, our world is an admixture of divine light and shards of the primordial vessels. Our task, say the Kabbalists, is to repair the cosmos—to piece it together again—through intentional acts of spiritual healing.[40]

Dr. Luchins noted that this concept was central to how Orthodox Rabbi Ahron Soloveitchik summarized Judaism in a sentence: "A perfect God dared to create an imperfect world and deigned to create the imperfect creature, and gave that imperfect creature the daunting task of perfecting his imperfect world."[41] Although many leaders I interviewed lamented that the modern term is often used simply as a synonym for social justice or even for isolated acts of service, *tikkun olam* comes from deep within the ancient Jewish tradition—it was most influentially articulated by Rabbi Isaac Luria, a sixteenth-century Jewish mystic—and contains "deep resonances" with a set of related religious ideas.[42] As Rabbi Saperstein clarified, "It conveys not just the social justice work but connection with God, connection with legal structures that need to work differently, and connection with the spiritual fulfillment of the mystical tradition."[43]

Central to the idea of *tikkun olam* is the realization that the world is broken and in need of healing and repair. One of the most moving aspects of doing these interviews was experiencing the sense of connectedness these leaders felt between deep human suffering on the one hand and the demands of authentic religion on the other. Rabbi Brous spoke eloquently about this connection:

> How do you live in a city where 86,000 people sleep on the streets every night when you're a religious person? It seemed to me that it was impossible to live an authentic religious life completely disconnected from what was happening out on the street. And it also seemed inauthentic to live a life that's about obligation toward other human beings in the world that's not rooted in a deep understanding and connection to our own traditions.[44]

Rabbi Michael Lerner, who named his influential progressive magazine *Tikkun*, also made the connection that *tikkun olam* is connected to a sense of hope that even in the midst of great suffering and injustice, transformation is possible:

> To believe in God, from the Jewish standpoint, is to believe that there is a power in the universe that makes for the possibility of transformation from that which is to that which ought to be. And that power in the universe makes it possible for us to look at any given existing reality and say that it can be changed and it can be healed and it can be transformed. That's what *tikkun* means, healing and transformation.[45]

While Rabbi Lerner emphasized the meaning of *tikkun*, Rabbi Gutow talked about the kind of world (*olam*) that such healing and transformation might bring about.

> I grew up thinking that one had to synthesize poetry and justice to create a life. . . . We're after a world, a whole world where people can love each other and care about each other. The first step to that world is making sure that people aren't starving and hungry and sick and don't have a chance to get to college and don't have a chance to appreciate music. . . . And when I hear some of the beauty of prayer or read Torah, I almost always connect back to that poetic piece. That's why social justice isn't alone. Poetry is essential to understanding what a really just world is.[46]

Like Rabbi Saperstein, Rabbis Brous, Lerner, and Gutow emphasized the religious resonances of *tikkun olam*, the essential connections between what Rabbi Gutow called "poetry and justice." These connections allow us to confront fully the real brokenness of the world while maintaining hope that transformation is possible.

Finally, there was considerable concern among most of the leaders I interviewed that the very success of the term *tikkun olam* threatened to cut its deep connections to Jewish tradition and its connections to systemic social change. Ruth Messinger noted with great irony, "There are Jews who are getting active in social justice around America who have been reported to say, 'How do you say *tikkun olam* in Hebrew?'"[47] And Rabbi Yoffie stressed the challenge of emphasizing that the term does not simply refer to "charity" or "acts of kindness" but rather to "establishing the conditions for justice":

> So it's not simply a matter of dealing with particular symptoms by extending kindness to a person in trouble, but it means repairing the world in order to establish conditions of justice. If we look at Leviticus and cancellation of debts, liberation of slaves and the return of ancestral property, we're not simply dealing with people who are poor, but we're helping them to avoid a situation in which poverty for them becomes inevitable.[48]

Like Rabbi Yoffie, many progressive religious leaders are working to reclaim, to reinvigorate the concept of *tikkun olam* so that it remains pregnant with its religious resonances and retains its connection not just to acts of service but to meaningful social change.

A Vote but Not a Veto: A Progressive Approach to Tradition

All progressive religious traditions must wrestle at some level with finding a balance between adherence to traditional texts and practices on the one hand and adaptation to contemporary understanding and needs on the other. Rabbi Saperstein argued that the central challenge for progressive religion in the twenty-first century is reclaiming the authenticity of progressive approaches to religious tradition.

> There clearly is a bias, not only deeply in American culture but I believe also in the world, to believe that the more fundamentalist people are, the more authentic they are. Even many people who are liberal themselves often deep down inside have a sense of this. Why is it that so much of the money that Chabad—one of the few missionary groupings within the Jewish community—gets for their missionizing activity, comes from Reform Jews, Conservative Jews, and even secular Jews that they often hold in disdain? Why is it that the media defaults to this notion of authenticity and equates "the religious vote" with those who are fundamentalist in our society? This is a very difficult challenge for genuinely religious, theologically liberal believers, especially over the last fifty years, and I think will remain in the twenty-first century a central challenge for progressive religion.[49]

This bias—that only fundamentalist religion is authentic—is often based on fundamentalists' ability (and willingness) to make absolute, black-and-white declarations about truth and to base these declarations on seemingly simple readings of ancient texts. Its continued persistence is also based on a failure of progressive religious leaders to clearly articulate alternative ways of understanding truth and to show how these truths are clearly rooted in the tradition. The leaders I interview here provide just this alternative response, demonstrating, for example, that abandoning a quest for absolute certainty does not mean settling for relativism and that listening for God's voice in contemporary experience is fully compatible with—indeed, it is a prerequisite for—faithfully engaging sacred texts.

A Progressive Approach to Truth: Hearing God's Voice

If, as Rabbi Saperstein argued, the central challenge of progressive Judaism and progressive religion is making the case for its authenticity, a key question is how progressive religious leaders relate ancient texts, beliefs, and practices to contemporary experience and problems. Rabbi Mordecai Kaplan, longtime teacher at the Conservative Jewish Theological Seminary and founder of the Reconstructionist movement, offered a famous aphorism that summed up many of the approaches I heard in the interviews: "The past has a vote but not a veto." In other words, progressive religious leaders seriously engage traditional texts, practices, and beliefs, but they also put them into conversation with contemporary experience and grant that experience real religious authority.

While Orthodox Judaism (which Kaplan left in favor of Reconstructionism) does not fully embrace this sentiment, it is worth noting that Dr. Luchins of the Orthodox Union not only clearly affirmed the human role in textual interpretation but (perhaps somewhat ironically) actually cited a divine mandate against being fundamentalist:

> We're not fundamentalists. We do not take the Bible literally. We're not allowed to. We're forbidden to. We have allegories, we have *midrash*, and Rabbi Joseph Soloveitchik paraphrases Maimonides and channels George Bernard Shaw to say that anyone that accepts *midrash* literally is brainless and anyone who rejects it out of hand is heartless. You can learn it with a teacher, with a tradition, within a *mesorah*. . . . Divine Torah tells me that human beings have to interpret.[50]

Rabbi Jonah Pesner, director of the Just Congregations Program for Reform Judaism, gave a compelling account of a progressive approach to grasping truth:

We should be less worried about truth and more worried about hearing God. God isn't so hung up on truth. I think I hear God's voice and what some might call truth—I know what to do—from the intersection of four places. I read my sacred texts and I take them seriously. And I distill that text through the experience of thousands of years of generations that lived after that text came to us: rabbis and lay people, and Christian and Muslim brothers and sisters who read those texts as well and interpreted them and wrestled with them. And then I mediate that through the third layer, which is my conscience, the voice that I hear from within. And finally, I distill all of those voices, the ancient text, the historical narrative, and my own conscience with the demands of my community. . . . I think the stories of the real lives [people in our community are living] call us to God's will as profoundly as the very ancient scriptures that started this all off. I hear God's voice in a member of our congregation's story about recycling his insulin needles [because he can't afford new ones] in the same way that I hear it in my wife Sarah's cry when she's trying to deliver a child.[51]

Several aspects of these accounts of progressive truth are worth noting. First, consistent with Rabbi Kaplan's call to give the past "a vote but not a veto," both Luchins and Pesner clearly embrace the necessity of human agency in hearing God's voice. Luchins describes the multilayered and creative act of interpretation through *midrash*. Pesner describes a complex dance of discernment that occurs amidst the winds of sacred texts, the great historical chain of interpretation (i.e., the *mesorah*), individual conscience, and communal norms and stories; God's voice, he argues, sometimes comes from unexpected places and is heard from within this whirlwind.

Rabbi Matalon, the charismatic senior rabbi at B'nai Jeshurun in New York, expressed a similar approach to hearing God's voice, noting that "through the give and the take in the dialectic, somehow God's voice is found in there."[52] Matalon also directly addressed a critical difficulty with this admittedly "messy" progressive approach to truth, its inability to have certainty about its conclusions.

God created a world that is messy, and we have to find our way in a world that is messy, and there are no certainties. So I am willing to live with the burden of this messiness, rather than embrace certainties that I know are false, because I know that nobody has the truth. The truth is discovered through hard work—through making mistakes also. Life takes us into lots of dark places, but we have lessons to learn there, and then we trace our steps back. I'm willing to live with this burden and this challenge of searching for the truth in this way, because I think it's the human way. It's the way God created us.[53]

Rabbi Yoffie, among others, noted that humility is perhaps the cardinal virtue of this more complex progressive approach to truth, and that this virtue may also make it challenging for progressives to articulate their positions with commitment and passion:

Religious progressives bring a certain humility to what they do. And does that mean we aren't quite as intense in all ways and quite as exuberant? Perhaps, but truly religious people, I think, don't overstate what they can do, and they don't overstate their own knowledge or certainty about God's will. . . . So maintaining some element of commitment and passion along with humility, that's the great challenge.[54]

Rabbi Marla Feldman, director of the Commission on Social Action for the Union of Reform Judaism, noted that because of this sense of humility, "liberals have had a hard time making their own arguments."[55] Rabbi Saperstein also indicated the contemporary need to recapture a powerful prophetic voice:

We have lost somewhat the deep religious grounding of the social gospel tradition in the Christian community, of the prophetic tradition in the Jewish community. These traditions understood that responding to the call of our religious texts as God's partners in creating a better world is a profoundly religious task. And working to recapture that with a positive robust embrace of our own tradition is I think the central challenge. . . . It's interesting to note that the two progressive religious groups in American society that have not declined over the last two generations are the Unitarian Universalist Churches and the Reform Jewish community. One of the profound reasons is that they've not backed off one iota from their embrace of social justice as a centerpiece of what God calls us to be engaged in.[56]

Although this more complex approach to truth certainly presents some challenges, these leaders are part of a reawakening of an authentic and progressive approach to truth that depends less on propositions and deductions and more on relationships both with God and fellow human beings. As Rabbi Feldman noted, progressive Jewish leaders are rediscovering how to "articulate with the same clarity [as fundamentalists] that there are rights and wrongs, . . . to say, 'I stood at Sinai and let me tell you what God said to me'" in a way that balances humility with clarity and passion.[57]

Being Progressive and Religious

Among the progressive Jewish leaders I interviewed, there was virtual consensus about two themes of significance for contemporary progressive Judaism: (1) the "reawakening" of the connections between religious ritual and study of religious texts on the one hand and work for social justice on the other; and (2) the importance, especially in the context of contemporary American group identity, of reclaiming a Jewish identity while working on social justice issues.

Many of the progressive Jewish leaders I interviewed talked about a growing movement to integrate an emphasis on the study of texts, a vibrant religious practice, and work for social justice. They described a palpable desire among progressive Jews over the last few decades to reclaim the study of sacred texts, ritual practice, and engagement with tradition. Rabbi Yoffie, for example, noted what he called a "religious revival" within the Reform movement:

> There's absolutely no question that there is a religious revival among all segments of American Jewry, . . . absolutely and unquestionably among those who are in the liberal camp. . . . What's very distinctive, noticeable in our ranks is a return to Jewish ritual. . . . In many ways, we are theologically radical; our people are experiencing a revival without identifying with Orthodox Judaism.[58]

Rabbi Sharon Brous talked about "an emergence of a progressive religious ethos" in her growing congregation that is declaring, "We're not giving up our religious lives just because there are a bunch of guys with black hats and long beards who tell us what it means to be Jewish; I'm not going to give up my Judaism because I have a certain set of beliefs that don't match theirs."[59] Likewise, Daniel Sokatch noted a similar broad reclaiming of Jewish tradition among his constituency of progressive Jewish activists who are engaged in community organizing.

> Part of what we try to provide for our community is a sense that these texts, this tradition, and this history are yours, whether you are a shul-going believer or whether you are sort of a Woody Allen–watching, bagel-eating, atheistic cultural Jew. No one has a monopoly on the Talmud. . . . So, our approach has been to say, "Before you go out and stand with the workers in the boycott line, you're going to sit in the park and study."[60]

In addition to this movement to reclaim Jewish tradition and texts for a progressive standpoint, many leaders I interviewed talked about a growing openness among nonreligious progressives to religious people and a corresponding comfort-level among the high number of progressive Jews who are working in progressive organizations to "come out as Jews," reclaiming the religious foundations of their work.

Engaging Sacred Texts

When I asked progressive Jewish leaders to identify particular sacred texts that grounded progressive social action, they often had trouble knowing where to begin because there are so many from which to choose. Rabbi Saperstein explained:

> There is hardly a classic text of Judaism that does not resound with both spiritual meaning and God's call for us to be engaged in creating a better world, the two major themes from my own life. So you can open up almost any story in the Bible—any psalm, any proverb, any of the stories of the prophets—and feel this deep spiritual reso-

nance that speaks across the centuries and embodies this call: that we are capable and called to create a more just and fair world for humanity. The same is true with the classic historical texts. The Talmud, in which the rabbis created one of the first social welfare states in the history of the world, describes a sense of ethics that permeated every aspect of life: the way we ran our businesses, we way we related to each other, the food we ate, the way we treated animals, the way we treated nature, the way we treated non-Jewish communities.[61]

Saperstein pointed especially to the Bible (the Jewish Bible, which consists of three sections: the Torah, the writings, and the prophets) and the Talmud (a collection of rabbinic teachings and commentaries on the Torah). But he also cited an unbroken chain of influential texts extending from the Talmud to the writings of *Sefer Hasidim* in the Middle Ages to the writings of Rabbi Abraham Joshua Heschel in the twentieth century.

Although there were dozens of texts mentioned across the interviews, three additional biblical texts were prominent: Genesis 1, the Exodus story, and Leviticus 19 (in conjunction with Isaiah 58). These texts revolve around three core ideas: the oneness and dignity of all people, the liberation of all people, and the essential connections between holiness and social justice.

Created in the Image of God: The Oneness and Dignity of All People (Genesis 1)

The most prominent theme that progressive Jewish leaders mentioned was the seminal message from the very beginning of the Torah that all human beings are created in the image of God.

> We're all created *b'tzelem elohim*, in the image of God. I think that more than anything is the root value that undergirds almost all social issues. In Jewish parlance, we are literally and figuratively and spiritually in the image of God. All creation and creatures are reflections of God, in all of our diversity and multifaceted nature and in all of our strengths and limitations. The way we live our lives needs to live up to that divine image because we're actually encountering God

through other people. And I think that almost everything comes back to that.[62]

For Rabbi Jennie Rosenn and many others, the truth that all of humanity is created in the image of God is foundational. As Rosenn notes, this belief has implications not just for charity and treatment of individuals but for evaluating and changing social systems and institutions. As Rabbi David Rosenn noted, "One of the things that grounds a Jewish theology of justice is the idea that we are called upon to preserve, protect, and enhance people's inherent dignity in the world, and when you have systems that really put that dignity in danger and threaten that dignity, especially through material degradation, it's very hard [to maintain human dignity]."[63]

Daniel Sokatch also cited a Talmudic text that expounds on an important meaning of the principle of being created in the divine image. Sokatch explained, "The Talmud says that if you destroy a single life, it's as if you've destroyed a universe. . . . Each individual is created in the image of the divine and thus is innately, inherently endowed with unique preciousness, full of potential."[64] This teaching was explicitly tied to the concept of *tikkun olam*, the responsibility to work as partners with God in transforming and healing the world.

Importantly, this teaching about the divine source of all people also has implications for protecting the other part of God's creation, the natural world. This insight also reinforces a broader understanding of *tikkun olam*; that is, "healing the world" means exactly that—working both for social conditions that protect the dignity of human beings and protecting the environment. Rabbi Or Rose explained these connections this way:

> While the teaching of *tzelem elohim* provides us with an essential lesson about the dignity of all human beings, we must also remember that *adam* ("the human being") emerges from and is a part of *adamah* ("the earth"). We cannot create a dichotomy between social justice and environmental activism. This is especially important because more often than not, it is the poor and the disadvantaged that suffer most from environmental degradation."[65]

Rose and many others made the clear connections between the flourishing of people and the flourishing of the earth and remembering the divine origin of each. To recall the mystical understanding of *tikkun olam*, the human task is not only to heal human lives, although this is essential, but to work to repair the cosmos itself, to remove barriers so that "God's presence or God's light can shine through" in each person and in the world as a whole.[66] And as Rabbi Rose reminds us, these are intimately related and mutually reinforcing tasks.

Liberation: The Exodus Story

Another formational text that progressive Jewish leaders cited was the central story of the Exodus from Egypt, which is retold each year during the Passover Seder. Rabbi Pesner described this story as "the one animating, ancient narrative of the Jewish people":

> I don't think it's a surprise that the Jewish community through all of its history has every year retold the story of our liberation from the slavery of Egypt. The Exodus narrative is not just a narrative about freedom, about redemption from some slavery, something terrible—it rather is about the redemption that happens when one enters collectively into a covenant to be a community that acts with values, that acts on a shared story and a love of God. The America that I imagine and the world that I yearn for is a world when we act like a covenantal community with each other, hearing God's will in different ways, but acting together to create that world.
>
> So for Jews, we retell that story every year at the Seder table. . . . Every year we repeat the words: "And you shall see yourself as if you yourself were brought out of Egypt with a mighty hand and an out-stretched arm so that you could be rescued by God to enter into covenant with God." We see ourselves as being part of that sacred master narrative. Our children learn that story from their earliest childhood and see themselves inside of it.[67]

As Pesner notes, one powerful aspect of the *haggadah* (literally, the "telling"; the document containing the order of the *seder*, the ritual Passover meal), is that it calls the participants to see themselves inside the "sacred master narrative" of being liberated from slavery and oppression in Egypt and standing at Sinai. Performing this logic, Pesner seamlessly maps Mount Sinai, the place where the original covenant was received, onto "the America that I imagine and the world that I yearn for," the place where its demands need to be lived out.

Rabbi Yoffie also emphasized the universal message in this particular narrative, which goes to the heart of progressive Judaism:

> We look at this text and we say, "Could there be any more convincing proof that religion is not on the side of established power? That religion is something where the oppressed and the persecuted look to God, and through God's prophets and representatives, by embracing God and following God's direction, liberate themselves from tyrants?"[68]

Here, Rabbi Yoffie locates in sacred text the powerful imperative to continue to work for liberation. The power of this reenacted drama is precisely in its repeated performance. This "animating ancient narrative" of liberation is etched into Jewish consciousness through numerous *seder* meals. As Rabbi Arthur Waskow's story at the beginning of the chapter demonstrates, this master narrative is a tributary that supplies a reservoir of sensitivity to injustice in the world that, at times, forcefully spills over into the very streets.

Holiness and Social Justice (Leviticus 19 / Isaiah 58)

Rabbi David Saperstein noted the prominence of the idea of holiness (*kadosh*) and its essential connection to social justice.

> Perhaps most of all, arguably the great defining chapter of the Hebrew scriptures, of the Christian Old Testament, is Leviticus 19, "You shall be holy because the eternal God is holy." And how does God tell us we're to be like God? By setting aside a corner of the field for the hungry, by removing the stumbling block before the blind, by creating courts of justice, by creating marketplaces that are fair, by observing the Sabbath, by honoring our parents. This is the amalgam of what holiness means. It means not only worshiping in a certain way, but honoring our parents, creating a just and fair world.[69]

This theme of the connection between holiness and social justice was also mentioned by several leaders I interviewed in connection with the message of Isaiah 58, cited by Rabbi Waskow above. For example, Rabbi Jennie Rosenn noted that God declares in Isaiah that ritual fasting without justice is empty:

> What is so powerful about this passage for me is the link between religious practice and the work that we do in the world. It's not enough to mournfully fast in a religious sort of pious ritualistic way. Our inner lives and our outer lives are connected, and the religious life is about what we actually do in the world and what we're called to do in the world—to do justice and respond to poverty and liberate people.[70]

From this perspective, holiness is not a kind of personal piety but a marriage of spirituality and an ethical orientation toward just acts. Moreover, while these acts include personal responsibilities such as removing stumbling blocks before the blind and honoring parents, they also mandate systematic institutional reforms that ensure just courts and marketplaces.

The Power of Religious Practice

One way of understanding religious traditions is to pay attention to the emphasis a particular tradition places on belief on the one hand and practice on the other. The accent in Judaism, especially as compared to Protestant Christianity, the dominant form of religion in America, is clearly on practice. Jack Chomsky, cantor at Congregation Tifereth Israel (Conservative), a leader in the congregation-based community organizing (CBCO) movement, and one of the leaders of the interfaith group "We Believe Ohio" in Columbus, stated this distinction provocatively:

> One of the things that distinguishes Jews from some other religious groups is that we don't really place any premium whatsoever on what you believe. We don't care what you believe. We say, "This is what we do," and from a certain routine of behavior may come a certain kind of belief or orientation in terms of how we approach the world. . . . You don't have to believe that God commanded us to keep kosher in

order for keeping kosher to become a powerful force in your life. Most of our traditions say, "This is what we do, and then we can argue about what we believe," but nobody's going to hell because they don't believe the right thing. I think that's a very Jewish view.[71]

In Judaism, as in most traditions that emphasize practice, ritual is often tied to time, such as the rhythms of the day, the lunar cycle, or the seasons of the year. In his elegant book *The Sabbath*, Rabbi Abraham Joshua Heschel, longtime professor of ethics and mysticism at Jewish Theological Seminary and an iconic civil rights leader, argued that "Judaism is a *religion of time* aiming at the *sanctification of time*." For Judaism, Heschel argued, "the Sabbaths are our great cathedrals," and most Jewish ritual can be understood as "architecture of time."[72] Rabbi Heschel was by far the most frequently cited Jewish figure in my interviews, and his influence on progressive Judaism would be difficult to overstate. The imprint of his understanding of the deep connections between religious practice and social justice was deep and ubiquitous. For Heschel, religious practice was the door through which we entered the holiness of time. In that temporal space, as Heschel described it, "the goal is not to have but to be, not to own but to give, not to control but to share, not to subdue but to be in accord"; there "we care for the seed of eternity planted in the soul."[73]

Reform Rabbi Jennie Rosenn, program officer for Jewish Life and Values at the Nathan Cummings Foundation, described the critical function and the power of ritual: "I think that it's often very, very hard to do what even sometimes we know is right. . . . Religious practice at its best can help cultivate a heart and mind that is able to recognize the moments when you can live out your beliefs."[74] Judaism's emphasis on embodied religious practice aims to transform time into sanctified time and to transpose everyday routines and yearly rhythms into acts with religious significance that have the potential to cultivate a particular consciousness that in turn leads to a life committed to healing the world.

Following the Path: Jewish Law (*Halacha*)

Rabbi Matalon talked about the primacy and power of religious practice and of the work within the progressive Jewish community to "unlock the meanings" of religious practice, including the daily practice of following Jewish law, or *Halacha*.

> We're always looking for the performance of ritual and the observance of Jewish law as a source of meaning and guidance. The Hebrew word for Jewish law is *Halacha*, a beautiful word, and it comes from the word "to go." It's the path that you follow. And as you go, meanings open. As you go, in some way God's presence comes through sometimes. . . . For example, [we have laws about how to treat the bodies of the deceased]. How could you say I'm going to wash this body and treat it carefully, but I don't care what they're doing in jails and prisons around the world, including what this country is doing in terms of mutilating and torturing people in wars that are crazy wars. . . . We don't separate here Jewish practice and prayer and social justice. It's all one. When we're doing social justice, we're observing Jewish law and it's a spiritual discipline, as much as *Shabbat* or the dietary laws. And *Shabbat* and the dietary laws are also a form of social justice.[75]

From Matalon's perspective, Jewish law—which many progressives who value autonomy (literally "self-law") might find problematic because of its seemingly heteronomous nature—is not an imposition but a path that opens to God's presence and leads to social justice. The specifics of religious practice not only connect us spiritually to God, but they sensitize us in concrete ways to broader events beyond ourselves—such as the connections between ritual body washings and the treatment of other bodies in the sanctioning of torture or unjust wars—where we are called to act for the healing and transformation of the world.

Engaging the Dream: *Shabbat*

When I asked about religious practices that ground engagement with progressive politics, the most frequently cited practice was what Rabbi Heschel saw as the cornerstone of Judaism's "great cathedrals" of time—the weekly observance of *Shabbat*, the Jewish Sabbath that runs from Friday sundown to Saturday sundown. In his book *Between God and Man*, Rabbi Heschel described the connection between holiness and *Shabbat*:

One of the most distinguishing words in the Bible is the word *kadosh*, holy; a word which more than any other is representative of the mystery and majesty of the divine. Now what was the first holy object in the history of the world? Was it a mountain? Was it an altar? It is, indeed, a unique occasion at which the distinguished word *kadosh* is used for the first time: in the book of Genesis at the end of the story of creation. How extremely significant is the fact that it is applied to time: "And God blessed the seventh *day* and made it *holy* (Genesis 2:3).[76]

Rabbi Sharon Brous described *Shabbat* as "the central spiritual practice that reinvigorates on a weekly basis the context for spiritual activism."[77] Tapping insights from Heschel and borrowing a phrase from Orthodox Rabbi Yitz Geenberg, Rabbi Brous described the observance of *Shabbat* as a "rhythm of perfection" that engages the dream of how the world should be in order to "lift the line of history" to match that dream:[78]

If we take seriously the core fundamental claims of our tradition that all human beings are created in the image of God and therefore have dignity, it's utterly impossible to live in the world we live in and to see the kind of devastation that we see on the streets on a daily basis, the degradation of humanity around us. So when your core religious teaching teaches you something that the reality of the world completely belies, it becomes [a question of] how you function.

Jewish tradition doesn't say the ideal would be [*Shabbat*] all the time. We say, "Go out and do the work of the world and kind of get your hands dirty; get out there and see what the world looks like, but don't allow yourself to believe that that's any more the reality than the dream is the reality." The dream is the world of human dignity, of infinite worth, of equality, and of uniqueness. That dream is what has sustained our people over the course of thousands of years of degradation.

So engage in the world for six days and then engage in the dream for one day a week, and just allow yourself to be in a place where you can sing and you can dance and you can hold someone you love and you can eat delicious food and you can dream of a world in which human dignity is real and the presence of God is around you. And then allow the inspiration from that experience to push you back into the world with a renewed commitment to go out and lift the line of history so that it matches the dream.[79]

When functioning correctly, this rhythm forces a consciousness about the way the world should be that carries concrete implications. On the one hand, Rabbi Brous noted that the engagement with *Shabbat* inoculates against the all-too-human tendency, especially for those of us who are fairly privileged, toward callousness and indifference in the face of suffering. As Brous provocatively put it, if we really grasp that the world is not supposed to look the way it does, "it's not possible to just go back to your carpools and your stress about your nannies."[80] On the other hand, dwelling in the day that God blessed as holy allows perspective and hope that protects us from despair and reinvigorates us for engagement with the work of transforming and healing the world.

Letting the Leopard Loose: Yom Kippur

In the Jewish cathedral of time, the rhythms of the week are also overlaid onto the rhythms of the year. One of the more intriguing accounts of the power of ritual and practice in Judaism came from Rabbi Arthur Waskow. When I asked him about religious practice, he told me a story:

> Franz Kafka wrote a bunch of *midrash*, a little book called *Parables and Paradoxes*,[81] and one of the tiny stories in there, which has been a kind of guideline to me ever since I discovered it, goes something like this. One day a leopard came stalking into the synagogue, roaring and lashing its tail. Three weeks later, it had become part of the liturgy. So for me, this was a powerful teaching of what is right and wrong about religious tradition—that we are constantly taking the leopard and taming it. So I decided part of my job in life is to untame the leopard whenever I can—whether it's sacred text or prayer or holiday ceremonies or for life cycle events—to look into what was going on for the people who shaped it and why were they drawn by its power, at least at first. And then to ask, "So, how do we let the leopard loose again?"[82]

Rabbi Waskow argued that the real power of liturgy is in both familiarity and disruption, what he called "a dance of mastery and mystery."[83] As the metaphor of the leopard indicates, the beginning of ritual is often a communal response to a powerful, often dangerous, formative event.[84] Over time, however, especially across multiple generations, the power of the ritual wanes along with the memory of its institution; if the ritual is to continue to have meaning, the power of that memory must be "reawakened" or unleashed through a renewed disruptive experience.[85] When I asked for an example of how this worked concretely, Rabbi Waskow told of a story about how he tries to keep the liturgy alive on Yom Kippur, the Day of Atonement and most solemn day of the Jewish High Holidays.

> The rabbis tell us to read the passage from Isaiah 58 on Yom Kipper morning in which Isaiah asks, "What is the fast that I, God, am demanding of you? You think it's to droop your head down like a bulrush and feel good because you're feeling bad because you're fasting? No, that's not the fast. Feed the poor, clothe the naked, bring the hungry and homeless to your own house, and break off the shackles on prisoners. That's the fast." All right. Isaiah seems, from his own description, to have walked into the middle of a crowd that was feeling good because they were feeling bad because they'd been fasting on Yom Kippur. He walks in and yells at them, "On the very day you fast, you lift your fist in violence." Then they're mad at him because he's interrupting the liturgy. And I'm sure I can hear them saying, "What are you doing? We're trying to listen to the Levites singing these beautiful songs. Shut up." So the rabbis figure this is really important for people to get about Yom Kippur. So what are they going to do? They put it to be read every Yom Kippur morning, and it becomes part of the liturgy.[86]

The irony of this story is that the rabbis have ritualized the disruption of ritual. As Isaiah's original radical interruption becomes part of the expected drama, it loses its potency. Rabbi Waskow continued to describe how he attempted to revitalize the liturgy by coupling Isaiah's reading with a disruption of his own, weaving into the traditional Yom Kippur readings contemporary newspaper stories about poverty and injustice: stories about an elderly man freezing to death in downtown Philadelphia and about Palestinian prisoners in Israeli prisons. With a knowing grin, Waskow described his congregation's reaction, "So, the temperature goes up, and the leopard comes out of the cage. And it turns out Isaiah is real, right?"[87]

A *Tzelem Elohim* Agenda

The Jewish religious leaders I interviewed spoke powerfully about the need to recover a progressive religious voice that reclaims a broad, aspirational agenda for inclusion and justice. Simon Greer of Jewish Funds for Justice argued that developing a "we're all created in the image of God agenda" would have far-reaching, profound implications if taken seriously and would be a powerful rallying point for a progressive religious voice. Greer also talked about the need to develop this agenda boldly as "a prophetic calling beyond the winnable issues."[88]

The Needy among You: Human Dignity and the Alleviation of Poverty

The centrality of a commitment to alleviate the conditions of the poor and establish conditions of justice in progressive Judaism by now are obvious. These priorities inhabit "the dream" of *Shabbat*, they fulfill the essence of the obligation to live a holy life, they are the very meaning of *tikkun olam*, they are echoed in the Exodus story of liberation from oppression, and they are central to the commitment to the human dignity of all. I want to highlight, however, how several leaders dealt with a notorious text, Deuteronomy 15:11 ("The poor shall never cease out of the land"), which is often used to dismiss strong proposals to eliminate poverty. Rabbi Gutow and Rabbi Jacobs among others explicitly discussed this text.

> God said something really interesting in Deuteronomy 15. God says [in verse 4], "There shall be no needy amongst you" [and then says in verse 8], "But when you find a needy person, treat them with an open heart and don't be haughty." And then [in verse 11], and it's always God talking: "There shall always be needy among you." God tells us

both what the Messianic world is, which is there shall be no needy, and then God tells us that we always are going to have to keep acting in this world.[89]

With echoes of the rhythms of *Shabbat*, where our task is to see within the architecture of time both "the dream" and the reality, the seemingly contradictory text of Deuteronomy first paints a portrait of what should be and then gives instructions about how to act in this world to move toward that vision. Far from serving as a text of complacency, the declaration that "there shall always be needy among you" is actually a call to ongoing action to "lift the line of history until it matches the dream."[90]

Lesbian, Gay, Bisexual, and Transgender (LGBT) Issues: The Implications of Being Created in God's Image

Although LGBT issues have been very divisive in the wider society and certainly have provided flashpoints of conflict within the Jewish community, particularly in the Orthodox and Conservative branches of Judaism, American Judaism as a whole is arriving at fairly open and affirming positions regarding gay, lesbian, bisexual, and transgender people. For example, in December 2006, after many years of struggle and debate, the Conservative denomination officially ended its ban on gay and lesbian rabbis and on same-sex unions.[91] Shortly thereafter, in March 2007, Jewish Theological Seminary, the flagship seminary of Conservative Judaism, began to accept openly gay and lesbian candidates into its rabbinical and cantorial schools.[92] Currently, Orthodox Judaism is the only branch of Judaism that opposes gay and lesbian rabbis and same-sex unions.

The least accommodating position among the leaders I interviewed on the role of LGBT persons was articulated, not surprisingly, by Dr. David Luchins of the Orthodox Union:

I'm not going to suggest that I think the Torah's rules on homosexuality can be changed one iota. They can't. But the fact that the Torah forbids certain behavior does not mean we should demonize, delegitimize, or write out of our religion or our humanity those who may fall short, as we all fall short in so many areas. . . . In the area of kindness to every human being, Jew and Gentile, white and black, gay and straight, even Republicans are created in the image of God.[93]

Even while upholding this strict interpretation of the Torah, however, Luchins affirmed that all are created in the image of God, and he noted that the Orthodox community is divided about how this *religious* conviction connects to *public policy* issues such as civil unions or marriage equality. He also affirmed the obligation to welcome all people in synagogues, even if homosexual activity is understood as sin.

Most of the leaders I interviewed, however, were fully supportive of LGBT equality. B'nai Jeshurun, a historically Conservative synagogue founded in 1825 on Manhattan's Upper West Side, has a long-standing record of not only being a welcoming congregation to gays and lesbians but of advocating as a congregation for LGBT rights. When I was there, on the walls of their temple offices there was an award from "AIDS Walk New York," and one of the three fliers on the "social action" bulletin board was a flier advocating for marriage equality headlined, "Why do New York same-sex couples want access to marriage?" In the interview, Rabbi Matalon noted that the congregation's current advocacy on LGBT issues was grounded in decisions the congregation made in the 1980s in response to the ostracization of people with HIV/AIDS:

> We were the first synagogue to start a spiritual program for people with AIDS, and we started getting to this program a large number of gay men, particularly, in many cases with their lovers, parents, and siblings. It was extremely moving, extremely moving. It was one of the most moving things we ever did here. Our message was, "We don't care what the Conservative movement says; you're welcome here. This is a synagogue that will welcome you and embrace you."[94]

Ultimately, Rabbi Matalon noted that his congregation's close, weekly relationships with gay and lesbian couples in the congregation provided the hermeneutical key to wrestling with the denomination and with the Torah. He summed up his approach as follows: "I am not of the school of playing endless games with the texts. At some point, you've got to make a choice and you've got to say, 'My sense of what God demands of me is this.'"[95]

Rabbi Brous also talked about the importance of contemporary understandings of humanity and sexuality along with the "core principle of human dignity" as a basis for affirming full inclusion for LGBT people in the community in spite of the texts condemning homosexual behavior, such as Leviticus 18.

> The text [Leviticus 18] isn't so straightforward, because the text that tells us that a man should not lie with a man, that it's "an abomination," is the same text that tells us that all human beings are created in the image of God. And we understand that to mean that all people have the capacity to love and be loved. So what does it mean if a person who is born in the image of God comes into the world a certain way? If that text is to remain relevant, we need to read it through new eyes. . . . Once we've realized that for most people homosexuality is not a choice, we have an obligation to make sure that they're not discriminated against, that they're given a context to engage in loving and dignified relationships. That's our obligation now as today's religious leaders.[96]

When I asked Rabbi Or Rose about dealing with these difficult texts, he told a story from the teaching of a nineteenth-century Polish Hasidic sage, Rabbi Menachem Mendel of Kotsk:

> When asked by his father why he joined the relatively new and still controversial mystical movement of Hasidism, young Menachem Mendel quoted the opening words of the *amidah* (the "standing") prayer: "Our God and the God of our ancestors. . . ." "Notice," said Menachem Mendel to his father, "that the words 'our God' precede the phrase 'the God of our ancestors.'"
>
> In other words, in each generation, people must work to renew their relationship with God based on their understanding of the spiritual and ethical demands of the hour. . . . We must seek to live on what my teacher, Rabbi Zalman Schachter-Shalomi calls "the growing edge" of life. The "growing edge" is different from "the cutting edge." We do not ignore the past, but we also do not let it determine the present or the future.[97]

This story and the approach I heard echoed by many on this issue reflected the perspective of giving tradition "a vote but not a veto." This approach allows texts to be read "through new eyes" that are refocused by the experience of gay and straight members of the congregation singing, dancing, praying, and eating together as a community. That experience, coupled with a commitment to uphold the human dignity of everyone, provides a new perspective on ancient texts. Engaging the Torah as "a living, breathing document" provides an authentic way to move beyond simply accepting what previous generations have declared the tradition or the text to say. Following this Jewish way, one can discern God's voice saying something new on the growing edge of Judaism in a way, for example, that says to all people, including LGBT people, "we will welcome you and embrace you."

Living the Dream:
New Initiatives by Progressive Jews

The "image of God" agenda is not only something for which progressive Jewish leaders are finding new language and ritual engagement; they are also, as Rabbi Heschel famously said, learning to "pray with their feet" by organizing for justice at the grassroots level. Ruth Messinger, a popular speaker at rabbinical schools, noted that she usually has one central message when she addresses future religious leaders:

> "We need prophets for our time." And then I say, "Actually on reflection, the prophets were totally miserable people; nobody listened to them. So we need something better than prophets. We need builders of activist, progressive religious communities who do a better job than the prophets at organizing."[98]

There is a palpable new energy among progressive Jewish leaders who are being both prophets and organizers. Two prominent examples that represent different types of organizing will help illustrate the current ferment. First, Rabbi Michael Lerner's Network of Spiritual Progressives has organized progressive Jews and others across the country with a para-denominational model grounded on a "politics of meaning" that calls for "a new bottom line."[99] Second, there is a mushrooming number of local congregations across all of the major Jewish denominations that are engaging in Congregation-Based Community Organizing (CBCO), a model of organizing members through their existing religious communities to engage in work not just for charity but for social justice. These movements have two things in common: they are interfaith, and they are initiatives that did not originate within the denominational hierarchies.

The Network of Spiritual Progressives (NSP)

Along with Rev. Jim Wallis of Sojourners, Rabbi Michael Lerner is one of the few contemporary progressive religious leaders with broad name recognition.[100] Like Wallis, Lerner has built his own movement on the foundation of decades of progressive activism as a religious leader, a progressive religious magazine that serves as a platform for disseminating ideas, and most recently a promotional/organizing tour based on a best-selling book opposing the over-reaching of the religious right in American politics.

One distinguishing attribute of Lerner's movement is that it is rooted in but reaches beyond Judaism. *Tikkun* magazine, for example, describes itself as a magazine "born of the Jewish Tradition but with a political perspective that attracts a far wider readership."[101] NSP is even more explicitly multireligious in its leadership; its three cochairs are Rabbi Lerner, Sister Joan Chittister, a Benedictine nun and longtime social justice advocate, and Dr. Cornel West, a well-known African American public intellectual and professor of religion at Princeton University.

Between the magazine, its companion website, and the local NSP local chapters, *Tikkun*/NSP has an impressive reach. In 2007, *Tikkun* had a circulation of 18,000 and an audience of 70,000; the magazine's website, www.tikkun.org, has 45,000 unique views per month.[102] NSP is a loose network of locally organized chapters in over one hundred cities in thirty states. Reflecting Rabbi Lerner's Berkeley-based headquarters, the NSP base of support is anchored on the West Coast, with nearly one-third of the chapters located in California.[103]

The central function of the local chapters is to build a local community of support and to engage in consciousness-raising acts such as taking part in "rallies, protests, demonstrations, or advocacy campaigns" with the caveat that "they do so in such a way that they raise consciousness among participants and fellow coalition members about the need to take into account spiritual needs as well as economic needs."[104] These networks are organized around four key goals developed in Rabbi Lerner's book:

1. Foster a new bottom line of love, generosity and ecological sensitivity in our economy, education, media, and government.
2. Foster a new global consciousness and solidarity.
3. Promote awe, radical amazement, gratitude and developing an inner spiritual life.
4. Challenge the misuse of God and religion by the religious right and religio-phobia on the left.[105]

The most concrete NSP calls to action are in the form of supporting two statements that are international in scope, a call for a "Global Marshall Plan" and a call for "an ethical way to end the war in Iraq," which had over 2,700 signatures in mid-November 2007. The "Global Marshall Plan" adopts "a 'strategy of generosity' to replace the 'strategy of domination' that currently informs our foreign policy" and argues that the only path forward to "a safe, sustainable, compassionate world" is "working together as a community of nations to eliminate poverty and solve the environmental crisis that threatens the existence of life on the planet."[106]

One of the most powerful aspects of Lerner's movement is a strong "spiritual critique of America" that results in a call to long-term political change, consistent with Greer's call above to move beyond short-term "winnable" issues.

> So we as a Network of Spiritual Progressives say, "What is being real-istic?" That's idolatry in a religious tradition. Because to be a spiritual person is to reject being realistic and instead to connect our vision to the transformative power of the universe. So in short, we say, "Screw realism." When I speak to younger people, I say, "Don't be realistic. Reject realism. Go for your highest ideals." When you do that, you will find that what is realistic changes dramatically. . . . This is what

I mean by God, that God is that force that makes possible this trans-formation. So we've seen right in front of our eyes [with the women's movement and the civil rights movement] the manifestation of God's presence in the universe through human beings struggling for unre-alistic goals and having an incredibly transformative impact. And I believe it will soon be true within the next several decades for those of us who want to see a new bottom line. The consciousness that our well-being depends on the well-being of every other person on this planet and on the well-being of the planet itself is more realistic than any of the programs put forward by the political forces out there today. And it will eventually triumph because it has to, because there is no alternative but the destruction of the planet and destruction of human life.[107]

Rabbi Lerner and the Network of Spiritual Progressives, then, are building a network that is committed to a new "spiritual politics" that calls us to our highest ideals, with faith that there is a force in the uni-verse to help effect that change, even if it seems in the present light of day unrealistic. This is not merely unreflective idealism, however. Rabbi Lerner notes that the women's movement and the civil rights movement both succeeded in lifting barriers that many thought impossible; more-over, even if it seems unrealistic in some sense, there is a necessity to it, since our current trajectory threatens not only our own flourishing but the very future of the planet. Lerner's objectives are measured not in short-term political gains but in changing the nature of the conversation over the next few decades.

Congregation-Based Community Organizing

A fall 2007 article in *The Nation*, titled simply "Progressive Jews Organize," featured what it called "a new wave of Jewish activists" who are leading a burgeoning nationwide movement to involve Jews in direct community organizing.[108] The most prominent model for this organizing is called "congregation-based community organizing" (CBCO). This model is used by about two hundred local community organizing groups of various kinds, which are in turn affiliated with four major national networks: the Industrial Areas Foundation (IAF), the Gameliel Foundation, the Direct Action and Research Training Center (DART), and the Pacific Institute for Community Organizing (PICO).[109] As the article notes, although the father of community organizing, Saul Alinsky, was Jewish, the model he began in Chicago in the 1930s primarily engaged Christian congregations, with synagogues playing marginal, mostly indirect supporting roles.[110] The *Nation* article, however, described the shifting landscape:

> But this picture is beginning to change. A growing number of rabbis and their congregations are no longer satisfied with the charity approach. A new wave of Jewish activists, from synagogues and other groups, seeks to challenge (and learn from) the rise of the religious right. They want to renew the Jewish ethic of *tikkun olam*—healing the world from social and economic injustice.[111]

The article notes the mushrooming growth in Jewish congregations' involvement with CBCO. The movement began less than a decade ago, in the late 1990s, and by 2000 there were twenty synagogues involved in these interfaith local activists groups. At the time of this writing in late 2007, there are more than one hundred synagogues involved, and the numbers are growing steadily.[112]

Under Simon Greer's leadership, Jewish Funds for Justice (JFSJ) has played a catalyzing role in helping this movement take root in the Jewish community. JFSJ brought together more than three hundred leaders at a conference to discuss and attend workshops on CBCO. JFSJ has also formed a partnership with four rabbinical schools—one each from Reform, Conservative, Orthodox, and Reconstructionist denominations—to allow students to receive academic credit for a course on community organizing.

Although most of the initial organization and affiliation has taken place at the local level, the Reform movement, the largest Jewish denomination, has taken notice and created a Just Congregations initiative to officially promote the CBCO model among Reform congregations. They tapped Rabbi Jonah Pesner, formerly associate rabbi at Temple Israel in Boston, a synagogue heavily involved in CBCO, as the founding director. Rabbi Pesner talked passionately about his experience at Temple Israel with the Greater Boston Interfaith Organization (GBIO), an affiliate of IAF:

My rabbinate was transformed by my work in the GBIO, which brought together more than fifty religious institutions: churches, synagogues, and some other institutions, a couple of labor unions and other nonprofits, to build power in Massachusetts to make change. We create relationships across lines of race, class, and faith, and we listen to hear in each other's lives concerns that we share about how the world is broken and how we need to fix it. Our signature victory was passing health reform in Massachusetts last year, which guarantees that just about every member of the Commonwealth will receive affordable quality health care.[113]

Pesner talked about the intense experience bringing a diverse group of people together with "listening campaigns" that help diverse congregations think together across lines of religion, race, and class about "what we need together," especially around struggles to have access to adequate health care. This foundation of shared stories has the potential to move beyond the model of "coalition" to "community," where diverse groups such as progressive Jews, black churches, and white Evangelicals are not talking past one another. Pesner passionately summarized his vision, "I hunger for an America where we are actually in relationship with each other, because then we have to hold each other accountable, and we have to work through stuff, and figure out what kind of America do we believe in together."[114]

When talking with Pesner, I was struck by the intensity and the ambitious potential he sees for a movement that clearly has momentum.

I realized how powerful and effective my synagogue could be in living out its deeply held belief that in the words of the prophet Micah, "We are to do justice, love mercy, and walk humbly with God." CBCO, which teaches folks in churches and synagogues and mosques how to build relationships with each other and then act powerfully together, can give us the tools to actually transform the Reform Jewish movement and to partner with other religious denominations to build power at the local level, one municipality at a time, one town at a time, one city at a time, to bring the churches and the synagogues and the mosques together to act powerfully for justice.[115]

Conclusion: A Progressive Jewish Movement?

There are clearly other signs of a new progressive movement afoot in Judaism. As Leonard Fein quipped, "I think the old line, 'Save your Confederate money, the South will rise again,' applies to Jewish liberalism. I think we are on the ascent."[116] Rabbi Sharon Brous concluded my interview with her by describing the emerging "progressive religious ethos" she sees not only in the Jewish community but in the Christian and Muslim community as well.

> I do believe that there is an emerging progressive religious ethos in Jewish and Christian and also segments of Muslim America—a fantastically, fabulously interesting array of people who are coming together. . . . There's this kickback happening right now. People are saying, "Wait a minute, I'm a religious observant Jew, and I am fighting to the death for immigration because that's what my Jewish life means to me; and I have a prayer life, and I can study Talmud, and all of that it deepens my belief in the unfairness of this system." There really is a progressive religious movement right now. What we're trying to do at IKAR with our three hundred families is the same thing that Ed Bacon [at All Saints Church in Pasadena] is doing with his three thousand families, and it's the same thing that BJ [B'nai Jeshurun in New York] is doing with their several thousand families. The voices aren't as strong, and we're not talking to each other as well, and we're not as organized as the conservatives are, but there is this emergence of a movement right now. If there ever is going to be something that's going to turn the course of our history, I believe it will be this group and this trend.[117]

Nearly all of the leaders I interviewed shared this sense of new energy, both in terms of a "religious revival" of reengagement with sacred texts and ritual and in terms of the emerging new forms of community organizing for social change. As Daniel Sokatch noted, before Jewish activists are standing with hotel workers, they are "studying Talmud in the park." Likewise, inside a growing number of congregations, members are taking their experience of *Shabbat*, the rhythms of the Jewish year, and engagement with sacred texts beyond the typical social action committee and beyond the walls of the synagogue into the streets.

In addition to the institutional energy and interconnectedness, there is an impressive intellectual coherency to the movement, captured for example in the recent, powerful collection of essays by progressive Jewish voices (many featured in this chapter) entitled *Righteous Indignation: A Jewish Call for Justice*.[118] There is perhaps room to disagree about whether this new ferment constitutes a full-blown movement. However, Rabbi Or Rose noted that there is no doubt that it constitutes an emerging *hevre* ("fellowship") that is embracing the full meaning of *tikkun olam* and changing not only the face of Judaism but also "the course of our history," the very face of American public life.[119]

CHAPTER 2

More Truth Breaking Out
How Progressive Christians Are Seeking the Reign of God on Earth

Introduction:
A Peek through the Window of Truth

"I'm going to crank up the car. You get in and stay warm while I clear off the snow." This was my introduction to the calm but intense seventy-seven-year-old Rev. Dr. James A. Forbes Jr., longtime senior minister at the historic Riverside Church in New York City and internationally recognized preacher. Waving away my repeated objections with a flourish of a small tool that was so clearly inadequate to the task that it struck me as comical, Rev. Forbes physically ushered me into his car, insisting that his Southern upbringing would not abide a guest—even one exactly half his age—scraping snow. So there I sat on this cold mid-March day, toasty warm, taking in the absurdity of watching this tall, impeccably dressed, graying African American man—one of *Newsweek* magazine's twelve most effective preachers in the English-speaking world, a person who gave a major address at the 2004 Democratic National Convention prior to Senator Barack Obama—clear the snow that obstructed the visibility of the front windshield.

As I sat there struggling with my discomfort with this display of hospitality, I realized I should not have been so surprised by this scene. This simple act was consistent with an ethic of servant leadership that Rev. Forbes has modeled throughout his career as pastor, scholar, community leader, and advisor to national and international leaders. Rev. Forbes has also been accustomed to dealing out surprises and breaking stereotypes. He served not only as the first African American but as the first Pentecostal minister to occupy the senior minister's role at the prestigious Riverside Church. This scene was also indicative of Dr. Forbes' unflagging energy. In addition to his duties at Riverside, Dr. Forbes keynoted most of the 2004 "Let Justice Roll" tour sponsored by the National Council of Churches in fifteen cities across the nation. At age seventy-seven, Dr. Forbes is "retiring" from his post at Riverside Church to start the Healing of the Nations Foundation, an organization designed to leverage Dr. Forbes' reputation and leadership to build a movement that will "help promote the spiritual revitalization of our country."[1]

Upon reflection, it occurred to me that Dr. Forbes' act of cleaning the snow from the windshield also held a metaphorical meaning. One of the most prominent themes expressed among the forty-one progressive Christian leaders I interviewed was a sense of humility about what we can accurately see as we clear—to the best of our ability but always with inadequate tools—the obstructions to seeing the truth clearly. Rev. Forbes summarized his approach to truth this way:

> Now *God* knows the truth, but we human beings, because of the nature of our perception, we get angles of things. So we cannot make the presumption that heartfelt convictions about something means that we finally got it. There's a humility that more truth can break out, but also that all the different people who are in the world are accessing [truth] as their limited perceiving makes possible. If God said, "So you want to know the truth? Let me give you the truth," it would blow our minds. What we get is a peek through the window of truth. We are not the receivers of the truth just because we hold a Bible in our hands. . . . Anybody who thinks that serving God allows them the gift of simplicity needs to get to know God a little bit better. And I think a liberal believes that to be invited into the mechanisms of relativity is God's inviting us into the complexity of the way God sees the world.[2]

Dr. Forbes reminds us that the best that limited human beings can hope for is "a peek through the window of truth." No amount of conjured certainty can change the fact that our vision always occurs at an angle, refracted in ways for which we cannot fully account. Even holding a reliable tool such as the Bible in our hands does not allow us to dislodge the distortions sufficiently to claim that we are in complete possession of the truth. Rather, our partial vision is an invitation into a dynamic relationship with both God and other people who are also using partial perspectives and their own dynamic relationships with God in order to grasp "the complexity of the way God sees the world."

American Christianity: An Overview

Christianity dominates the American religious landscape, with nearly eight in ten Americans identifying with some form of Christianity.[3] Unlike Judaism, Islam, or Buddhism, where one can count on one hand the major subgroups that constitute the religion, Christianity in America is mind-bogglingly complex. In addition to the Roman Catholic Church, which accounts for approximately one-fourth of the general population, sociologists regularly catalogue well over 150 different Protestant denominations, which make up fully half of the general population.[4] Although these groups are tied together by the Christian Bible (although even this commonality is not absolute—Catholics and Protestants use slightly different versions) and a shared history, the differences between some of these groups are so great that an anthropologist from Mars might categorize the various denominational families as different religions. In order to make the analysis manageable, I concentrate here primarily on the two largest Christian families, Roman Catholicism and the Protestant denominations; where especially relevant, I will distinguish between the main Protestant subgroups: white evangelicals, mainline Protestants, and black Protestants.[5]

Basic Christian Subgroups: A Primer

While a full description of Christian denominational diversity is beyond my purposes, a few introductory comments may help illuminate the basic

TABLE 2.1 American religious affiliation

AFFILIATION	POPULATION %
CHRISTIAN (ALL)	78.4
Protestant (all)	51.3
White Evangelicals	26.3
Mainline Protestants	18.1
Black Protestants	6.9
Roman Catholic	23.9
Mormon	1.7
Orthodox	0.6
NON-CHRISTIAN	
Other Religions	4.7
Unaffiliated	16.1
Total	*100.0*

Source: Pew Forum on Religion and Public Life, "The U.S. Religious Landscape Survey," 2008; religions.pewforum.org/reports.

frames that shape the worldviews and imaginative infrastructure between the two major divisions of Christians, Catholics and Protestants.

Sociologist Andrew Greeley has usefully described the Catholic religious imagination as "sacramental":

> Catholics live in an enchanted world, a world of statues and holy water, stained glass and votive candles, saints and religious medals, rosary beads and holy pictures. But these Catholic paraphernalia are merely hints of a deeper and more pervasive religious sensibility which inclines Catholics to see the Holy lurking in creation. As Catholics, we find our houses and our world haunted by a sense that the objects, events, and persons of daily life are revelations of grace.[6]

Sr. Joan Chittister echoed these sentiments in her own description of the "smells and bells" of Catholicism, a common shorthand that captures this Catholic sense of God lurking in tangible elements of embodied experience.[7] One other major Catholic distinction is the strong emphasis on community, an attribute that can be seen in such disparate cultural expressions as Martin Scorsese films such as *Mean Streets* and the tradition of Catholic social teaching, a long tradition of papal encyclicals that hold up the idea of the common good, a holistic vision of human flourishing within community.[8] As a result, Catholicism has preserved a strong social conscience, with an emphasis on reforming social institutions and protecting the integrity of local communities.

While the Protestant tradition is not devoid of these sensibilities, by and large the Protestant imagination is less "enchanted" than the Catholic.[9] The roots of the emergence of a distinctively Protestant branch of Christianity in the sixteenth century found nourishment in a variety of sources, but at least one component of the break was the objection that the Catholic sacramental imagination had not sufficiently guarded against superstition among the common people of Europe and that the community or church had been interposed artificially between God and human beings.

As a result, the Protestant imagination downplayed metaphorical ways of talking about God that brought God too near or made God too familiar. For example, marriage, with its metaphorical overlay of erotic and divine love, never became a sacrament in Protestant theology; the belief in the actual presence of the body and blood of Christ in the Eucharist was transformed in Protestantism into a rational symbol and memorial. Protestantism also rejected a notion of an individual beholden to the official church community and rituals, and through its emphasis on individual salvation, embraced and participated in the emergence of the Enlightenment notion of the autonomous individual.[10] As a result, Protestantism has emphasized individual rights and liberties, such as human rights and freedom of conscience, which serve as the foundation of the democratic cornerstone of separation of church and state.

As David Tracy rightly points out in *The Analogical Imagination*, the Protestant and Catholic imaginations each contain valid Christian sensibilities; moreover, they need each other and are mutually correcting.[11] If the Catholic imagination errs toward superstition and stifling of individuals, the Protestant imagination errs toward stripping the world of the divine presence and sacrificing communal well-being to individual success (usually of the privileged few). The progressive Catholic and Protestant leaders featured in this chapter demonstrate that a productive cross-fertilization between these two sensibilities is occurring.

The Restructuring of American Christianity

American Christianity was in considerable flux during the twentieth century, especially following World War II. In the early twentieth century, ideological fault lines mostly ran *between* Christian denominations, and each denomination had fairly high boundaries. This was especially true between Catholics and Protestants. For example, Sr. Joan Chittister talked about the strong formative impact that being the child of a "mixed marriage" (e.g., a Catholic mother and a Presbyterian father), especially the strong objections from both sides of her extended family, had on her own spirituality.[12] It is a sign of the times that talking about a Catholic-Presbyterian wedding as a "mixed marriage" would have a strange ring in most circles today.

Leading sociologist Robert Wuthnow has documented this "declining significance of denominationalism" since World War II.[13] Christian denominations have been becoming more homogeneous due to intermarriage, mobility, and education; this homogenization has in turn led to unprecedented denominational switching as interdenominational barriers have decreased. During this same period, American civil society saw the rise of pan-denominational special purpose groups (SPGs) that served as an interface between an expanding state bureaucracy and the denominations. These SPGs, as the name implies, formed around narrow issue agendas and thus tended to cluster around ideological extremes. With the historic tensions *between* Christian denominations eroding, these SPGs served as a gravitational force, stretching denominations from within between liberal and conservative poles, largely along class and especially educational lines.

As a result of these trends, knowing a person's denominational affiliation in today's religious market is less important than knowing, for example, what SPG mailing list he or she is on or his or her educational background. Conservative Catholics who are members of National Right to Life, the national anti-abortion group, may feel more kinship with Presbyterian members of National Right to Life than with their fellow Catholics sitting on the other end of the same pew who are members of Pax Christi, a Catholic antiwar group. The result, as Wuthnow provocatively summarized it, is that American Christianity has developed two increasingly divergent civic orientations, each claiming parts of the promise of America: a conservative one centered on the phrase "one nation under God" and a liberal or progressive one centered on the phrase "with liberty and justice for all."[14]

Finding Progressive Christians

The central implication of this intra-denominational polarization, as I noted in the introduction, is that progressive Christians are scattered across the denominational spectrum. As table 2.2 shows, Christians as a whole are split evenly in their support for Democrats and Republicans, and in terms of political ideology, nearly half of Christians (48 percent) consider themselves political moderates. Among the half of Christians who lean ideologically to one side or the other, political conservatives outnumber political liberals nearly two to one (35 percent to 16 percent). The high number of conservatives is disproportionately due to white evangelicals, who make up a quarter of the general population and who are overwhelmingly conservative (57 percent).[15]

The internal polarization within denominations is also evident on purely religious measures, such as the composite measure of "religious orientation" developed by Dr. John Green, senior fellow at the Pew Forum on Religion and

TABLE 2.2 Vote and political ideology by Christian denominational families

	2006 HOUSE VOTE		POLITICAL IDEOLOGY		
	DEM	REP	LIB	MOD	CONS
Black Protestant	90	8	28	49	23
Catholic	54	44	17	56	27
White Mainline	47	50	19	54	27
White Evangelical	26	71	8	36	57
All Christians	*47*	*50*	*16*	*48*	*35*
General Population	*52*	*45*	*21*	*47*	*31*

Source: National Election Pool Exit Poll, 2006.

Public Life.[16] Using five items of belief and practice, this measure sorts respondents into three groups: religious traditionalists who, for example, attend religious services weekly and have more literalistic approaches to the Bible; religious centrists who attend services monthly and have less literalistic understandings of the Bible; and religious modernists who attend services once in a while and have more critical and fluid understandings of the Bible. This analysis reveals that the majority of Christians are religious centrists. While there are still more Christian traditionalists (26 percent) than Christian modernists (20 percent), these groups are actually fairly balanced, a fact that is often lost because of the disproportional public presence that more-conservative Christian groups have been able to garner in the last few decades.[17]

The upshot of this analysis is that with the possible exceptions of black Protestants (who are progressive on most political issues and vote overwhelmingly for Democratic candidates) and white evangelicals (who are conservative on most political issues and vote overwhelmingly for Republican candidates), it is difficult to find an identifiable Christian denominational family that aligns solidly on one side of the ideological spectrum. And even in those cases, the generalizations break down quickly. Black Protestants have been historically conservative on many so-called cultural issues such as gay and lesbian issues, and white evangelicals are becoming more progressive on issues like the environment and poverty and are showing signs, especially among younger evangelicals, of loosening their allegiance to a single political party.[18] While progressive Christians have been outmaneuvered, outnetworked, and outspent in the public arena, new institutions are forming

TABLE 2.3 Religious orientation by Christian denominational families

	Traditionalist	Centrist	Modernist
Black Protestant	34	56	10
Catholic	11	64	25
White Mainline	15	54	31
White Evangelical	44	46	11
All Christians	*26*	*55*	*20*
General Population	*22*	*50*	*18*

Source: Robert P. Jones, The American Values Survey (Washington, DC: Center for American Values in Public Life, People for the American Way Foundation, 2006).

connective tissue between the progressive Christians spread across the denominational landscape, and they are beginning to find a collective voice.

In the introduction to this book, I noted the illuminating Barna study, *Unchristian: What a New Generation Really Thinks About Christianity . . . And Why it Matters*, which showed the dim view a majority of young Americans have of Christianity. These youth, who have come of age during the reign of the Christian right, saw Christianity as antigay, judgmental, and hypocritical.[19] The progressive Christian leaders I interviewed provide a hopeful antidote to the stark findings. Among these leaders, there was a distinct absence of the bombastic, harsh pronouncements against other groups that so many of the young Americans in the Barna study associated with contemporary Christianity. While there was a range of opinion on the complex issue of homosexuality, not a single one of the forty-one leaders I interviewed could be classified as antihomosexual. None of these leaders are waving the banner for banning same-sex marriage or excluding gay and lesbian people from protection against discrimination in the workplace. And many of these leaders are explicitly working for full inclusion and rights for LGBT persons both in the church and society.

Rather than championing defensive and negative causes, the progressive Christian leaders I interviewed offer a different voice. These leaders talked about the dangerous temptation of American empire and the challenge of working for the "reign of God" on earth—a vision not of Christian domination but of Christian service to a broken world in need of healing. They talked of a relational and humble approach to truth that makes room for the idea that God is still speaking. They described the power of Christian practices such as an open table theology that includes all, and they laid out a common good agenda that flows from a commitment to seeing the image of God in everyone. These voices offer a different image of Christianity, one that is sorely needed to correct the tattered public image that three decades of narrow politicization has created.

The Idolatry of Empire:
The Responsibilities of a Majority Religion

The Christian leaders I interviewed were very aware of their special responsibilities as members of the majority religion in the most powerful country in the world at a time when America has increasingly imperialistic ambitions. These leaders expressed a clear love for the best of American ideals, along with a sharp critique of American excesses and hubris. I interviewed Rev. Jim Wallis, evangelical CEO of Sojourners/Call to Renewal, on September 11, 2007, the sixth anniversary of the terrorist attacks in New York, Pennsylvania, and Washington, D.C. He spoke powerfully about the dangerous temptation that nationalism presents to authentic faith and about the particular effect of September 11 on America and American Christianity.

> Nationalism is a lethal disease for Christians. It destroys Christians' faith. . . . At the recent World Vision conference in Singapore I said to a crowd of five hundred evangelical Christians that we are to be Christians first and members of our tribes second or third or fourth or fifth. No Christian in the world could dispute that theological affirmation. Yet if it ever became true, it would transform American church life and politics, utterly transform our lives. . . . So I'm in favor of keeping an American flag in the churches because it tells the [lamentable] truth, that we are Americans first and Christians second, third, fourth, or fifth. . . . We need to repent of American nationalism.
>
> I love this country. I love the landscapes. I love the beauty of it. I love so much of the culture and the history. And to love and serve the place where you have been planted, and to follow Jeremiah in seeking the welfare of the city you're in because in its welfare will you find your own, that's a good thing. I don't hate America like some people on the left seem to. But nationalism, the idea of America as the indispensable nation, which the Democrats and Republicans agree to, is heresy.[20]

For Wallis, nationalism is a lethal disease that threatens to unmake authentic Christian faith. Its "pretentious claims and demands for ultimate allegiances" are a direct affront to Christians, who owe this ultimate loyalty only to God.

Dr. Rosemary Radford Ruether, groundbreaking Catholic feminist theologian, echoed this critique of empire, noting the growing body of biblical scholarship and theologically based social critiques coming from the developing world against American unilateralism and militarism.[21] As

Ruether bluntly put it, "You cannot read pro-empire out of the Bible. You can't read support for the wealthy out of the Bible. It's not there."[22] Like Wallis, Ruether also noted that there was no inherent conflict between social critique and love of country. "Patriotism" and authentic loyalty, she declared, entail criticizing "the follies, the oppressiveness, the mistakes of your country and your church. . . . Any serious concern for a better America and better world has to grapple with the way the national security state promotes continual patterns of violence."[23]

Along with Ruether and others, Wallis also noted that September 11 exposed another kind of idolatry to which white, middle-class American Christians were especially prone: the worship of a government that will use any means necessary to guarantee our "illusion of invulnerability."

> Today is the day: 9/11. It was a teachable moment. We could've joined the rest of the world in its vulnerability. They know vulnerability in Sarajevo, in Cape Town, in San Salvador, in Tel Aviv. They know how random violence can come from anywhere at any moment and take your loved ones, and you can't stop it. That's what it means to be human, to be vulnerable. Christians trust God in the midst of their vulnerability. We have this illusion of invulnerability that got shattered on 9/11. And so the government says, "I'll protect you. I will erase your vulnerability with a war on terrorism." That's idolatry. We could've joined the international community and brought these criminals to justice. Rather we launched a war, the first war that killed quickly many more innocents in Afghanistan than died on 9/11, and then an utterly unrelated war in Iraq. Now we've lost the moral high ground. Nobody believes our word. Nobody believes in our vision for the world, and we've lost our soul in Iraq.[24]

The problem of a desperate, futile quest for invulnerability was also noted by Ruether. Ruether talked about developing a "theology of letting go"—what she called "the other side of the theology of liberation"—which "starts with the people who are the most oppressed in the present system and then essentially calls other people to be in solidarity with them, which means to in some way renounce their own unjust privileges."[25] She elaborated this theology as follows:

Any liberation which is somebody's else's disaster is false liberation. . . .
When you let go and allow other people to flourish, then you can
construct a system in which both people, in which the whole community is able to mutually benefit, rather than being based on the
assumption that my up is your down. In fact, I would say you only
have responsible government when it's based on the assumption there
must be at least minimum mutual benefit for everybody.[26]

Wallis and Ruether expressed a theme here that I heard in a number of
interviews: a conviction that Christians, as members of the dominant religion in the country, bear a special responsibility for curbing the tempta-
tions toward American empire, with its drive to dominate the world
economically and militarily.[27] Moreover, as Wallis and Ruether put it,
Christians are called not to set up an impregnable security state but "to trust
God in the midst of vulnerability" and to embrace a "theology of letting
go" that might bring us into a relationship of mutual trust and respect with
the rest of the world. This act of faithful trust need not be naive, but it
would keep Christians from overreaching for a guarantee of security that
can only be achieved at the expense of others. This unending quest for
invulnerability is nothing less than an act of idolatry that clearly runs contrary to the central message of the gospel.

Jesus and the Reign of God

To many non-Christian (and many Christian!) ears, the idea of "the reign of
God" or "the kingdom of God" has an ominous ring today. It conjures up
images of the Crusades or campaigns to supplant democracy with theocracy. In the New Testament, however, despite the militaristic and patriarchal challenges of the language, this idea is closely connected to the Jewish
idea of *shalom*, a time of peace. And this peace is not some kind of enforced
Pax Americana, where peace is brought by military dominance of the strong
over the weak, but rather a holistic vision of a new era where "the lion lays
down with the lamb" and "the last are first." And many progressive Christians are rehabilitating this language to reflect this latter vision of justice,
equality, and peace.

Telling the Story of Jesus

One of the most significant passages in the New Testament is found in the sixteenth chapter of the Gospel of Matthew, where Jesus asks his band of followers, "And who do you say that I am?" Two thousand years later, Christians are still struggling to grasp the full identity of Jesus and the depths of his message, the gospel, or "good news." The following is a representative sample of the range of responses the progressive leaders I interviewed gave to who Jesus was.

> Jesus put people first, made the poor central, made every attempt to connect the daily-ness of people's lives with the temple.[28]
>
> —*Sr. Joan Chittister, OSB, author; cochair, Global Peace Initiative for Women; cochair, Network of Spiritual Progressives*

> I've come to the conclusion that the only thing you can say for sure about Jesus is that he was nonviolent.[29]
>
> —*Fr. John Dear, SJ, author; peace activist*

> At the center of Jesus' life is the message of the kingdom of God, and that is all about justice and overturning of our assumptions about power.[30]
>
> —*Rev. Brian McLaren, evangelical author; leader in the emerging church movement*

> Jesus was always concerned about the least of these in society, those who were the most disenfranchised—the poor, outcasts, the untouchables. He was turning things upside down, and that upset people at the time.[31]
>
> —*Rev. Jennifer Butler, director, Faith in Public Life*

> The central question for me is, "Why was Jesus crucified?" It's because he gave voice to the poor and to women. It's because he had the audacity to go against the grain. So Jesus is more than

somebody we just put on some gold cross. He identifies with those
who are oppressed.[32]

> —Rev. Timothy McDonald III, pastor; chair,
> African American Ministers in Action

New Testament scholar Marcus Borg begins his remarkable book on
Jesus by borrowing an image from Southern writer Walker Percy, who
provocatively described the United States as a "Christ-haunted" culture. As
Borg emphasizes, "for Christians, Jesus is utterly central" because he is
believed to be "the decisive revelation of God."[33] Borg notes, however, that
American Christians tell the story of Jesus in very different ways, and these
different stories about Jesus provide different lenses that lead to often con-
flicting understandings of God, the Christian life, and moral and political
issues. Borg insightfully argues that these divisions "illustrate sharp disagreements among American Christians about what it means to take Jesus seriously. Our culture wars are to a large extent Jesus wars."[34]

Dr. Ron Sider, president of Evangelicals for Social Action and author
of the best-selling book *Rich Christians in an Age of Hunger*,[35] discussed
how the message and role of Jesus has been bifurcated within the broad
evangelical world.

> Part of what's happened in the evangelical world is that we've reduced
> the gospel and salvation to a kind of individualistic, privatistic, per-
> sonal relationship between me and Jesus. And, thank God, that's part
> of it. . . . But it's not just personal; the gospel of the kingdom means
> that the new Messianic order is breaking into history. Jesus formed a
> new community and gathered a circle of disciples. And that new com-
> munity began to live differently, began to challenge the status quo the
> way Jesus did; they began to care about the poor the way Jesus did.
> And the New Testament understanding of salvation is not just me and
> Jesus walking in the garden alone—it's partly that—but it's also this
> new community where there's economic sharing, and slaves and Gen-
> tiles and women receive a new dignity. That's all part of what the New
> Testament means by salvation.[36]

As Sider suggests, the contribution of progressive Christianity across
the denominational spectrum has been to emphasize the central social

aspects of Jesus' ministry and message. When the progressive Christians I interviewed were asked about their understanding of Jesus, their responses created a kaleidoscope of variations on this theme. The portrait of Jesus that emerged was that of a master teacher who strongly identified with the poor, the sick, women, and the outcasts at the bottom of the social and political ladder. The leaders I interviewed frequently talked about the significance of how Jesus announced his public ministry and the heart of his own message by reading from the book of Isaiah that proclaimed "good news to the poor." Jesus "put people first," favoring compassion and attention to the needs of those around him over ritual purity and religious rules. Jesus strongly challenged the status quo, went "against the grain," "turned things upside down," and "overturned assumptions of power"—but always with nonviolent means.

Finally, it is worth noting what these leaders did not emphasize: atonement theology, with its singular emphasis on the death and crucifixion of Jesus as vicarious payment for the sins of humanity. Atonement theology, which has dominated evangelical circles, radically narrows the relevant part of the story of Jesus to his death. For example, even during Advent, the period leading up to Christmas that emphasizes the birth of Jesus, an evangelical church near my house in Maryland trumped Advent with atonement on their marquee, declaring, "Jesus was born to die." In sharp contrast, when progressive leaders talked about Jesus, they emphasized his life, example, and teachings; they might say, "Jesus was killed because of the radical way he lived." And when they spoke of his death, they most often connected it to his radical politics that upset the status quo by calling on his followers to stand with the poor and the oppressed and taking the privileged to task for their apathy and complicity in the injustices of society.

The Reign of God

From the perspective of the progressive leaders I interviewed, then, Jesus was not simply born to die but to show humanity how to live. The central image Jesus used to describe this new era he was calling into being was "the kingdom of God" or "the reign of God." When Jesus invoked the reign of God, he was appealing to a nexus of ideas with deep roots in his own Jewish tradition. Jesus' reading from the book of Isaiah to announce his ministry took place in the synagogue he regularly attended in his hometown of Nazareth. The passage he chose was Isaiah 61, which is a message of good news to the poor, healing for the broken-hearted, and freedom for prisoners. This text also evokes the year of jubilee, a time every fifty years when debts were forgiven, prisoners set free, and land redistributed back to its original owners. He declares, much to his hometown's surprise, that his movement is the fulfillment of that promise of an emerging era of peace, liberty, and equality.

Rev. Dr. Tony Campolo, evangelical leader, author of thirty books, and professor of sociology at Eastern University, talked passionately about the centrality of the idea of the reign of God and its contemporary implications.

> We all know why Jesus came into the world: to declare that the kingdom of God is at hand. It's the first thing he says in Matthew, Mark, and Luke. . . . If you want a good description of what the kingdom looks like, it's very, very concrete in Isaiah 65. People have decent houses and jobs. Children do not die in infancy. Old people live out their lives in health. All of this implies that we're not going to let elderly people suffer because they can't afford medicine because the U.S. governmental pharmaceutical plan is so inadequate. Everybody is going to have a decent job and get the benefits from those labors. When children are born, mothers are not going to have to worry whether their children will grow up to calamity, to become drug pushers or gang members. The last verse of that passage, "none shall hurt the earth anymore," implies that we're going to be an environmentally concerned people. So when we pray for the kingdom of God, we're praying for all of these things.[37]

For Campolo, the reign of God provides a powerful image by which we can measure how our current society embodies God's priorities. The reign of God is an ideal, but it provides a concrete metric by which economic policies concerning housing and jobs, health care policies for children and the elderly, and environmental policies can be measured.

Fr. John Dear emphasized the real demands of the ideal represented by the reign of God.

Christ is calling us to be citizens of the reign of God, first and foremost. We're voting, if you will, with Christ. Our citizenship is real and political, and in that reign, there's no war, there's no poverty, there's no executions, there's no starvation, there's no nuclear weapons, there's no global warming. Everyone sees one another as a sister and brother, and you love all creation itself. We're supposed to believe Jesus when he says the reign is at hand here and now. I want something far more than a Democrat or Republican in the White House. I want a new world.[38]

When I objected in our interview that this vision was too utopian to be practical, Fr. Dear replied that many people thought the abolitionists were utopian as well because slavery was as old as recorded human history and was even in the Bible itself. Fr. Dear argued that contemporary Christians need to follow the heroic example of those past followers of Jesus who declared against all odds that "a new world is coming" and who were willing to give their lives for it.[39]

For Rev. Alexia Salvatierra, an ordained Lutheran minister and director of Clergy and Laity United for Economic Justice (CLUE), the idea of the reign of God was a sustaining reminder that Christians live in two kingdoms. One kingdom is "this world of really terrible dog-eat-dog realities where scarcity is a daily experience." On the other hand, Christians are reminded that "we have the breaking in of this other kingdom where you can turn the other cheek and transform people."[40] As a seasoned leader from the rough-and-tumble world of labor organizing, Salvatierra talked about "a dance of discernment of the spirit" that sometimes requires "having to watch your ass because otherwise you'll get knifed in the back." Even in those situations, however, the kingdom of God may "break in" and allow nonviolent resistance to "create something amazingly new."[41]

The Very Rev. Tracy Lind, an openly lesbian Episcopalian priest who is dean of Trinity Episcopal Cathedral in Cleveland and on the executive committee of We Believe Ohio, gave the most moving account of the reign of God I heard. As we sat in the backyard of her home sipping lemonade on a warm spring day, she leaned forward and, with an intensity usually reserved for a great secret, talked about the connection between the reign of God and the Jewish concept of *shalom*, or peace:

This is what Jesus says to us. It's right there; it's so close. If we can all hear and follow God's voice—whether we hear it through Torah or the Qur'an or the gospels or all the other ways we hear God's voice—if we could hear the voice of God, which I believe is the voice of universal love and justice and mercy for all creation, and if we're willing to follow that voice, I believe that *shalom* is as close as our fingertips and will ultimately be a reality.[42]

For these leaders, the reign of God provided a powerful vision of God's ideal for human community. While this ideal often seems far off amidst the brokenness of the world, these leaders remind Christians that if they are faithful and available as God's instruments in the world, the reign of God is always nearby, ready to break in to bring peace and healing.

"Truer than That": Engaging the Bible and Tradition

As I noted above, the late twentieth century witnessed a polarization *within* Christian denominations rather than between them. And without a doubt, among the Protestant denominations that dominate the American religious scene, the most divisive internal issue has been the battle over the Bible. Specifically, the battle lines have been drawn over how to read the Bible— literalist versus more critical approaches.

This battle took on epic proportions because, at a deeper level, it was a battle over how to deal with the uncertainties of modernity. For example, the nineteenth century birthed an emerging modern science that gave us alternative ways to understand human origins that relied on natural selection rather than divine intervention, and other spheres of life—such as politics, business, and the arts—were all developing their own values and demands for allegiances as they increasingly moved out from under the auspices of the church. These shifts and their implications for religion, for example, were a major preoccupation of early sociologists such as Max Weber and Karl Marx. Weber noted that these competing allegiances resulted in a kind of disconcerting "value polytheism."[43] And his contemporary Marx famously declared that these industrial and cultural disruptions had left many with the uneasy feeling that "all that is solid melts into air, all that is holy is profaned."[44]

The main reason the battles over how to read the Bible have been so brutal is that they were at their heart about how to find a stable source of truth and guidance for life in the rapidly changing modern world. This problem is more acute in the Protestant Christian context than in the Catholic context, which shares a more explicit interpretive tradition with Judaism and Islam. In Catholicism, Judaism, and even Islam (where the Qur'an is considered the actual revelation of God), the sacred text is understood through the lens of centuries of recorded layers of interpretation between the present and the text. One of the foundational instincts of Protestantism, however, was the insistence on *sola scriptura* ("only scripture") as the basis for Christian belief and practice. While the Protestant reformers such as Martin Luther clearly had a complex relationship to scripture and were not themselves biblical literalists, the *sola scriptura* assertion provided fertile ground for a modern reactionary biblical fundamentalism, which insisted that clinging to a wooden reading of the text was the only way to find truth.

Beyond Biblical Literalism

In recent years, the battle over the Bible has been not only theological but increasingly political. In my interview with Rev. Dr. Susan Thistlethwaite, president of Chicago Theological Seminary, she noted the double significance of the Bible: "The Bible is probably the most significant American religious symbol, and it is now a partisan political symbol as well."[45] The progressive Christians I interviewed had a variety of critical responses to the emergence of a neoconservative literalism, the particular form of biblical literalism that weds an ostensibly literalist reading to conservative politics focused on a few narrow issues.

On the one hand, several leaders pointed out that even if one accepts the premise of literalism as a valid approach to the text, such a reading would not lead to a politics focused narrowly on abortion, same-sex marriage, and unfettered free market capitalism. Rev. Jennifer Butler, director of Faith in Public Life, put it this way:

If people really took the Bible literally, there are times that I would welcome that. Because if they looked at all the passages about the poor and "the first and the last" and applied those to our tax system here in America or our social welfare system, they would have to change how they're voting and the kind of policies they advocate. If they took the Bible literally, there are very few mentions of homosexuality, and even of those that exist, it's not clear what those passages mean. There's not enough mandate there to spend all of their time worried about what gay people are doing. There is no mention of abortion. Now they might say there are certain texts about life. Okay, well, let's talk about life and about the whole spectrum of life from birth to death.[46]

Thistlethwaite concurred that one clear response to a political strategy that claims to be based on a literal reading of the Bible is "more Bible study for everybody."[47] A reading that was literal enough to note the overwhelming emphasis on the poor in the Bible, for example, would translate into a radical shift in politics for those who claim to be literalists.

On the whole, however, the progressive Christian leaders I interviewed argued that Christians ought to move beyond the myth that a consistent literal reading of the Bible in its entirety is even possible. A number of leaders argued that a more honest approach would be to embrace the inevitability that everyone is selective, favoring some passages over others, and that the way to read the text responsibly and authentically is to consciously develop and critically use an explicit reading strategy. For example, Rev. Jennifer Kottler, deputy director of Protestants for the Common Good, [48] clearly described how she holds together an embrace of biblical authority with a rejection of literalism:

Do I believe the Bible is the inspired word of God? I absolutely do. And is there truth to be found within those pages? Absolutely. Do I take verbatim what the Bible says? *Heaven forbid!* It also said if my child speaks back to me, I should kill them. I don't know any fundamentalists who would use that as a justification for murder. We all have a selective literalism. As people of faith, we have a responsibility to understand as best we can the heart of God and to allow God to continue to reveal God's self through the scriptures and through the community and prayer.[49]

Rev. Brian McLaren, evangelical author and leader in the emerging church movement, noted that there is a kind of intellectual dishonesty in many literalist churches. When they encounter a text like the one Rev. Kottler mentioned, or a challenging positive text such as the passage in the book of Acts that demands that the followers of Jesus give all that they have to the poor, they do not take it literally. For example, Thistlethwaite noted, "If James Dobson sold everything owned by Focus on the Family and gave it to the poor, I would pay more attention to his views on biblical literalism than I do now, because he doesn't take the Bible literally."[50]

McLaren emphasized the importance of noticing why self-avowed Biblical literalists in fact know not to take certain passages literally: "They're a part of an interpretive community that teaches them not to take it literally. Unfortunately, that community lies to them and tells them that they are taking it literally."[51] Noting that this duplicity was propped up by a conservative political alliance with evangelical Christianity that is now eroding, McLaren predicted: "Twenty-five years from now, the vast majority of Christians will say that literalism is a primitive and sub-Christian way of reading the text."[52]

A Relational Approach to Truth

Rev. Thistlethwaite said that one of her favorite quotes about the shallowness of biblical literalism came from Reinhold Niebuhr:

> Certainly the way the issue presents is that literalism equals truth. I love to quote Reinhold Niebuhr, who was asked if the story of Adam and Eve in Genesis in the garden was literally true. And Reinhold Niebuhr replied, "No, I think it's truer than that."[53]

Thistlethwaite noted that the problem with literal truth is that it tends to get caught up into superficialities rather than dealing with the deep truths of the Bible, which wrestle with "the human condition in relationship to God."[54]

If biblical literalism is untenable, and Christians are looking in the Bible for deep truths, how exactly does one find them? In my interviews, a strong theme emerged that I call "a relational approach to truth." Although this theme showed up across the denominational spectrum, it was notably strong among leaders who were women, racial minorities, gay, or lesbian—all groups that have been on the underside of social or economic power dynamics. For example, as Rev. Dr. Kenneth Samuel, pastor of Victory Baptist Church in Stone Mountain, Georgia, and cochair of the African American Ministers Leadership Council, noted, "Black Christians are still pretty much people of the book" and have some struggles with literalism. However, having learned through hard lessons of history that purely literal readings of the Bible, for example on slavery, did not capture God's truth for our day, African Americans also developed ways of bringing their own experience of God into conversation with the text.[55]

Rev. Harry Knox, an openly gay ordained UCC minister and director of the Religion and Faith Program at the Human Rights Campaign, talked movingly about the primacy of relationship with God in approaching the Bible. It merits citing him at length.

> The Bible is holy, it is powerful for me, it is normative for me. I can trust it as a relevant document that really is both revelatory of God and also messy enough to be relevant in my life.
>
> What we've done is embrace the Holy Spirit and built a relationship with God that is truly a relationship. Some of the many metaphors that the Bible uses for our connection to God are parent to child, bride to bridegroom, et cetera. I am able to trust a relationship more than I can trust a set of rules, because I can trust my partner to be in relationship with me—whether it's a friend or my dad and mom or my brothers and sisters or an employer—even if I can't trust them to follow the rules all the time. Because I'm not able to live up to the rules all the time.
>
> So, I don't think we give up certainty when we give the Bible up as a rulebook. What we do is embrace the relationship with a God who loves us, cares for us, and wants to guide us through God's Holy Spirit. What disappoints me with my fundamentalist sisters and brothers is that they talk a lot *about* the Holy Spirit, but they don't

seem to want to talk *with* the Holy Spirit. God is knocking and begging for this conversation, and we're saying, "Just give us a rule to live by. And could I please find it in this book in a way that I already understand. I don't want to work at this, God." And God says, "Geez, this doesn't feel like much of a relationship anymore. This feels like something else."[56]

Rev. Alexia Salvatierra echoed these concerns, noting that most "white male North Americans don't trust relational truth, but the Bible is a relational book."[57] Salvatierra noted that grasping truth in this way required a long-term investment. "Relationship is a pattern," she noted, that is formed over time as two people "create a dance together." The patterns formed by this dance, not propositions, teach each who the other is. According to Salvatierra, we learn about God and God's desires for our lives by learning to recognize God through our own experience and through the story of the Bible, which is itself "the story of the relationship between God and God's people."[58]

The emphasis on dynamic relationship with God recalls Rev. James Forbes' noting that God invites us into relationship, and from this vantage point, we get "a peak through the window of truth." Because our understanding of truth is always partial, there is always room, as Forbes put it, that "more truth can break out."[59] Rev. Thistlethwaite also emphasized that these ideas of relational truth and ongoing revelation have long history in American Christianity:

> When you walk into Chicago Theological Seminary, you actually walk right past a carving on the side of the building that quotes John Robinson from his famous sermon to the pilgrims. . . . Robinson said, "God hath more light and truth yet to break forth from his holy word." We always bring the questions of our existential situation to the text, and the text itself has questions for us. It's not just the literalists' approach: "I've got a question; the Bible's got an answer." But we also have commitments within our contemporary life about human rights, about justice, for which the Bible does not sometimes have a good answer. So we need also to be interrogating the text. This is to me a lifelong argument that I am involved with. It's kind of a love relationship.[60]

Thistlethwaite's emphasis on the relational aspect of truth allows the relationship with God and the quest for understanding to continue even when the text seems to fail us, such as when we trip and come face to face with the biblical support for slavery and other "texts of terror" that advocate the killing of disobedient children or the exploitation of women.[61] As Knox pointed out, this method is precisely the way in which the great leaders of the past such as Augustine or Luther or King in the Christian tradition have reformed and reawakened Christianity when it had lost its way.

> The people that we study now as great thinkers were all revolutionary in their time. They were all radical, they all pushed the limits, they all listened to God first, and then made what they were hearing bump up against the text and bump up against the tradition of the church. And they found that maybe the text and the tradition weren't big enough to hold what they were hearing from God, and so they said some new things.[62]

Like the great reformers of the past, Knox argues, contemporary Christians should "listen to God first." If one finds that the current interpretations of the Bible and the tradition are not "big enough" to hold the new word coming from God through experience, the responsibility of Christians is to have the courage to say something new. As Knox notes, saying something new is always controversial and requires courage at the time, but it is the responsibility of faithful Christians to be the instruments through which more of God's light can break through.

The Power of Religious Practice

Many of the progressive Christian leaders I interviewed talked about the importance of religious ritual for embodying the truth of a religious tradition. As Rita Nakashima Brock, director of Faith Voices for the Common Good, described it, "Religious ritual is how a tradition's best ideas are lived out as embodied practices."[63] Religion is often inculcated in "people of faith" less by their "faith" than by their bodies. Religious ideas are internalized powerfully by what we do as we move through space: whether singing, kneeling, smelling, chanting, or reciting. With our movements, we internalize more than the content of the words; the religious ideas actually become part of us in a deeper way, as part of our kinetic memory.

Fr. John Dear gave a compelling account of the purpose of ritual in the face of dehumanizing forces in the world:

> You're talking about how to become human in an inhuman world. How to be peaceful, loving, compassionate and nonviolent in a world of war, violence, injustice, and hatred. Well, it's very hard to do. You need a text, you need community, and you need a practice: daily meditations and worship.[64]

Religious ritual, indeed, can be powerful in helping us internalize the best ideas from the text and our community. The best of religion is about shaping human beings to live beyond themselves, a task that is hindered by both internal and external forces.

I asked each leader I interviewed to tell me about specific religious practices that sustained them and that helped orient people toward a Christianity with a progressive social outlook. Three practices came to the fore. By far, the most frequently cited practice was prayer, in both its individual and communal forms. Secondly, a number of leaders talked about the importance of a theology of radical welcome in the context of observing communion or the Eucharist. Finally, many leaders talked about the importance of activism, especially living in proximity to the poor, as a transformative religious practice.

Prayer

I was amazed at the depth and the variety of prayer described in my interviews. It became clear that prayer was not only an anchoring and transformative individual practice but a practice that was sustaining a variety of initiatives. Just a few examples will illustrate this richness. First, leaders talked about prayer that follows the rhythms of the day: "centering prayer" at the beginning of the day that allows "the spirit of Christ to flow into my being" and "prayers of examine" at the end of the day to remember the good and the bad of the day;[65] and saying "table grace" at meals to remember that "I do not get my food ultimately from the economy, I get my food from the earth, and that's God's gift."[66]

Second, many talked about trying to follow the New Testament command to "pray without ceasing"—to make oneself "more permeable to God," "to breathe God in and out" in order to "live with every breath in God."[67] Rev. Steven Baines, senior organizer of the Faith Action Network at People for the American Way Foundation, described it as a "state of being." For Baines, this heightened awareness means "walking the streets of Washington, D.C., and not turning your head when you see a homeless person" and noticing the juxtaposition of abundance and wealth with "great poverty and hunger and alienation." In short, Baines explained, prayer can help us "be aware that God is around us and that there are needs that we can meet even as we are walking home in the evening."[68]

Finally, Rev. Tim Ahrens described how prayer had served as a foundation for We Believe Ohio, the interfaith religious movement in Ohio that formed in the wake of the 2004 elections to give an alternative moderate/progressive voice to religion in the public square:

> What grounds me, and what I find every time We Believe Ohio is together is that the inspiration of our movement is prayer. When we gathered as a Sikh, Christian, Muslim, and Jewish gathering on the National Day of Prayer in my sanctuary and then marched to the State House to speak to the legislators, the power of that day was the prayer. When we met with each legislator, the power of that time was the prayer. One of the Senate leaders here said, "You know, no one has ever prayed for me that way." We begin each meeting, whether by telephone or steering committee or whatever, we begin it with prayer. We truly believe that the spirit of God is present and that God will lead us through these things. And it's a mystery in many, many ways.[69]

For Ahrens, prayer has been part of the mystery of the success of We Believe Ohio. With no staff and small contributions, this diverse group of religious leaders is transforming the public face of religion in Ohio away from narrow, divisive politics to politics of the common good.

Radical Hospitality: An Open Table Theology

One of the central practices of Christian worship is the Eucharist or communion, the participation in and commemoration of the last supper of

Jesus with his disciples before his death. This ritual is a sacrament in Catholicism and the centerpiece of Catholic worship. In Protestant circles, practices vary by denomination, but it remains a central Christian ritual. Common elements of the ritual are a table on which bread and wine are present. During the ceremony, usually presided over by a priest or minister who acts in the place of Jesus, congregants come to the table to receive the elements, reenacting the breaking of the bread and drinking of the wine by the disciples. Although there have been numerous theological disagreements about the meaning of different aspects of the ceremony, a basic shared view is that this common meal is a powerful sign of unity. In its traditional form, bread is broken from a single loaf and wine is drunk from a common cup, symbolizing the receiving of God's grace equally by all.

The leaders I interviewed emphasized not only the unity inherent in this ritual but what might be called an "open table theology," which emphasizes that all are welcome at the table. Alexia Kelley, director of Catholics in Alliance for the Common Good, described this basic insight of the Eucharist.

> Urban Catholic cathedrals have always been a draw to me. The cathedral is in the city with all its troubles and sin, and it's right there. Jesus called everyone to the table. And I think the Eucharist in the Catholic tradition has that emphasis. And that's why using the Eucharist as a political weapon or lever has been so painful; within the church community, this has been so distressing and destructive. It's not what Jesus would've done. Jesus didn't say, "Sorry, you're a prostitute, go away. Sorry, you're a tax collector, see you later. Can't come to communion." It's really contrary to Jesus' own practice.[70]

For Kelley, there is a strong affinity between the presence of the cathedral in the middle of the city with all of its problems and the way Jesus conducted his own ministry, as the New Testament notes, in the questionable company of tax collectors and sinners. Kelley's reference to the painful experience of the Eucharist being used as a political weapon refers to a controversial edict in February 2004 by St. Louis Archbishop Raymond Burke forbidding Senator John Kerry to take communion while campaigning for president in the area because of Kerry's stance on abortion.[71]

For Kelley, the power of the symbol of the church in the world is diminished by the act of excluding a practicing Catholic from communion over a single issue and contradicts the example of Jesus, who welcomed all to the table.

Rev. Tracy Lind echoed this emphasis on the open communion table, what she called "Jesus' radical table politics":

> Central for me is the concept of the table and the great banquet and Jesus' radical table politics, which emphasized table fellowship, a sense of community, and the invitation to everybody. I really believe that the good news of Jesus Christ is very simple: that God loves all of us unconditionally, without qualification, and that he proclaimed that over and over and over again.[72]

Lind's connection of Jesus' radical table politics to the simple good news that God loves us all unconditionally was a theme that many others expressed as well. Connecting this idea to the "God Is Still Speaking" media campaign sponsored by the United Church of Christ (UCC), Rev. Ron Stief, director of the Office of Public Life and Social Policy for the UCC, noted, "Jesus didn't turn people away, and neither should we; we call it our radical welcome, our extravagant welcome."[73]

Finally, Rev. Steven Baines told a moving story of the power of an open table theology to experience Christian fellowship and community, even in the midst of strong disagreements:

> At National City Christian Church, there are those sitting on the same pew as me who think I am an abomination to God. They make no bones about it. But I have been really blessed that I have found a community that's not based so much on whether we agree or disagree but on the unity we find around the Lord's table. Because when we come to the table, we're all worthy of God's love and grace. The man who thinks I'm an abomination takes holy communion and believes in the empowerment of God's spirit as much as me, the gay man, who has a life partner of nine years. But at that moment that doesn't divide us; holy communion brings us together. I find great comfort in that.[74]

Activism as a Religious Practice

Beyond the traditional religious practices that normally come to mind such as prayer, communion, and communal worship, many religious leaders also talked about the importance of activism as a religious practice, particularly the act of living in proximity to the poor. Fr. John Dear noted that the emphasis on activism was not something external to Christianity but embedded in the example of Jesus himself:

> You have to actually engage in some public action for justice and peace. If we're not, I don't see how we can claim to follow Jesus, who by and large is doing things. He's healing people, he's teaching people, he's condemning injustice, he's traveling, he's always doing something. Christians can't go to church on Sunday and then just go to work and ignore it. No, you have to be involved in some public work, whether with the homeless locally or working to end the death penalty or the war in Iraq or involvement in larger campaigns to abolish nuclear weapons and starvation. This is critical to the Christian life, given the world today.[75]

Dr. Ron Sider and Rev. Jim Wallis, two longtime activists on poverty issues in the evangelical community, also emphasized activism not only as a matter of obedience to the model of the life of Jesus but as a transformative act for middle-class Christians. For Sider, without some regular contact with the poor—whether making a strong commitment as he has to live among the poor or spending even as little as a few hours a week tutoring or going to church with poor people—middle-class Christians "don't really get it" and are bound to be "seduced by consumerism and materialism," two enormously powerful forces in American culture.[76]

Wallis, another leader who has intentionally lived among the poor, also told a challenging, moving story about the necessity of "living around yellow tape":

> One thing that changes American Christians is direct proximity, relationship to poor people. Revival is going to be triggered when the relationship to the poor on the part of the churches reaches a critical mass.

When people go into poor neighborhoods and start doing stuff and meeting poor families, we hear, "My goodness, I never knew that. I never understood that. I never saw, tasted, smelled this before." I lived in a poor neighborhood not because I thought I was the salvation of a poor neighborhood, but it's a spiritual discipline to teach me, particularly when you get treated like a rock star. For example, I go into a first-ever White House conference on youth violence with the First Lady, Hillary Clinton, brand new in town—"We've got to stop youth homicide." I go home, and there's yellow tape outside my house. A kid across the street was shot during the meeting. I know that no one else but me [from that meeting] is going home to yellow tape. So you've got to live around yellow tape.[77]

For many of the progressive religious leaders I interviewed, doing justice and working for peace were preconditions that must be in place, as Fr. Dear put it, "before you can really get into an authentic Christian theology and spirituality."[78] For Sider and Wallis, living in proximity to the poor is absolutely essential for living an authentic Christian life. Without seeing, smelling, and tasting the problems of poverty and living in proximity to the violence that often accompanies it, Christians simply "don't get it" in a way that allows them to live faithful lives that are authentically connected to their fellow human beings.

An *Imago Dei* Agenda

If there was one theological theme that was an undercurrent across all of the interviews with progressive Christian leaders, it was the conviction that all people are created *imago dei*, "in the image of God," and that God has a particular concern for what Jesus called "the least of these," the poor and disadvantaged in society. It would be nearly impossible to overstate the importance of this idea as a foundation for Christian engagement with progressive politics. Rev. Dr. Kenneth L. Samuel captured this sentiment eloquently:

To be uncommitted to caring for those people who find themselves at the bottom rungs of our socioeconomic ladder will eventually spell havoc for all of us. To not be intentionally inclusive of all people will damage the whole because, in God's providential design, we are one human family. We make a mistake when we neglect to make the needs of "the least of these" our priority because it really is going to take all of us to move forward. We really are one body, one nation under God. One of the lessons that we learned from one of our greatest national leaders, Abraham Lincoln, is that a house divided cannot stand. It just cannot stand. He learned it from Jesus. America is a house that is greatly divided, and it will ultimately lead to our detriment, if we do not reassess and begin to build the bridges and make the connections to bring us, as a people, back together.[79]

Samuel noted that this insight is at the root of Martin Luther King's notion of "the beloved community," which itself is based on the vision of the coming reign of God. The affirmation that all are created in the image of God is, in many ways, a simple affirmation. But it confronts, as Rev. Salvatierra put it, "the big lie" that some are more important than others. As these leaders declare, this affirmation has radical implications across many prominent issues such as poverty, peace, the environment, and issues of equality and inclusion of gay and lesbian persons.

Poverty, Peace, and Planet Earth

Bob Edgar is the general secretary of the National Council of Churches, the umbrella group representing thirty-five denominations (largely mainline Protestant) and forty-five million people in the United States.[80] In his recent book *Middle Church: Reclaiming the Moral Values of the Faithful Majority from the Religious Right*, Rev. Edgar provocatively formulated a summary of three key issues for a progressive Christian agenda: "The shorthand of what we're about is confronting fear, fundamentalism, and Fox News with a commitment to peace, poverty, and planet Earth."[81]

The issue of poverty was by far the most frequently mentioned issue in my interviews. As this chapter has illustrated already, concerns about the poor are not far below the surface in discussions on a number of topics. Dr. Ron Sider, whose book *Rich Christians in an Age of Hunger* has helped keep the issue of poverty squarely on the evangelical agenda for nearly three decades now, noted that Christians engaging in politics must ask, "What does God care about?"[82] While Sider notes that there are a number of issues that should make up what he calls "a biblically balanced agenda," if Christians care about "defining the gospel the way Jesus did," poverty must be near the top of the list.[83]

Tony Campolo, another evangelical who has been deeply concerned with poverty issues for decades, confirmed that concern for the poor is not some sideline to Christian faith.

> The twenty-fifth chapter of Matthew is the only description that Jesus gives of judgment day. And on that day he says, "Did you feed the hungry, did you clothe the naked, did you take care of the sick, did you welcome the alien, did you visit those who are in prison?" And then he says this, "Whatever you do to the least of these, you do to me." What we try to do in our preaching is to make it clear that Jesus uses the poor sacramentally, that in a sense he becomes a presence in each of them to be loved and to be served. And when they say, "But you're an evangelical and you say you can only be saved by a personal relationship with Jesus," my answer is, "Exactly. And what Jesus says is you can't have a personal relationship with me unless you have a personal relationship with the poor and the oppressed of the world."[84]

Campolo notes here a remarkable passage where Jesus identifies himself with "the least of these"—he sacramentally becomes the poor—and makes the outcome of judgment day dependent not upon belief but upon how one treats the outcasts. Sider also noted this same passage and emphasized the stark implications of this passage: "It says that if we don't feed the hungry and clothe the naked, we go to hell. That's just exactly what it says." With a gift for understatement, Sider concluded, "If you think that the Bible is God's word in any significant sense at all, you have to take that pretty seriously."[85] This powerful insight pushes back to the idea of the oneness of humanity; Jesus declares that it is impossible to maintain a relationship with God without a relationship with and care for the poor and oppressed.

The second central issue for progressive Christian leaders was the issue of peacemaking. Like poverty, peacemaking was linked to a number of other issues in the interviews, particularly to the idea of solidarity with all humanity. Citing the prominent teachings from the Sermon on the Mount in the

New Testament, Fr. John Dear talked about helping Christians regain a vision of peace and take seriously their biblically mandated role as peacemakers. Fr. Dear talked about his own dramatic awakening to this truth when he was in Israel during a time of fighting between Israel and Lebanon in 1982, an experience that began his journey as a peace activist:

> I was camping out at the Sea of Galilee and reading the Sermon on the Mount really for the first time. The place was empty, and I was really, really deep into reflection and the meaning of all this when I saw a lot of jets swoop down and kill a lot of people at the Sea of Galilee, at the place where Jesus said "Love your enemies." I was shocked into being awake to the reality of the teachings of Jesus, which is love your enemies—don't kill them, don't bomb them, don't nuke them—love them, and blessed are the peacemakers.[86]

Fr. Dear continued by noting the difficulty of grasping this radical vision of peace for contemporary American Christians, who have largely accepted violence—especially violence from which we remain largely disconnected—as a normal way of life. One crucial task Dear has committed himself to work for is the reclaiming of a Christian vision of peace that takes seriously Jesus' call to "love your enemies."

> So we're talking helping people reclaim their vision and the imagination of peace because we're also blind. That's a very biblical challenge of Jesus, to help people see one another, to see Christ in each other, to see the coming of the reign of God. And then to work for it, to say no and resist injustice for it, and even to lay down their lives nonviolently, in love for the coming of that vision, as Dr. King did and Mahatma Gandhi did, knowing that we may not live to see it but that it will come true one day because that's what Jesus calls for.[87]

Significantly, reclaiming a vision of peace is deeply connected to the theme of the oneness of humanity. As Dear describes it, renewing this imagination requires that people see one other, "see Christ in each other." When that vision has become real, Christians will have the courage to act for real change.

Third, concern for the environment has increasingly become a consensus issue. While mainline Protestant and Catholic leaders have had long-standing commitments to the environment, one of the most exciting new developments has been the explosion of environmental concern among evangelicals. Dr. Ron Sider was one of the early leaders of this movement, and housed the Evangelical Environment Network (EEN) as a program of Evangelicals for Social action in the early 1990s. EEN was active on endangered species concerns and had as their first big public campaign the "what would Jesus drive" campaign, which challenged evangelical Christians to drive fuel-efficient cars.

In February 2006, EEN brought together a group of eighty-six centrist and progressive evangelicals to endorse what became the Evangelical Climate Initiative, which coined the term "Creation Care" as an evangelical approach to the environment.[88] Tapping existing concerns about poverty, the statement explicitly tied concern for the environment to the poor, who would be disproportionately affected by climate change. The document boldly declared, "Love of God, love of neighbor, and the demands of stewardship are more than enough reason for evangelical Christians to respond to the climate change problem with moral passion and concrete action."[89]

Finally, the leaders interviewed noted that these issues were deeply intertwined. Fr. Dear talked passionately about the need to "make the connections" between these issues:

> We have to keep making the connections. War is connected to racism, and it's connected to the environment, and it's connected to poverty. If you're working on the environment, but you're saying nothing about nuclear weapons or depleted uranium in Iraq, then I don't believe you; I don't think you care about the earth. On the other hand, if you're working on war, and you're not making the connections with starving people, then you're not seeing the full picture. The money that goes into these weapons belongs with starving people. And the same with death row and sexism—it's all one. We have to keep making those connections and bridging the movements for peace and justice.[90]

As Dear makes clear, Christians need to keep working to bridge the movements for peace, poverty, and planet Earth. Because all are created equally in the image of God, Christians cannot stand for policies that perpetuate "the big lie" that some lives are more important than others.

LGBT Issues: Becoming a "Whosoever" Church

There is good evidence to show that the issue of homosexuality is becoming a defining issue within Christianity, as David Kinnaman's study of young Americans' views of Christianity—aptly titled *Unchristian*—demonstrated. Recall Kinnaman's stark findings: The most frequently identified attribute of present-day Christianity, selected by more than nine in ten young "outsiders," was that it was antihomosexual, and the other top attributes were that it was judgmental and hypocritical. Moreover, Kinnaman also found that even four out of five young churchgoers say that Christianity is antihomosexual, and "half regard it as judgmental, too involved in politics, hypocritical, and confusing."[91]

The proposed solution to this problem put forward by Kinnaman and the thirty evangelical contributors to *Unchristian* is basically to "reshape the negative images" by "helping to articulate a 'kinder, gentler' faith—one that engages people but does not compromise its passion for Jesus or its theological understanding of him."[92] To be sure, there are some hopeful recommendations from Kinnaman on this front that, if adopted, would represent real progress, especially among white evangelicals. Kinnaman calls for Christians to be guided in all their actions by grace and compassion; to take seriously the fact that we are all sinners and no sin is greater than any other; and to remember that being against homosexual acts does not justify being against homosexual persons. Moreover, Kinnaman warns against seeking inappropriate political solutions that allow the government to regulate adult sex lives, and he admonishes Christians to work side by side with gays and lesbians to address HIV/AIDS issues and "to end workplace discrimination in nonreligious settings."[93] These are all significant recommendations.

Given all the hate-mongering that has been done in the name of Christianity in America, this call for a "kinder, gentler" faith is certainly to be applauded and supported. But when Christians have behaved so shamefully that the gospel (literally, the "good news") has now become synonymous with being antigay, judgmental, and hypocritical, many progressive Christian leaders are arguing that a more substantive shift in the church's approach to the issue of homosexuality is necessary. Many of the progressive Christian leaders interviewed here, for example, propose that the solution to being perceived to be antihomosexual might entail more than driving a wedge (one that never ceases to slip out) between sin and sinner. Rather, many progressive Christians argue that an uncompromising "passion for Jesus"—a Jesus who never once mentioned homosexuality but who embraced those at the margins of society—leads them to a more straightforward response. These progressive Christian voices propose that a more appropriate response to the distortions of Christian faith that have made it synonymous with being antihomosexual is, to put it simply, to reclaim a gospel message that is not antihomosexual.

In addition to the issues of peace, poverty, and planet Earth, issues surrounding the equality and inclusion of lesbian, gay, bisexual, and transgender (LGBT) persons, both in society and within the church, were central. This issue created a broader spread of opinions among the leaders I interviewed than the other issues, where there was virtual unanimity. Generally speaking, mainline Protestant leaders, especially those associated with the United Church of Christ, which has a denominational policy of welcome and inclusion, were more supportive of full welcome and inclusion in the church and full equal rights in society. Even among the minority of leaders who held reservations on some aspects of LGBT welcome and justice, there was clear consensus that the radical narrowing of Christian political engagement to issues like same-sex marriage and abortion—the cause of so many young people seeing Christianity primarily as antihomosexual and even un-Christian—was deeply misguided and unjustifiable from a biblical standpoint. Among the larger number of leaders who held more affirming positions regarding LGBT persons, the affirmation that all are created in the image of God and the "extravagant welcome" of Jesus, who did not exclude anyone from the table, were foundational.

No one that I interviewed denied that there were six biblical "clobber texts" that are unequivocally negative about particular sexual acts between members of the same sex. Many were quick to point out, however, that these texts are extremely scarce in the biblical canon, that most Christians regularly ignore other purity texts such as not eating pork, and that none of these texts address homosexual orientation, a concept that did not exist in the biblical world.[94]

For example, Rev. Thistlethwaite pointed out that even within certain interpretations of the text, there is what she called "biblical breathing room" that can be created in honest conversations with people:

> You can certainly help people see that there's more room within their own expressed views of how they interpret the Bible. While you may say that there are six texts that are anti-homosexuality, what about what Jesus teaches us, which is also in the Hebrew Bible, to love God with your whole heart and your neighbor as yourself? Well, does the homosexual person not get to qualify as your neighbor? Is there some litmus test of morality for the neighbor? Jesus didn't put one in.[95]

The central appeal, however, for progressive Christian leaders who held full welcoming and affirming positions was a return to a relational understanding of truth that emphasized that "God is still speaking." These leaders embraced the idea that through our lived experience there is yet more truth to break out, and they accepted the fact that this truth may be larger than our past understanding of revelation can hold. Walking this path is certainly a matter of difficult discernment, especially when these issues have become so charged and politicized. Two African American ministers who have been leading both local and national conversations about welcoming gay and lesbian persons in the black church, Rev. Timothy McDonald and Rev. Kenneth Samuel, talked honestly and movingly about their own exemplary journeys on this issue.

Both McDonald and Samuel talked about their experience of not being able to escape the pull of one of the most fundamental verses in the New Testament for evangelical and black Christians (the one often seen on placards at televised football games!): "For God so loved the world, that he gave his only begotten Son, that whosoever believed in him should not perish, but have everlasting life" (John 3:16, KJV). Both ministers talked of the resonance of the "whosoever" in that verse and how that reverberation had challenged them to become "a whosoever church."[96]

Rev. McDonald noted that his personal experiences as a young minister first pushed him to "back off of this vileness against homosexuality and to ask God, 'What are you doing? What are you saying? What are you trying to teach us?'"[97] He summarized his own journey for answers as follows:

I do not get to choose whom I pastor. Whoever God sends, that's whom I have to pastor. And whether they are legal or illegal, whether they are gay, whether they're straight, whether they're black, whether they're white, I have to pastor them. Everybody needs a pastor. So I'm still evolving, and I'm still questioning. I'm still trying to discover, but I don't hate like I used to. I don't use those labels like I used to. And I see that God is a God of love, and God is a God of compassion, that the church is a healing station, not a hurting station. And that means that whosoever will, let him come. I do not get to define what "whosoever will" is.[98]

Rev. Samuel also noted that a personal experience in his youth had shaped his own journey toward more inclusivity and welcome of gay and lesbian persons. When he was fourteen years old, a church friend told him that he was gay and felt that no one, not even God, loved him because he was gay. A week later, his friend killed himself. He described his thoughts at the funeral as follows:

I sat there saying to myself, "There is something wrong with this picture—that this church could preach that God hates homosexuals and then cry at the funeral of a homosexual." Something just wasn't meshing with me, that the church could contribute to the death of a person in the name of Jesus, and then lament about it after his death, but never really acknowledge what internal strife drove him to commit suicide.[99]

As Samuel described it, he did not have the theological tools to fully come to terms with that experience until seminary, and even now is striving to live out a ministry that "embraces social justice across the board for all people, not just black people."[100] He has gradually led his church in this direction, a move that initially cost him nearly half of his seven-thousand-member congregation. The message he now strives to put forward echoes McDonald's emphasis on being a "whosoever church":

The whole Bible is a narrative about the story of a God who is so extravagant and so unbiased in God's love for humanity that God extravagantly offers God's self as a sacrifice not just for some but for the whole wide world. The whole story is that God so loved the world that *whosoever*. . . . That's got to reverberate and that's got to have deep religious and theological foundations in the psyche of the Christian body.[101]

The emphasis on the "extravagant" here conjures not only the extravagant welcome of all but also the extravagant offering of God's very self to the entire world. It also echoes the "open table" theology described above, which offers a radical welcome to all to come to the Lord's table. As they are struggling to become a "whosoever" church, these leaders are hearing more truth break out. As they are trusting what they hear, they are not only embracing an affirming Christian response toward gay and lesbian people, but they are also demonstrating an alternative vision of what a "passion for Jesus" might mean in light of this truth—one that might seem to many to be more "Christian."

Working for the Reign of God: New Initiatives by Progressive Christians

The national elections in 2004 were a wake-up call for progressive Christians. While many had noted and lamented the dominance of the Christian right, few had anticipated the success with which this vocal minority would claim to be the exclusive voice not only of Christianity but of faith in America. But 2004 also represented a tipping point, as this aging group of far-right leaders overreached in two ways: first, by becoming explicitly identified with the Republican Party; and second, by insisting that Christians ought to only be concerned with a radically narrow agenda of abortion, same-sex marriage, and embryonic stem cell research. These bald political strategies revealed to many Christians that the leaders who had held the megaphone for nearly three decades had become more concerned with power than principle, more enamored with backroom access than biblical agendas. Over the past four years, there has been enormous organizing activity and outreach in progressive Christian circles nationally, in Washington, D.C., and in the heartland to amplify a progressive Christian public voice.

"Getting It": Establishing a Different Voice on "Moral Values" and Politics

Among the established national Christian organizations, Rev. Jim Wallis's Sojourners/Call to Renewal, established over thirty years ago in the early 1970s, is perhaps the strongest example of an organization that has tapped the new energy among Christians outraged by the excesses of the religious right. In 2005, Wallis's book, *God's Politics: Why the Right Gets It Wrong and the Left Doesn't Get It*, became a national phenomenon, staying on the *New York Times* bestseller list for four straight months.[102] Looking back from the perspective of late 2007, Wallis explained the success of the book:

> It was the right book at the right time. There were millions of American Christians, and others, who didn't feel represented by the voices that were predominant in the culture, in the media, in the public square. They said, "Wait a minute; I'm a Christian too, and I don't agree with that. Wait, I care about moral values, too, but I think there's more than two of them." So they were ready to hear another voice. From the first week the book was out, I knew something was happening. You don't normally have at a book-signing event one, two, three, four thousand people. We had that everyplace we went: in the South, in the Midwest, around the country. We were saying that the monologue of the religious right is over. They're not dead, they're not gone, but they're not the only voice anymore. And that's the way it should be.[103]

Leveraging the success of the book, Sojourners has grown significantly over the past few years. Subscriptions to *Sojourners Magazine*, the award-winning magazine for which the organization is best known, nearly doubled between 2002 and 2006, increasing from 24,000 to 46,000, with combined print and Internet readership now exceeding 250,000. Revenue has also nearly doubled over the past few years, rising from $2.4 million in 2004 to $4.6 million in 2006.[104] One clear sign of its growing clout was its ability to spearhead high-profile events such as a June 2007 forum on "Faith, Values, and Poverty," which featured the three leading Democratic presidential candidates—Senator Hillary Clinton (NY), former Senator John Edwards (NC), and Senator Barack Obama (IL).[105] Sojourners has also used its increased assets to produce resources like their "Voting God's

Politics" voter's guide in 2006 (over 300,000 distributed) and their recent "Covenant for a New America," an antipoverty policy vision and platform. Through efforts like these, Rev. Wallis and Sojourners have become one of the leading national voices reasserting the link between faith and social justices issues.

Good News from the Beltway

The flurry of activity following the presidential elections of 2004 included a number of strategy sessions with key progressive leaders. These meetings resulted in new initiatives at older, established advocacy groups and birthed a number of independent initiatives. Among the established organizations, new projects such as the Center for American Values at People for the American Way Foundation (PFAW), the Program on Religion and Belief at the American Civil Liberties Union (ACLU), and the Religion and Faith Program at the Human Rights Campaign (HRC) sprang up. This milieu also ensured that organizations such as John Podesta's Center for American Progress (CAP), which was founded during this same period, began with religion programs.[106]

These programs and others represented by the leaders interviewed above are important, but a brief snapshot of two new initiatives—one explicitly Catholic, one representing a broad array of faith voices—provides a good illustration of the new energy and spirit operative among progressive Christian leaders in the nation's capital. Each of these organizations, Catholics in Alliance for the Common Good and Faith in Public Life, was modeled on a new, collaborative "open source" model that sought not to build a competitive brand or to work in single-issue silos—strategies that have often led to gridlock among progressive social movements—but to foster and amplify a variety of neglected voices. Started from scratch in the wake of the 2004 elections, the reach and effectiveness of these new organizations are remarkable and a sign that something new is happening.

Catholics in Alliance for the Common Good (CACG), a nonprofit, nonpartisan organization was founded in 2005 to "promote awareness of Catholic social teaching and its core values of justice, dignity, and the common good."[107] For founding director Alexia Kelley, being a holistic Catholic means embracing both the moral tradition and the social tradition of the church, which has been too often neglected in recent years. CACG began in order to remind Catholics that being a "cafeteria Catholic"—that is, following the moral teachings on issues like abortion while leaving aside the social teachings on issues like poverty and war—was inadequate. Proper attention to Catholic social teaching would broaden and balance the Catholic political agenda in important ways from the overemphasis on issues like abortion that many Catholics presently feel. Kelley summarized her basic argument as follows:

> We disagree with this line of argument that says we can disagree on the policy prescriptions to reduce poverty and whether or not to engage in war. Actually we cannot. There is unambiguous Catholic teaching on just war. And it's not confusing. This war is an unjust war—the bishops said so—and there should be no arguments among Catholics. . . . Catholic social teaching is pretty clear about the role of government in ensuring a basic level of human dignity across the board in terms of access to health care, not living in hunger, and not being homeless.[108]

This perspective is captured in their "Common Good Voter Pledge," which will be the centerpiece of organizing in 2008; the pledge states, "Vote out poverty, vote out war, and vote in the common good."[109]

CACG, along with their 501(c)4 partner, Catholics United, have become a strong voice for Catholic social teaching. Just a few examples are indicative of the major contributions they have made in a short period of time. First, Alexia Kelley and Catholics United Director Chris Korzen have recently written *A Nation for All: How the Catholic Vision of the Common Good Can Save America from the Politics of Division*, a promising book that combines popular Catholic theology with a political vision of the common good.[110] In 2007, their media outreach served as a pro bono public relations firm for the Catholic social justice movement, producing over one thousand media hits that reached over twenty million Americans. As a result, they have become a central media source for TV, radio, and print journalists who are looking for a Catholic social justice voice on public issues. Finally, showing that social justice advocates can also use the media aggressively, Catholics United produced a series of hard-hitting ads that ran in the local districts of ten "pro-life" members of Congress who opposed the State Children's Health

Insurance Program (SCHIP), which provides health coverage to poor children. The ads feature a mother of three children saying, "I'm concerned that Congressman ———— says he's pro-life but votes against health care for poor children. That's not pro-life. That's not pro-family."[111]

Faith in Public Life (FPL), which often partners with Catholics in Alliance for the Common Good, also began in 2005 and has made an impressive impact in just two short years under the leadership of founding director Rev. Jennifer Butler. FPL aims to strengthen "the effectiveness, collaboration, and reach of faith movements that share a call to pursue justice and the common good."[112] FPL has produced results in three main areas: amplifying a broader faith agenda, bridging ideological divides, and building a progressive faith movement. Serving as an increasingly popular resource with the media, FPL delivered more than $1.5 million in pro bono media support for progressive faith leaders and coalitions, securing more than six hundred media hits on high-profile media such as the *New York Times*, CNN, and Fox. FPL has also assisted leading nonreligious think tanks such as The Third Way on crucial projects to bridge the gap between political progressives and evangelicals on cultural issues.[113]

Finally, FPL has launched a number of projects to help build much-needed infrastructure for the progressive faith movement. They launched "Mapping Faith," a growing online Google Maps–powered database of over three thousand faith-based groups that are working on "compassion issues including poverty, the environment, human rights, peace, race, and immigration."[114] Additionally, they host Faithful America, an e-advocacy community of more than 70 thousand activists, and have provided critical guidance and media support for coalitions on the ground such as We Believe Ohio, a group I return to in more detail in the book's conclusion.

These are just a few examples of the dozens of major new initiatives that are growing among progressive Christians. Other important examples of new life, which space prohibits extensive treatment of here, are the mushrooming online communities such as www.streetprophets.org, run by the progressive UCC pastor and blogger "Pastor Dan" and www.crossleft.org; strategic advising of progressive candidates by Mara Vanderslice and Eric Sapp of Common Good Strategies; important organizing among African American ministers such as the African American Ministers Leadership Council at People for the American Way Foundation and the Samuel DeWitt Proctor Conference; and the organizing of clergy who support full inclusion of gay and lesbian Americans in public and church life, such as the Religion and Faith Program at the Human Rights Campaign and the Institute for Welcoming Resources, an umbrella group for mainline Protestant welcoming and affirming groups. Additionally, congregation-based community organizing (CBCO) groups are alive and well within Christian congregations across the denominational spectrum, aided by organizations such as Clergy and Laity United for Economic Justice (CLUE) in Los Angeles and Interfaith Worker Justice (IWJ) in Chicago.

Conclusion:
A Progressive Christian Movement?

A key question is whether this clear surge of new energy and initiatives constitutes a progressive Christian movement. As I noted in the introduction, there was some uneasiness with labels in general among these leaders. Many noted the baggage the words "liberal" and "left" have come to have, and some even expressed concerns about the term "progressive." But beyond semantics, there is a clear set of leaders and organizations coalescing around a broader faith agenda that headlines issues of poverty, peacemaking, the environment, and social justice. The social justice agenda also increasingly includes commitments of welcome, inclusion, and equality for LGBT persons.

This emerging community is also showing signs of maturing and broadening from a reactionary movement against the religious right to a more proactive stance that is beginning to change the way faith is perceived in public life. Rev. Jim Wallis captured this new stage of development in his new book, *The Great Awakening: Reviving Faith and Politics in a Post-Religious Right America*.[115] He noted that this book "is not about taking back the faith—we've done that now—it's about what our faith needs to mean, what we do, how our faith could change the wind on the big issues: climate change, global poverty, HIV/AIDS. About how faith could change the really big issues of our time."[116] As the title indicates, Wallis is both seeing and helping to call into being a "great awakening" that goes beyond the left-right dichotomies of politics and says, "don't go left, don't go right, go deeper."[117]

The twin convictions that we are in the midst of a real renewal among progressive Christians and that this renewal is going beyond the old, one-dimensional boundaries of left and right were confirmed by a majority of leaders I interviewed. For example, Diana Butler Bass, an independent scholar of American religion and culture, has recently shown that despite the conventional wisdom that mainline Protestant churches are dying, there are a growing number of vital mainline Protestant churches that represent "an emerging shape of Protestant Christianity."[118] These churches were rediscovering a "transformative" engagement with tradition that was nourishing a politically active "radical center," which embraces a number of progressive political issues such as poverty while simultaneously transcending traditional ideological and partisan assumptions.

Finally, one anecdotal piece of firsthand reporting I can offer about the growth of a progressive Christian movement is an epiphany I had at an informal gathering of people of faith, mostly younger Christian leaders under forty, who are playing leading roles in shaping progressive policies in the nation's capital. Over the past two years, this growing group has been meeting regularly reflect on how faith should impact public policy. The group has begun to form a kind of *koinonia*, or fellowship, that shares Christian practices such as prayer and singing. As we stood in a circle on a Sunday morning and sang "Lift Ev'ry Voice and Sing," I was struck by just how much the picture had changed since 2004. The vast majority of leaders in the room, including myself, were not working in their current capacities then, and a number of the organizations at which these leaders now worked were not even in existence three years ago.

I realized then that the words of "Lift Ev'ry Voice," the song so prominent in the civil rights movement, are also appropriate to the present moment, one infused with a sense of new possibilities:

> Lift ev'ry voice and sing,
> Till earth and heaven ring.
> Ring with the harmonies of Liberty;
> Let our rejoicing rise,
> High as the list'ning skies,
> Let it resound loud as the rolling sea.
> Sing a song full of the faith that the dark past has taught us,
> Sing a song full of the hope that the present has brought us;
> Facing the rising sun of our new day begun,
> Let us march on till victory is won.[119]

The leaders that I interviewed here made no claim to be the only faith voices in the public sphere, but they are announcing a new day dawning. In the place of the shrill, divisive monotone of the religious right, the present is revealing a diverse but harmonious chorus of new voices. Victory for these voices does not mean left trumping right or Democrats defeating Republicans. Rather, these voices are moving beyond the old political divides and are marching toward a more inclusive common good agenda that honors the image of God in all. The new public face of Christianity that these leaders are bringing forth will be known less for whom it is against and more for declaring that the reign of God may indeed be as close as our fingertips, as we come together to work for the good of all our neighbors.

CHAPTER 3

Knowing One Another
How Progressive Muslims Are Fostering Justice, Beauty, and Pluralism

Listening for Beauty in a "Conference of the Books"

I arrived at Dr. Khaled Abou El Fadl's house mid-evening, a bit early for our appointment, after a long day of interviews in Los Angeles. His wife Grace and two dogs led me into the den, and Grace left to retrieve some tea. As I settled into the couch, I was struck by the floor-to-ceiling bookshelves filled with Islamic texts surrounding me on three sides, illuminated by the fireplace on the fourth wall. Some were clearly ancient, with aged bindings. Some were new, with proud red leather spines embossed precisely such that stylized Arabic script could be read across the line of volumes on the shelf. Clearly a lover of texts, Dr. Abou El Fadl, the Omar and Azmeralda Alfi Distinguished Fellow in Islamic Law at the UCLA School of Law and himself author of numerous books, is one of the most widely respected authorities on the development of Islamic law. He also has a remarkable grasp of the text of the Qur'an, having memorized it fully by the time he was 14 years old in his home country of Egypt. During the interview, Dr. Abou El Fadl explained that he had "gone to great expense and effort" acquiring these sources on Islamic law from around the world. He collects these sources, he explained, as testimony to Islam as a living, breathing tradition.

From my perch in the shadow of the towers of books, the metaphor of a "conference of books" that Dr. Abou El Fadl used in his own writings came alive. Abou El Fadl used this metaphor to talk about his engagement with ancient texts, which stand in for the greatest Muslim intellects of history, and the modern Muslim community. Prior to September 11, Abou El Fadl had written about what he called the "ugliness after ugliness after ugliness" that had come to plague corners of the Muslim world, and sitting both metaphorically and literally among this conference of books, he had attempted to reclaim a core moral value in Islam—the value of beauty.[1]

In an interview for PBS's *Faith and Doubt at Ground Zero*, he noted that when he first saw the news on September 11, 2001, he immediately walked away from the television and uttered "a prayer, a wish, a plea: 'Please, God, not Muslims. [Do not let it be] Muslims who have done this, or anyone who is calling themselves a Muslim.'"[2] He returned to find the resources to sustain what he called "my burden and privilege and virtue to go out and try to create beauty, as much beauty that is reflective of the beauty of God."[3] And since that time, Abou El Fadl has spoken and written prolifically of an inspiring vision of Islam. When I asked specifically about engaging sacred texts, Abou El Fadl leaned toward me, and explained with a tone of reverence, "[We must] enter into conversation with the text and ask the text, so to speak, [pauses]'Okay, what is it? How did you fit in the fulfillment of God's beauty?'"[4] This search for beauty that guides a deep engagement with Islamic tradition is central to the progressive Muslim voices represented here.

Middle Class and Mainstream: A Portrait of Muslim Americans

Muslim Americans are one of the fastest-growing and most complex religious groups in American society. The latest Pew survey, the most extensive to date, estimates that there are approximately 2.4 million Muslims in the United States.[5] The headline from the report announced that despite

TABLE 3.1 American Islam at a glance

Basic Demographics

Population:

    1.5 million adults (0.6% of adult general population)

    2.35 million total

77% U.S. citizens

Immigrants:

    65% first generation (39% arrived since 1990)

    Arrived from more than 68 different countries

Major Divisions

Ethnicity:

    80% Immigrant Islam

    20% African American Islam

Religious affiliation:

    50% Sunni

    16% Shia

    22% "Just Muslim"

Politics

Political ideology:

    24% liberal

    38% moderate

    19% conservative

2004 vote:

    71% Kerry

    14% Bush

Party identification:

    63% Democrat/lean Dem.

    26% Independent

    11% Republican/lean Rep.

Source: Pew Research Center for the People and the Press, *Muslim Americans: Middle Class and Mostly Mainstream,* (Washington, DC: Pew Research Center for the People and the Press, 2007).

the relatively recent arrival of most Muslims in America—fully two-thirds are first generation—Muslim Americans were "middle class and mostly mainstream" and bear the signs of a "community in the process of assimilating with the larger society."[6]

Success and Integration

A 2007 *Newsweek* "Special Report on Islam in America" concluded, "The story of Muslims in America is one of overwhelming success. . . . Muslim Americans represent the most affluent, integrated, politically engaged Muslim community in the Western world."[7] Indeed, the Pew survey showed that Muslim Americans look remarkably like the general population in terms of income and education. Nearly a quarter of Muslim Americans have a college or graduate degree (14 percent college and 10 percent graduate), compared with virtually the same number in the general population (16 percent college and 9 percent graduate). Like the general population, about half of Muslims are middle class, with incomes between $30,000 and $100,000.[8]

Muslim Americans are also highly integrated in terms of identity. The Pew survey offered this summary of Muslim integration into American society:

> Although many Muslims are relative newcomers to the U.S., they are highly assimilated into American society. With the exception of very recent immigrants, most report that a large proportion of their closest friend are non-Muslims. On balance, they believe that Muslims coming to the U.S. should try and adopt American customs rather than trying to remain distinct from the larger society.[9]

Muslims, however, like most immigrant groups today, are not simply blending in to the old melting pot. Nearly half of Muslims in the United States (47 percent) also say they think of themselves first as Muslim rather than as American.[10] They are engaging in a dance of adoption and adaptation, adopting American customs and at the same time adapting American culture to fit their Muslim identity.

Representative Keith Ellison (D-MN), an African American who made history in 2006 by becoming the first Muslim elected to the U.S. Congress, noted that for most Muslim Americans, "the idea of America is an amazing thing—a society organized around a set of principles instead of around racial or cultural identity."[11] The existence of a set of principles rather than a particular culture as the center of gravity of American identity, coupled with freedom of religion that protects minority religions, has provided fertile ground for the flourishing of an integrated Muslim community in America.

Religion and Politics

In terms of religion, the Pew report also concluded that "Islam resembles the mainstream of American religious life."[12] For example, approximately the same number of Muslims and Christians in the United States say that they attend religious services at least once a week (40 percent and 45 percent, respectively). While Muslims are slightly less likely than Christians to report that they pray every day (61 percent vs. 70 percent respectively),[13] more Muslims than Christians say that religion is "very important" to their lives (72 percent vs. 60 percent).[14]

Politically speaking, American Muslims are surprisingly progressive. More than seven out of ten Muslims voted for Democratic candidate Senator John Kerry over Republican candidate President George W. Bush in 2004, and nearly two-thirds (63 percent) of American Muslims identify with or lean toward the Democratic Party. As noted above, Rep. Keith Ellison, the only Muslim ever elected to Congress, is a Democrat from Minnesota; moreover, Ellison ran an unapologetically progressive campaign reminiscent of the late Senator Paul Wellstone, declaring boldly, "Democrats have to rediscover and re-embrace liberalism. I would say that every good thing about this country came out of the mind of a liberal. Absolutely, I'll say that."[15]

In terms of political ideology, a quarter of Muslims identify as liberal, outnumbering the number of Muslim conservatives; in the general population, conservatives outnumber liberals by a margin of 34 percent to 19 percent.[16] Moreover, for Muslims, ideology and party identification are not tightly linked as they are in the general population; even among self-identified conservatives, 60 percent align with the Democratic Party. Finally, the Pew survey found that "by nearly two-to-one, Muslim Americans do not see a conflict between being a devout Muslim and living in a modern society."[17]

In the Shadow of September 11: Shifting Muslim American Identity and Engagement

According to Dr. M. A. Muqtedar Khan, associate professor of political science at the University of Delaware, prior to the events of September 11, 2001, American Muslims were on a steady, if low-profile, path toward both becoming more established in the United States and becoming more socially and politically progressive.[18] Since September 11, this trend has become more complicated as Muslims struggle with the experience of increased prejudice and sometimes outright hostility against their own Muslim identity and Islam in general. In an interview with *Newsweek*, Raze Mohiuddin, a successful entrepreneur in Silicon Valley, reflected the experience of many Muslims: "[The September 11 attacks] forced people to say, 'Where do I stand? Either I walk away from the faith or I become more involved in defending the faith, which is under assault.'"[19]

The progressive leaders I interviewed generally characterized their outlook as cautiously optimistic. On the one hand, there are some troubling signs of retrenchment. Many of the leaders I interviewed noted that many mosques, which are predominantly led by imams trained outside the United States and tend to be more conservative than American Muslims as a whole, have taken a measured inward defensive turn as many perceived their religion and values to be under attack. Moreover, there is also some indication that some Muslim American youth are more conservative and less inclined to embrace integration than their older counterparts. For example, Muslims age eighteen to twenty-nine are much more likely than their parents to go to mosque every week (50 percent vs. 35 percent of Muslims over thirty) and are significantly more likely to think of themselves as "Muslim first" (60 percent vs. 40 percent of Muslims over thirty).[20] Of more serious concern, more than twice as many younger Muslims as older Muslims believe that suicide bombings can be "often or sometimes justified" (15 percent vs. 6 percent respectively).[21]

On the other hand, there are hopeful signs of more open civic engagement and integration. The largest Muslim organization, the Islamic Society of North America (ISNA), which represents the vast majority of the immigrant Muslim community that makes up 80 percent of U.S. Muslims, has embarked on a self-conscious campaign among its 100,000 members and 1,000 affiliated organizations to improve the public image of Islam and to engage positively in American civil society in broader ways. The theme of its 2007 convention—"Upholding Faith, Serving Humanity"—reflected this dual focus, and the cover of the convention program linked this emphasis with a verse from the Qur'an: "To those who believe and do righteous deeds, God has promised fogiveness and great reward."[22]

These themes, especially the emphasis on the need to engage American society more broadly, ran strongly through the sessions at the conference. In the two sessions I attended, several speakers exhorted individual Muslims to see themselves as ambassadors for Islam to the wider American community. The following comments by Salam al-Maryati, director of the Muslim Public Affairs Council and Committee Member of Multifaith Voices for Peace and Justice, were typical:

> What is the value we as representatives of the faith have to America? And how do we serve humanity? And this is not a matter of issuing a press release; this is a matter of working side-by-side with other Americans on these issues. . . . Now we have gone from the level of individuals to the level of institutions. Even the Prophet Muhammad was told to say he was following the way of God, he and his followers, so there was an institutional approach to this issue. I say for us today, we cannot wait for saviors to solve our problems. It is our institutional responsibility. And when we talk about civic and political integration here around this table, what we mean is now we have to be part of an American society when they get concerned about the affairs of our country, no matter what those issues. . . . We are here. We have something to offer. Let us take advantage of the opportunity and let us become relevant to American society, and that will make the extremist voice irrelevant. That is the day of victory for all of us.[23]

Of the seventy-five individual sessions at the conference, more than one-third addressed issues of broad social justice and civic engagement.[24] Given the relatively recent establishment of the Muslim community in

America, and the needs of attending to community and institution building this stage of development entails, a commitment of one-third of the
sessions to broad social justice and civic engagement issues is significant.

The Growing Role of Women in American Islam

The ISNA conference was also an indicator of another feature in the emerging public identity of Islam in America: the prominent role of women in
leadership. In 2006, Dr. Ingrid Mattson, professor of Islamic Studies and
Christian-Muslim Relations at Hartford Seminary, was the first women to
be elected president of ISNA.[25] As I discuss below, the prominence of female
leadership has certainly not been without strong controversy. The initiatives
to promote an Islamic Bill of Rights for Women in the Mosque and the
woman-led prayer movement, while somewhat successful, were met with
strong opposition, and even death threats from some fringe elements. However, the move for women's full equality is taking root, especially among the
second generation of Muslim women who have grown up in America with
equal political rights. And the emerging group of progressive Muslim voices
is declaring squarely that "the Muslim community as a whole cannot achieve
justice unless justice is guaranteed for Muslim women."[26]

The Emergence of Progressive Muslim Voices in America

The experience of September 11 catalyzed a loose collection of leaders to begin
organizing a progressive Muslim movement in the United States. This progressive network had been growing organically and informally, but did not yet
have an institutional presence when the events of September 11 precipitated
the need for a public progressive voice. These needs brought two organizations
into being, an edgy e-zine called Muslim WakeUp! (www.muslimwakeup.com)
and the Progressive Muslim Union (www.pmuna.org). Because these organizations came into being somewhat abruptly, they created considerable tensions
within the mainstream Muslim organizations such as ISNA, and the leaders
of these organizations themselves had competing goals.

The most lasting contribution of this movement was the book *Progressive Muslims: On Justice, Gender, and Pluralism*, which not only served to
bring together for the first time in print a group of progressive Muslim voices

but succeeded in naming a set of core issues around which progressive Muslim voices were organizing.[27] Citing Bob Dylan's "The Times They Are A-Changin'," Dr. Omid Safi, associate professor of religious studies at the University of North Carolina and former cochair of the Progressive Muslim Union, summarized the heart of the progressive Muslim movement:[28]

> We realize the urgency of the changin' times in which we live, and seek to implement the Divine injunction to enact the justice ('adl) and goodness-and-beauty (ihsan) that lie at the heart of the Islamic tradition. . . . At the heart of the progressive Muslim interpretation is a simple yet radical idea: every human life, female and male, Muslim and non-Muslim, rich or poor, Northern or Southern, has exactly the same intrinsic worth . . . because, as the Qur'an reminds us, each of us has the breath of God breathed into our being.[29]

This emphasis on the oneness and equality of humanity served as the basis for new thinking about three prominent themes that emerged from the writings of these progressive Muslims: social justice, gender justice, and pluralism. Like other religious progressives, Safi and his colleagues in the book explicitly affirm that this commitment to the oneness and equality of humanity "changes the way we think about God, and vice versa."[30] For progressive Muslims, the Qur'an and the tradition are not simply starting places, but they are partners in a conversation that makes possible "going beyond older interpretations of Islam" by bringing together egalitarian commitments with critical engagement with the tradition.[31]

Ijtihad: The Principle of Independent Thinking and the Pursuit of Truth

One of the key growth edges for progressive Islam in America is the revival and development of the Islamic concept of *ijtihad*, or independent thinking about the tradition in light of contemporary issues.[32] While a method of thinking about truth may not seem sexy, an authentic theological method is crucial for providing space for creative engagement with the tradition in which new understandings of truth can flourish. Dr. M. A. Muqtedar Khan—author of both the website www.ijtihad.org and the book *American*

Muslims: Bridging Faith and Freedom—noted that the fruits of a progressive reclaiming of *ijtihad* are quite significant:

> We can see the product of American *ijtihad* in the progressive role that women play in the American Muslim community and in Islamic scholarship. Another important indicator is the absence of embedded radicalism in American Islam and the enormous appetite that American Muslims and their organizations express for democracy, civil rights, pluralism, and civic engagement.[33]

The great strength of this critical engagement with tradition is that it wrestles with the tradition in light of contemporary experience not to "graft Secular Humanism onto the tree of Islam," but to develop new, progressive interpretations that are authentic outgrowths of the tradition.[34]

Dr. Khan noted that one of the fault lines between progressive Muslims and more conservative Muslims is demarcated by two competing notions of *ijtihad*. Historically, *ijtihad* had a fairly circumscribed usage:

> One [conception of *ijtihad*] is a very narrow, legalistic notion of it as a process of juristic reasoning employed to determine the permissibility of an action when primary sources, namely the Qur'an and Sunnah (Tradition of the Prophet), are silent and earlier scholars of *shari'a* (Islamic law) had not ruled on the matter.[35]

In other words, *ijtihad* was a necessary concession in the face of new situations, a technique for filling in the gaps where revelation and established tradition were silent or unclear. Moreover, historically, only certain qualified jurists were authorized to engage in *ijtihad*. Dr. Khan went on to note that this view—where *ijtihad* was only admissible in a narrow set of circumstances and only accessible to an elite few—"stifled independent thought among Muslims."[36]

Getting There: Recovering *Ijtihad* and Independent Thinking

Dr. Abdullahi Ahmed An-Na'im, professor at Emory University Law School and internationally known human rights activist, noted that although such a limitation may have been appropriate in previous historical times, a broader approach to *ijtihad*—what Dr. An-Na'im calls "persuasive *ijtihad*"— is the only justifiable approach in the contemporary age.

> What I say is that now we live in a different environment where the possibility of *ijtihad* is much wider in its scope and methodology and outcomes than ever before in Muslim history. The fact that more Muslims are now able to read the sources for themselves, the fact that they can communicate among themselves, marginalizes the traditional craft of the scholars who used to monopolize Islamic knowledge. At this point we cannot prescribe what is legitimate *ijtihad* in a preemptive way. We have no way of knowing until we hear what it has to say. And for that reason, I say that we have to open the door completely. There is not even a door to open. . . . It is simply the responsibility of every Muslim to apply themselves to the sources to the best of their ability to make up their own mind.[37]

For An-Na'im, the current age, which is marked by the rise of literacy and mass communication tools such as the Internet, represents a new era that demands a more democratic approach to tradition. This approach "opens the door" to all interpretations pending argument and persuasion, which are the only legitimate means by which truth can be discerned. This approach builds on and extends the approach of his mentor Mahmoud Muhammad Taha, an unorthodox mystic in An-Na'im's home country of Sudan, who was ultimately executed in 1985 by the state for his attempts to reform *shari'a* (Islamic law) there.[38] Dr. An-Na'im himself was jailed and then exiled, and he has devoted the last two decades of his life to retrieving a more open approach to tradition that builds bridges between the ancient traditions of Islam and the modern ideals of human rights and democracy by means of persuasive *ijtihad*.

One challenge that a more open, persuasive *ijtihad* faces is an often-cited strong warning attributed to the Prophet Muhammad against *bid'ah* (innovation) in religion. Saleemah Abdul-Ghafur is a second-generation African American Muslim, former advisory board member of the Progressive Muslim Union, and author of *Living Islam Out Loud: American Muslim Women Speak*.[39] As she put it, however, too often people pose as "the *bid'ah* police" simply in order "to keep you from thinking or expanding or considering something in a different way, but there should be a very vigorous and aggressive plurality of thought and dialogue in our community; we've lost that and we're bringing it back."[40]

Progressive Muslims remind their fellow Muslims that the warnings against *bid'ah* do not stand alone. Dr. Khan, for example, pointed to other sayings of the Prophet that strongly encourage *ijtihad*, which he called "a license to think and rethink":

> There's a tradition of the Prophet, peace be upon him, that says that there are two rewards for those who do *ijtihad* and get it right, and there is one reward for those who do *ijtihad* and get it wrong. So when I read this tradition, I said, "Wow! This is license to think. God is encouraging Muslims, or everybody, to think." So even if you get it wrong, you will get rewarded. He just wants us to exert our intellectual faculties.[41]

From this more inviting perspective, *ijtihad* is encouraged by the Prophet Muhammad himself and, by extension, by God. The emphasis here is less on the correct outcome and more on the proper use of God-given human intellectual capacity. There is a sense that God takes pleasure in seeing the exercise of these gifts, and therefore rewards the effort, the learning, and the creativity even if the outcome is not strictly speaking correct. The biggest concern in this approach to the tradition is not illegitimate innovation but the stifling of human spirit and the ossification of religion into antiquated irrelevance. Far from being un-Islamic, this tradition of *ijtihad*, Dr. Khan argued, is "an appeal to an authentic aspect of Islam; even this aspect of rethinking is an Islamic thing to do."[42]

A Symphonic Approach to Finding Truth

Consistent with Abou El Fadl's admonition to enter into a creative conversation with a text in order to "listen" for how texts "fit in the fulfillment of God's beauty," Dr. Omid Safi evoked a musical metaphor for understanding truth:

> People like me who think musically are very interested in this resonance of modern international secular human rights norms and tra-

ditional Islamic values. At a musical level, how do these two notes resonate with each other, without saying that one derives from the other one or that they must be collapsed into one another? It's a symphonic approach. It doesn't mean that the text is so open as to say whatever the heck we want it to say, but it does mean that human beings are involved and that the text, the audience, and the revealer of the text form a kind of holy triangle.[43]

The metaphor of musical resonance is a vivid way of describing the interplay of a "holy triangle" involving individual and communal experience, religious tradition, and God. Contrary to the common notion that tradition simply trumps experience, this progressive understanding allows the note of experience to sound first and then listens for the legitimacy of a particular interpretation of Islam.[44]

In my interviews with progressive Muslim leaders about the nature of truth, three other related ideas also emerged. The first concept, closely related to the more open interpretation of *ijtihad*, was ironically the positive and even necessary role of dissent in finding truth. The second pair of concepts strongly echoed themes I heard among the progressive leaders I interviewed across religious traditions: the concept of humility in accessing truth and the importance of experience in assessing the authenticity and legitimacy of claims to truth.

The opposite of truth is commonly understood to be heresy, and so I was especially struck when Dr. An-Na'im provocatively characterized his current book project, "The Future of *Shari'a*: Secularism from an Islamic Perspective," as "a celebration of heresy."[45] As An-Na'im notes, "within every religion, every view that came to prevail was at some point a heresy to the previously prevailing view. To keep the possibility of heresy alive is critical to the development of the tradition itself."[46] In a creative move that is designed to make his own scholarship embody the principles of persuasive *ijtihad*, An-Na'im is publishing "The Future of *Shari'a*" on the Internet in the eight major languages of the Muslim world and inviting critique from around the globe as he writes. So, from An-Na'im's perspective, protecting or even celebrating dissent—"the possibility of heresy"—is integral to a religious tradition finding its way to truth, to an authentic expression of Islam for the contemporary scene.

This idea is also closely related to a prominent theme of humility in discerning the truth, especially about what God requires of particular people and societies in particular historical circumstances. As Dr. Safi notes, the Islamic tradition has a particular view of "Truth":

> If anyone tells you that Islam is "the Truth" with a capital T, they have actually committed the cardinal theological sin of idolatry. When you look at classical Islamic thought, they had this word for "Truth" with a capital T, and the word was *al-haqq*. The interesting thing is that in Islam, Truth with a capital T is the name of God. So when we speak of truth, in fact, when you read classical medieval mysticism or philosophy and they say "Truth," that's God. It's not Islam, it's not my interpretation, it's not this verse, it's not even the Qur'an—"Truth" as such is God.[47]

According to Safi, Islam reserves "Truth with a capital T" as an attribute of God, something not directly accessible to human beings. Even if one holds a high view of the Qur'an as a divinely revealed text, the Qur'an itself is not the "Truth."

Safi also expressed the foundation of humility in his description of the connections between general affirmations of the existence of truth and the methods by which we grasp the content of those affirmations: "Ultimately there is God; and there is truth and beauty and justice in the world. How we manage to find it is also part of how we find our own selves."[48] As this quote implies, affirmations of the existence of God and ideals such as truth, beauty, and justice in the world still leave open the question of how we humans gain an understanding of God or grasp these ideals. Moreover, the way in which we find these things also influences the way in which we experience ourselves. If we find God and truth as something external to ourselves, we find ourselves disempowered, passive recipients. If, on the other hand, we find God and truth through a more active engagement with sacred texts and tradition, we find ourselves empowered, active partners with God on a journey to help truth break into our contemporary world. Dr. Khan summarized this latter view as connecting "the word of God" with the "intuitive feelings of conscience" and noted that this path "is how you ultimately become a progressive Muslim: you begin to rely on your rational and conscience-related instincts, as opposed to shutting yourself down as a person and trying to practice somebody else's ideas that are hundreds of years old."[49]

This curious combination of humility in what truth we can know and confidence that the only way we can know it is through our own consciences points to the critical role of experience in assessing claims to truth. This theme, not surprisingly, was especially prominent in my interviews with progressive Muslim leaders who were women. Saleemah Abdul-Ghafur characterized some of the changes she has witnessed recently in the American Muslim community the following way:

> [The changes] we're witnessing right now are particularly because Muslims like me have grown up in the West and have access to Emory University and Harvard University, and we can travel to al-Azhar to study for a summer. When we come back, we already have the expectation of freedom of speech, of human rights, of access to education, when we read and engage sacred texts. We say, "Okay, I went to school. I learned Arabic. So now I can access that sacred text. . . . And I'm going to read the freedom iteration of [the text] because that's my foundation." And so what we're experiencing now is more women and men engaging sacred texts in really public ways, reclaiming Islam and uncovering or excavating things that have been lost in our tradition.[50]

Abdul-Ghafur notes that when Western Muslims like herself gain access to Arabic texts, they also bring their commitment to democratic values such as of freedom of speech, human rights, and access to education to that engagement. And when those values clash with certain patriarchal interpretations of the text, Muslims like her are weaving together a new "freedom iteration" of the tradition.

Abdul-Ghafur emphasized that this reclaiming of the progressive strands of Islamic tradition was especially prevalent among younger, second-generation Muslims like herself.

> We were born and raised in this country, and we don't have the same baggage that my parents do coming through Jim Crow and the civil

rights era, or an immigrant's experience living in India before it split into India and Pakistan and having a really hard middle passage coming to this country and really struggling to survive. No, we were raised in a Detroit suburb and had the best of everything and had an Ivy League education.

The second generation is saying, "These things don't work for us. . . ." We came up against this notion that we could not have Islam expressed through us, but rather we had to conform ourselves into Islam. . . . But God doesn't want us to be Muslim robots that follow a particular way. Islam is supposed to be expressed through individuals and through communities, and we should leave a space for that and welcome that. Many of the women in my book would've just walked away from Islam at another time because it was too difficult. But now what we're saying is, "No, we're Muslim, and we have the right to that just like anybody else does, and furthermore, you don't have the right to tell me that I'm not Muslim just because I don't practice the way you think I should." And that's a much more powerful place to be in.[51]

For Abdul-Ghafur, the second generation has a more confident hold not only on what "works" for them but on their own legitimate standing to reclaim an Islam that they can express through their own lives and communities.

Women particularly are drawing on their own experiences and identities to reclaim their space both figuratively and literally. Abdul-Ghafur, for example, lived out this principle with her involvement as co-organizer of the controversial "Woman-Led Prayer Initiative." At this event, which had to be rescheduled several times due to bomb threats, Dr. Amina Wadud, African American activist and well-known professor of Islamic studies at Virginia Commonwealth University, led a mixed gender group of about one hundred Muslims in Friday prayer at the Cathedral of St. John the Divine in New York City on March 18, 2005.[52] Abdul-Ghafur compared the experience to Sojourner Truth's courageous, controversial preaching in Christian churches and summed up her experience of hearing Dr. Wadud's sermon at the service, saying, "I had just heard freedom. . . . Through Dr. Wadud, God offered me another vision of Islam and Muslims. One where I belonged, and it belonged to me."[53]

Like Safi, Abdul-Ghafur evoked the imagery of "resonance" as a way of putting experience into conversation with tradition:

> It resonates within me that God is beyond gender. . . . That's something that gives me goose bumps, this whole notion that God is like me. When God is creator, God is the all-knowing, the all-powerful, the all-forgiving, the all-merciful, the most subtle, all the attributes of God, why would God then be a gender? If God is loving to all people, why then would God be one and not the other, and then have it set up in our minds so that it would be one over the other? It doesn't work for me, so what resonates within me is that God is supernatural.[54]

For Abdul-Ghafur, the teachings she inherited about a patriarchal God clashed both with her increasing knowledge of the broader tradition and with her own embodied experience as a woman. Ultimately, she determined that the patriarchal, hierarchical teaching did not "work" for her, and she claimed other strands in the tradition that "resonated" with her conscience.

With this progressive approach to tradition, Muslims need not simply "conform into" a preconceived notion of Islam but rather can take a "more holistic" approach to the Qur'an in order to claim an authentic Islam that is "expressed through" empowered individuals and communities.

Sacred Texts: Unity and Diversity in the Qur'an

Progressive Muslims bring a variety of tools to the encounter with the text of the Qur'an. They begin, as Abou El Fadl described, with what might be called an aesthetic approach to the tradition that links justice and beauty and privileges the fulfillment of divine beauty in the world as a criterion for discerning truth. This approach necessitates engaging in a creative conversation between contemporary experience and texts, a method that operates more in the realm of aesthetics than in the realm of deductive logic.

One of the clear characteristics of progressive Muslims that emerged in my interviews was the prominence of direct appeals to the Qur'an and the mystical Sufi tradition as a foundation for progressive stands and approaches. As Dr. Safi explained:

> Progressives are extremely well-versed in and tend to go to two places as our security blanket. One may surprise people and the other one should not. The first one is the Qur'an, and the second is the example of Islamic mysticism or Sufism. Progressives in many ways are actually remarkably Qur'an-centric Muslims. And this might be a way in which progressive Muslims might be substantially different from progressive Christians or progressive Jews, in the extent to which they haven't ceded the Qur'an as a source of authority to literalist exclusivists.[55]

As Safi notes, the prominence of the Sufi mystical tradition is not so surprising, since the mystical approach is consistent with the progressive emphasis on creative interpretations of texts and the authority of direct, contemporary experience.[56] However, the emphasis on direct appeals to the Qur'an at first glance may seem unusual. As many of the leaders I interviewed pointed out, however, this emphasis is understandable because, in addition to the Qur'an being the supreme authority that virtually all Muslims accept, the Qur'anic texts are often more open to progressive interpretation than the writings of Muslim jurists, especially conservative Muslim jurists who wrote from a defensive posture in the context of Western colonialism over the last few hundred years.[57]

When I asked progressive Muslim leaders for specific Qur'anic texts that grounded their own work, they most frequently cited passages that emphasized the unity and equality of all people and the goodness of diversity. Dr. Najir Khaja, a practicing physician and chairman of Islamic Information Services, a nonprofit media company reaching 2.5 million people in two hundred U.S. cities and seven countries through its flagship program, "The American Muslim Hour," paraphrased two passages from the Qur'an that I heard repeated numerous times during the interviews.

> There is a passage in the Qur'an that starts, "we have made you from a single soul," so the gender issue is addressed there by a sense of equality. Then there is another passage that says, "Mankind, we have made you into nations and tribes, so that you understand the differences between one another."[58]

The tension between unity and diversity, from this perspective, is built into the very fabric of creation. On the one hand, all of humanity is descended not only from a single set of ancestors but from a single soul; on the other hand, diversity becomes one of the ways through which God ordained that unity be realized.

Dr. Kecia Ali, assistant professor at Boston University and author of *Sexual Ethics and Islam: Feminist Reflections on Qur'an, Hadith, and Jurisprudence*,[59] elaborated on the importance of the verse about the unity of humanity, especially for establishing the equality of women:

> The beginning of the fourth chapter of the Qur'an talks about creation, and for feminist scholarship in particular, this is tremendously important. It says, "[speaks Arabic] Oh people, be conscious of your Lord who created you from a single soul and created from it,"—literally "from her," because "soul" is grammatically feminine in Arabic—"her mate, and from the two of them, many men and women scattered far and wide." Here you start from a single entity. And to me, this trip from singularity to duality is tremendously important and useful. . . . We move from God creating to human reproduction, and I think that that contrast between divine power, divine self-sufficiency and human interdependence is very important. And that theological move is important for feminists.[60]

Dr. Ali, who is also distinguished by being the first female officiant at a Muslim marriage in America, emphasized that "there's no rib in this story"—the well-known biblical account of Eve being created from Adam's rib that has been used to justify patriarchal ideas and institutional arrangements.[61] In this Qur'anic account, there is no hierarchical gender relationship, no ontological priority in creation order, but rather a radically egalitarian story of creation from a single "soul," a word that is grammatically feminine in Arabic.

Dr. Umar Faruq Abd-Allah, chairman of the board and scholar in residence of the Nawawi Foundation, a Chicago-based foundation dedicated to building a successful American Muslim cultural identity, noted that the unity of humanity was also reflected in a well-known saying of the Prophet Muhammad found in the *Hadith* (a collection of the sayings and deeds of the Prophet):

The Nawawi Foundation is named after a great Sufi scholar. One of his great compilations is called "The Forty *Hadith*," which contains the forty *hadiths* that he felt were the most important to teach people if you couldn't teach them anything else. One of those is regarded by all Muslims to be authentic: "None of you believes until he loves for his brother what he loves for himself." Nawawi himself in his commentary says that "his brother" here is not "his brother *Muslim*"—it's all human beings.[62]

In this saying, the Prophet Muhammad specifies the implications of shared human origins, declaring that religious belief is inauthentic without a universal ethic of love. This sentiment of reciprocity is present in all the major world religions and is most familiar in American society as "the Golden Rule." Just as Jesus specifies that one's "neighbor" extends far beyond one's coreligionists, Nawawi clarifies that the Prophet's declaration here also is not limited to fellow Muslims or to men but, consistent with the creation story above, the word "brother" is to be understood in the most expansive sense to mean "all humanity."

One perhaps unique contribution of the Qur'an is its coupling of the unity of all humanity with an explicit affirmation of diversity as a positive part of the divine plan for humanity. Simply put, unity in the Qur'an does not imply sameness. Dr. Abou El Fadl noted the clarity and prominence of this idea in the Qur'an:

> Quite contrary to the common perception, the Qur'an is actually quite insistent that the world will never be all Muslim. It is just a fact of creation that there will always be Muslims and non-Muslims and that people will be very different. And then the Qur'an has this famous expression, "Behold, We have created you from a male and a female and have made you into nations and tribes so that you might come to know one another."[63]

From the perspective of the Qur'an, there is a unity in human origins that is nonetheless expressed in a plurality of ways. Moreover, the diversity of expressions is the means by which humans come to know one another and ultimately come to know truth.

Dr. Eboo Patel, founder and director of Interfaith Youth Core, a Chicago-based organization that brings together youth from different religious traditions in common dialogue and service, also noted the centrality of the affirmation of pluralism in Islam. Dr. Patel related another account of creation from the Qur'an to make this point.

> In Chapter 2 of the Holy Qur'an we are told this story, that God created Adam, the first human being and the representative of all humankind, with a lump of clay and his breath. And God made Adam his *abd* and *khalifa*, his servant and representative. . . . And then God says to Adam, "I want you to name the different parts of creation," and Adam can name them. So Adam has the ability to do what even the angels don't have the ability to do, and that is to name diversity. And so how we engage with that diversity, how we use language, how we build relationships amidst diversity, I think is a central aspect of what it means to be human. And of course Muslims believe that Adam was the first prophet, the first of God's messengers carrying God's message of monotheism and mercy, which is the core of Islam and the core of all the Abrahamic faiths.[64]

From this perspective, unity and diversity are not competing concepts; diversity is actually an appropriate expression of this unity and part of God's will for creation. This diversity is a means through which humans "might come to know one other." And as Dr. Patel notes, the ability to engage this diversity and build relationships amidst diversity is a central way in which we become fully human, and in fact, share in the divine nature.

Because the word "diversity" is merely descriptive of a varied landscape, many progressive Muslim leaders also specified that the Islamic vision of diversity might better be captured by the concept of pluralism. As Dr. Diana Eck, director of the Pluralism Project at Harvard University and author of *A New Religious America: How a "Christian Country" Has Become the World's Most Diverse Nation*, has noted, diversity describes a state of affairs, while pluralism represents "an achievement" based on an affirmation of diversity.[65] Dr. An-Na'im picked up this distinction, "We can have a situation where a society is diverse but not pluralistic. To be pluralistic, there has to be self-conscious choice of promoting and accepting difference."[66]

One other corollary that I heard consistently was that the positive affirmation of diversity required by this conception of pluralism does not entail relativism (believing all religious traditions are equal) or secularism (believing all religious traditions are equally bad). Dr. Patel summarized what it means to be a religious pluralist:

> A religious pluralist is somebody who may well believe very, very deeply in their own tradition, who may even be an exclusivist and believe that their own tradition is the only "right" tradition, but who fundamentally believes in a society where people from different backgrounds have the freedom and the right to live by their own traditions and where they can live together in equal dignity and mutual loyalty.[67]

For Patel and other progressive leaders, then, their commitment to the equality of all human beings and to pluralism is not something they bring to Islam from the outside but something that is rooted in the Qur'an, the very foundation of Islam; it is thus a core part of what it means to live an authentically religious life as a Muslim.

The Power of Religious Practice: The Five Pillars of Islam

Traditionally, Muslims belief and practice have been defined around "five pillars" of Islam: the *shahada* (profession of faith that "there is no God but God and Muhammad is the Prophet of God"), *salat* (ritual prayer), *zakat* (giving of alms), *sawm* (fasting), and the *hajj* (pilgrimage to Mecca). It is notable that four of the five pillars of Islam are practices; like Judaism and Buddhism, Islam is better understood primarily as an "orthopraxy" rather than an "orthodoxy." As Reza Aslan notes in his excellent, accessible introduction to contemporary Islam, "the primary purpose of the Five Pillars is to assist the believer in articulating, through actions, his or her membership in the Muslim community [the *ummah*]."[68]

Each of these four major practices was mentioned frequently during my interviews with progressive Muslim leaders. Dr. Ali captured a sense of the basic approach that progressive leaders are taking to these traditional practices:

One of the things that's been remarkable to me in terms of progressive Muslim activism is the extent to which it hasn't sought to disrupt any of the established sets of practices. And I think that's a good thing and that's praiseworthy and laudable. My concern, when it comes to the Five Pillars, is not about changing any of them, but one, deepening and improving my own practice, and two, perhaps thinking about more inclusiveness.[69]

This approach of deepening authentic practice and opening traditional practices to be more inclusive, especially of women, was a prominent theme. Progressive Muslim leaders emphasized deepening practice not only as a way of putting forward an authentically Muslim perspective, but, as Rabia Terri Harris, director of the Muslim Peace Fellowship, put it, as "the wellspring of my existence"—a necessary part of grounding their own lives and guiding their own work.[70] For these progressive Muslims, the sustaining role of religious practice is essential for having the enlarged vision to see what work needs to be done to enhance justice and beauty in the world, the energy to do it often against great odds, and the wholeness of heart to persevere in the right spirit.

Religious Practice in Unusual Places

One striking aspect of Muslim religious practice—at least from the standpoint of the dominant form of religion in America, Protestant Christianity, where practices tend to center on worship services at churches—is that none of these four major Pillars of Islamic practice are centered on attending mosques. While in many majority Muslim societies, the mosque is more prominent—it is at the center of town and daily calls to prayer can be heard over loudspeakers from its minaret—the mosque is fairly decentered in American life, especially among progressive Muslims.[71] In fact, *most* of the progressive Muslim leaders I interviewed expressed disappointment and frustration about their experience of American mosques, noting their conservative, often insular nature. The following comment by Dr. Khan was typical:

The people who control the mosque, they control everything in the community. So there is gender segregation, there are restrictions on the nature of topics that can be discussed, the kind of speakers who can be brought. It's a very tyrannical environment, and so the community is intellectually restricted by the [lack of] enlightenment of the people associated with the mosque.[72]

Although many progressive Muslim leaders acknowledged and lamented the lack of a thick web of other Muslim institutions that might serve as a hub of Muslim communities, a number nonetheless talked with excitement about a new movement of informal gatherings. Abdul-Ghafur described her own experience:

I've done this here in Atlanta—in my desire to want fellowship but just not being able to stand mosque culture—from time to time, create a prayer space in your house and invite like-minded people into your home. And that's happening all over, particularly the people who wanted to do woman-led prayers but their local mosque wouldn't allow it. They'd just rent out a community center. They'd do it in their house. They'd do it above their store.[73]

Dr. An-Na'im also noted that after experiencing local mosques being either too "superficial," "partisan," or "narrow," he and some like-minded Muslims "created a sort of parallel or alternative social network, which is evolving into our [religious] practice."[74]

A number of leaders also talked about broadening religious practices in other ways. In addition to making practices more inclusive of women, as with the woman-led prayer initiative, several leaders talked about expanding the range of what counts as a religious practice. Many leaders were quick to remind me that the careful reading and interpretation of sacred texts was itself an authentic religious practice in Islam. Additionally, other leaders noted the need to expand religious practice to include a range of contemporary practices that may show up in unexpected places:

For some, there is a very deliberate and intentional daily spiritual practice, and for others there is not. Their spiritual practice is like Starbucks and blogging. If you have a Muslim blog, and you do it ten hours a day, that is spiritual. One woman in *Living Islam Out Loud* talks about how dealing with her autistic son is what changed her practice of Islam. That is a calling. That is your expression of Islam in the world. And we need to understand that that's okay.[75]

For Abdul-Ghafur, practices embraced by younger Muslims such as blogging or practices engendered by particular lived experience such as caring for an autistic child should be understood as Muslim religious practices that are authentic "expressions of Islam in the world" and thus authentic ways of participating actively in and shaping the contemporary *ummah*, the Muslim community in the world.

Remembering the Disadvantaged: Fasting and Giving Alms

Sarah Eltantawi, former Communications Director for the Progressive Muslim Union and one of the co-organizers of the woman-led prayer, spoke powerfully about the interconnections between two practices that connected her to a consciousness of and solidarity with the poor:

> Two practices that really jump out for me are fasting during the month of Ramadan and *zakat*. During Ramadan, the entire community theoretically has to go without eating or drinking for thirty days from sunup to sunset; and you're told as a little child that we do this so that we can understand what it's like not to have food and water, so that you can know how poor people feel. That really is a profound experience. The other practice is *zakat*, which is almsgiving. In Islam it's not the tithe; you don't give it to the church. You give it to poor people. You have to seek out people who are less fortunate than you. For most Muslims, it's around 2½ percent of your wealth.[76]

The twin acts of voluntary deprivation for the sake of consciousness raising and the required proper use of wealth are powerful religious practices that, as Rabia Terri Harris noted, remind Muslims that "the rich owe the poor" and that "if you don't recognize the right of the poor in your wealth, your wealth is an offense before God."[77] It is worth noting also that because *zakat* is calculated from wealth rather than an income (the basis of the Christian tithe), it can be quite demanding, particularly for the wealthy. Moreover, *zakat* is not seen as a voluntary contribution but rather as a religious obligation that is concerned with a just circulation and distribution of wealth in society. In this way, *zakat* is also connected to establishing the social conditions for basic human dignity described in the Qur'an.

The *Hajj* : The Liberating Power of the Story of Hajar

All able-bodied Muslims are expected to make the *Hajj*, the pilgrimage to Mecca, at least once in their lifetime. One of the most powerful themes from the *Hajj* that emerged among progressive women leaders was the story of Hajar, a figure they described as "a strong-willed woman who was the historical mother of Islam."[78] Hajar may be more familiar to most Americans as "Hagar" in the English translation of the Christian Old Testament, the servant of Abraham and mother of Ishmael who was banished by Abraham at the bidding of his jealous wife Sarah after the birth of her son Isaac. After being banished, Hajar searched frantically for food and water and finally cried out to God, who rewarded her faithfulness by creating a spring that sustained her. During the *Hajj*, pilgrims reenact the story of Hajar's desperate search for life-giving water and food for herself and Ishmael by hurrying seven times between two small hills.[79]

Drawing on the imagery of strong female leadership as represented by Hajar, a group of Muslim feminists founded the Daughters of Hajar, a group dedicated to women's equality in Islam in the American context.[80] In 2004 the group began demanding equal access to mosques for women, action that culminated on March 1, 2005, when Asra Nomani, the founder of the group, posted her "Ninety-Nine Precepts for Opening Hearts, Minds, and Doors in the Muslim World" on her local mosque door in Morgantown, West Virginia.[81] This action represented a creative expression of Islam in the American cultural context. Substantively, it recalled the traditional ninety-nine names of God in Islam; and performatively, it conjured up the image of the sixteenth-century Protestant reformer Martin Luther's nailing of his "Ninety-Five Theses" to the church door in Wittenburg. The Daughters of Hajar were instrumental in organizing a "Take Back the Mosque" freedom tour (of which the woman-led prayer in New York was a part) to equalize women's access to American mosques and also published an "Islamic Bill of Rights for Women in the Mosque" and an "Islamic Bill of Rights for Women in the Bedroom."

Two of the leaders I interviewed, Sarah Eltantawi and Saleema Abdul-Ghafur, were members of the Daughters of Hajar. For these women, the story of Hajar was central. Eltantawi noted:

> For the women-led prayer, the story of Hajar—who was banished by Sarah into the desert and had to live on her own for 40 days and would run from well to well until finally God created a spring for her—animates the movement. This notion of the outcasted, struggling woman who finally finds redemption was something people brought up.[82]

Likewise, Abdul-Ghafur said:

> No one ever taught me about Hajar. I went on *Hajj*, and you run between two mountains seven times on *Hajj*, and I was just like, "Okay, I guess we're doing that; that's the ritual." But what are you really doing? I discovered this story of Hajar, who was left in the desert by her husband, who was a prophet of God, with a baby, and she didn't disintegrate and say, "Oh my God, my man has left me, what am I going to do?" She was like, "I'm going to pray. I'm going to call on my faith, and I'm going to muster everything that I can so that I can survive and my child can survive." What we typically see in sacred texts is the woman who is pious, but it's relative to a man somehow. And so she creates her life—it's incredibly powerful—she's a change agent in her own life, and she does that directly as a result of her relationship with God.[83]

For these women, the experience of the *Hajj*—the only major Muslim ritual in which men and women participate with no gender separation—with its broad messages of unity and equality, combined with the particular prominence of the story of Hajar as the mother of the faith, were particularly powerful, transformative foundations for working for women's equality in Islam.[84] In this ancient story, the patriarch—whom Abdul-Ghafur noted with some incredulity was "a prophet of God"—abandoned Hajar and her son, who then by her relationship with God finds redemption, salvages a covenant, and ultimately saves a people. This example of a "strong-willed woman" empowered these women leaders with an authentic Islamic precedent to draw on their own relationships with God in order to be "change agents" in pushing for women's equality.

An Agenda of Justice and Beauty

A number of leaders I interviewed made the link between beauty and justice—what might be called an aesthetics of justice in the Qur'an. Justice in Islam is linked to beauty, and one of the tasks of humanity is to play a role in bringing about the realization of that beauty in the world. Beauty also serves as a kind of hermeneutical key; asking how a particular interpretation of a text contributes to the establishment of beauty in the world provides a way of judging the legitimacy of particular interpretations.[85]

"The Qur'an," noted Dr. Khan, "says God loves those who do beautiful things: who establish beautiful behavior, who establish beautiful societies, societies that are compassionate."[86] All forms of tyranny and oppression are a blight on that ideal, and a central role of the Qur'an is to chart a path toward a society where all can live together in the absence of oppression.

This basic theme of justice—an aspect of beauty that is reflected in a well-ordered, fair society—ran through the most frequently mentioned issues during the interviews: terrorism/war, democracy/pluralism/human rights, and women's issues.[87] Because American Muslims have been under such scrutiny in America since September 11, the conversations about the relationship between Islam and terrorism/war and between Islam and democracy were particularly animated.

Not in My Name: Terrorism and War

Every single leader I interviewed unequivocally denounced terrorism and religious extremism. The following declaration by Omid Safi in the introduction to *Progressive Muslims Speak* captures these sentiments eloquently and passionately.

Not in my name, not in the name of my God will you commit this hatred, this violence. We stand by the Qur'anic teaching (5:32) that to save the life of one human being is to have saved the life of all humanity, and to take the life of one human being is to have taken the life of all humanity. That what you do to my fellow human beings, you do to me.[88]

Virtually all talked of the need to face up to the problems of the fringe elements of Muslim extremists within the Muslim community, and none of these leaders denied that, as in the Bible, there are passages in the Qur'an that can be used to support armed conflict in certain circumstances. They also went beyond the now-familiar assertions that Islam is "a religion of peace" to make strong arguments, all deeply rooted in Islamic tradition, against the use of violence, which ranged from the theological to the ethical to the practical. Finally, they declared in various ways that the time has come for mainstream and progressive Muslims to stand up and be counted.[89]

In our post–September 11 society, the issue of terrorism is not far beneath the surface of any conversation about Islam, and Muslim leaders constantly must deal with the stereotype of all Muslims as armed religious extremists. Like many others, Dr. Eboo Patel expressed his indignation at the way some "aggressive atheists," such as Christopher Hitchens, have painted all religious people, particularly Muslims, as fanatics and zealots:[90]

Are you crazy?! Are you kidding me that the 1.2 billion Muslims in the world really have something in common with the Muslims who behead people on television?! What do I have in common with those people?[91]

A'isha Samad, an African American Muslim woman and member of the executive committee of We Believe Ohio, also talked about how these stereotypes permeated her everyday life in Cleveland:

September 11 is an obstacle in every area of Muslims' lives now, especially for African American Muslims. We've seen an entirely different shift in how we're accepted or perceived. It used to be if you had chosen Islam as a way of life, you were looked upon as someone who chose a faith—you're living a disciplined life, you're okay, a good, godly person. After 9/11, even we became looked upon as suspicious in our own country. People say things. They didn't used to say things. People will say rude and harsh things. So prayer is what keeps me on track, and fasting.[92]

Despite grappling with the larger problem of Islamophobia and the everyday problem of prejudice, progressive Muslim leaders spoke of two constructive trends that have developed in the aftermath of September 11. First, the shared experience of prejudice fostered a sense of solidarity between the larger, generally more privileged immigrant Muslim community and the smaller African American Muslim community. Sara Eltantawi described this dynamic as follows:

After 9/11 there was a lot of justifiable comments from African American Muslims toward the immigrant Muslim community, which has been hegemonic in the American Muslim scene. A lot of comments along the lines of, "Now you finally get it. You came here, you thought you were 'white'—meaning you thought you didn't have social problems—and now you do and so now you're sort of 'black.'"[93]

This sense of being mapped onto American racial history—moving from a privileged "white" status to a clear minority "black" status—was talked about as a negative consequence that nonetheless gave two very different Muslim communities a common social experience and a common cause.

Second, as the ISNA conference theme ("Upholding Faith, Serving Humanity") discussed above demonstrates, the cultural crucible formed by the experience of September 11 produced the beginnings of a common Muslim American consciousness and a sense of urgency in putting forth a more public face of Islam. Dr. Khaja explained that the central effect of September 11 for many Muslims was a conviction that "we need to get involved because we have a stake in America."[94]

One prominent way of getting involved was speaking out for peace and against the war in Iraq. Saleema Abdul-Ghafur, for example, argued that the oneness of humanity reflected in the shared image of God provides a basic presumption against war itself:

God says in Qur'an that every person possesses the divine breath of God, and we should treat all people like that. And waging preemptive war? No. Because, really, what would a person of faith go to war over? If you believe we're connected, that every single person possesses that divine breath of God, could you go to war with them over resources? If you were a person of faith, you would not believe that resources are scarce; you believe resources are abundant.[95]

Abdul-Ghafur argues that a person of faith rejects one of the common premises of war—that there is a scarcity of resources worth killing for. A person of faith, rather, operates out of a sense of shared humanity and shared stewardship of resources. A person of faith, Abdul-Ghafur argues, sees an environment of abundance where those who share God's very breath can share the resources of the rest of God's creation.

One of the oldest Muslim organizations that responded early to September 11 was the Muslim Peace Fellowship, founded in 1994 as an affiliated organization of the Fellowship of Reconciliation, the largest and oldest (founded 1915) interfaith peace organization in the United States. When I asked Rabia Terri Harris, the founder of the organization, about the justification for a Muslim Peace Fellowship, she quoted without hesitation a verse from the Qur'an that captures the essence of a Muslim peacemaker: "The servants of the All-Compassionate are those who walk on the earth with humbleness, and when the ignorant address them, say 'Peace.'"[96]

Harris also evoked aspects of what might be called, to borrow a term from Christianity, the Islamic "just war" tradition.

Now, *jihad* doesn't mean "military engagement." *Jihad* means "struggle," it means "effort," and the word was used in the Qur'an and in prophetic practice long before there was any military dimension to it at all. So armed struggle is a subset of *jihad*. Contemporary armed struggle cannot qualify as *jihad* because of the limits that the Prophet, peace and blessings be upon him, placed on military engagement such as not harming noncombatants, not destroying the environment. There are no modern weapons that do not endanger noncombatants. Even [an] ordinary sidearm, if it's an automatic weapon, is really *haraam* [forbidden] because it can hit anybody. If you're engaging in armed struggle according to the prophetic example, you can't hit just anybody. You can only hit a combatant.[97]

Harris invokes two important ideas in this passage: the meaning of the infamous term *jihad* and the moral limits on armed conflict. As Harris notes, despite its ubiquitous connection with armed conflict and even terrorism in the post–September 11 American consciousness, the term *jihad* literally means "struggle." Muhammad himself is recorded in the Hadith as specifying that "the most excellent *jihad* is that for the conquest of the self" and that *jihad* in the sense of armed struggle was considered the "lesser" meaning of *jihad*.[98]

Moreover, like Christianity's "just war" tradition, Islamic tradition contains a set of moral criteria for the conduct of *jihad* as armed struggle, which have been developed over centuries. In the quote above, Harris invokes one of the most foundational principles of just warfare from an Islamic perspective: the prohibition on harming noncombatants. For Harris, this strong prohibition not only obviously rules out acts of terrorism that intentionally target innocent civilians, but it also rules out war by modern weapons of mass destruction, including even automatic weapons that indiscriminately kill combatants and noncombatants alike. Thus, far from the common public perception, even *jihad* as armed struggle must be understood not as unlimited war by unlimited means but war that must be morally justified and conducted within moral limits.

Finally, Dr. Safi invoked the legacy of Martin Luther King Jr. to make a straightforward moral argument about war and military spending in America.

Look, if we're spending $2 billion a week on this God-forsaken war, that's $2 billion that we don't have to build homes in this country. That's $2 billion a week that we don't have to actually take care of our children's health insurance. That's $2 billion a week that we don't have to actually put good teachers in schools and to take care of our students. This is what Martin [Luther King Jr.] was so amazing at helping people see: that a war that was literally on the other side of the world was responsible for an exacerbated poverty in this country. I think this is one of the things that we have to keep doing and saying and preaching, that there is no reason why we as the United States should be spending more on our military than the next thirty countries combined.[99]

According to Safi, progressive religious leaders must make the connections between bloated, escalating military spending demanded by the growing appetite of "American imperialism" and the lack of resources to invest in children's health care and education. For Safi, the current unjustified, literally God-forsaken war with Iraq was indicative of moral failing and misplaced national priorities that progressive Muslims are opposing.[100]

Islam and Democracy: What's Right with Islam Is What's Right with America

Imam Feisal Abdul Rauf is the imam of Masjid al-Farah in New York City and the founder of the American Society for Muslim Advancement (ASMA) and the Cordoba Initiative, two organizations that are designed to build bridges and heal relationships between American Muslims and the American public and between the Muslim world and America respectively. Like many progressive Muslim leaders with whom I spoke, Imam Abdul Rauf was thrust into action in the wake of the attacks on September 11, 2001:

> The attacks on the World Trade Center and the Pentagon also changed me personally. Before September 11, I was an Islamic teacher focusing on the theological, spiritual, and jurisprudential side of my faith and active in interfaith work in New York City. I went from refusing to get dragged into politics because I saw it as a no-win situation to being forced to explain myself and defend my faith. The events of that day in 2001 pulled me out of the warm mahogany pulpit at my mosque twelve blocks from ground zero in New York City.[101]

As Imam Abdul Rauf responded to hundreds of speaking requests, he realized that he had to address the strong misperception among many Americans that "Islamic values are antithetical to American values."[102] Imam Abdul Rauf's message, in his speaking and writing, connects the American social contract as embodied in the founding documents such as the Declaration of Independence and the Bill of Rights with a broad

"Abrahamic ethic." This shared ethic of the oneness and equality of humanity is, he reminds audiences, "a fundamental Islamic value."[103]

The compatibility of Islam and democracy was clearly established among the progressive leaders I interviewed. Dr. Abou El Fadl referred to the "amazing parallels" between the thought of Locke and Rousseau in the Western philosophical tradition and "the Qur'anic command that no one govern Muslims unless they freely give them their vote of endorsement."[104] Several referred to the concept of *shura* ("consultation"), which functioned in the Islamic legal tradition basically as a principle of consent of the governed. As Dr. Khan convincingly argued, "Look, the Qur'an is the only religious text among all religious texts that has a chapter on democracy. It has a chapter on *shura*, and *shura* is democracy; the Prophet had a constitution when he established the state in Medina."[105]

As a way of invoking this legacy of consultative government and an affirmation of pluralism, Imam Abdul Rauf named the Cordoba Initiative after the period of 800 to 1200 CE, when the Cordoba Caliphate ruled much of today's Spain, creating "what was, in its era, the most enlightened, pluralistic and tolerant society on earth" during the time of the so-called "dark ages" in much of Christian Europe.[106] Despite the monolithic tendencies of many Muslim countries in the postcolonial context of the last few centuries, Abdul Rauf has made a mission of reminding Muslims that the vast majority of Islamic history was pluralistic in terms of ethnicity, competing schools of interpretation of Islamic law, and religion. Abdul Rauf concluded with a point that he noted is critically important for creating the connections between the Islamic tradition and American democracy: "So except for the very recent history, the first thirteen or fourteen centuries of our history were very, very similar to the American social contract."[107]

Dr. An-Na'im also noted the contrast between classical Muslim societies, which from a place of relative security embodied a much more open, pluralistic form of Islam, and colonial and postcolonial Muslim societies, which from a place of external rule and embattlement developed a more rigid, closed form of Islam. One key result of colonialism, An-Na'im argued, is that "the state that we live with now is not an organic outgrowth of our societies. . . . Muslims in these societies have not been through the process of negotiating these questions for themselves."[108] This renegotiation of Islam with democracy involves both retrieving an earlier tradition of nascent democratic and pluralistic principles and making the case that modern democratic foundations, such as religious freedom, can be grounded authentically in the Islamic tradition. Both of these tasks are necessary to create the space where contemporary Muslims are able to see the organic connections between deeply held religious beliefs and modern democracy.

One clear example of such a project is Dr. An-Na'im's work to establish a reinterpretation of *shari'a* that fully embraces religious freedom and affirms what he calls "secularism from an Islamic perspective."[109] Dr. An-Na'im's stated his argument emphatically:

> My claim is not that we need to secularize the state in order to be modern. My claim is that we need a secular state to be better Muslims. We need to keep religion out of the state so that people can practice religion out of conviction, not coercion. And also so that we can debate religious doctrine.[110]

For An-Na'im, the work to legitimize a secular, democratic state from an Islamic perspective is not some external task imposed upon Muslims; rather, An-Na'im argues that Muslims have internal reasons for supporting democracy and religious freedom.

> In Islam, there's this notion of *niyya*, which means intent. No act can be religious unless intended to be so. And intention cannot be coerced. So, for example, if I go to pray in the mosque because these morality police force people to close their shops to go to the mosque as they do in Saudi Arabia, then the state is taking away the possibility of my intent being genuine, because then I'm praying to the state, not to God. I'm praying because the state said so, not because God says so. So the secular state is necessary, actually, for the possibility of being a pious Muslim—to be able to form the choice autonomously, independently, without any coercion to observe or not to observe. Belief requires the possibility of disbelief.[111]

The possibility of being "a pious Muslim," then, for An-Na'im is linked to a secular state, because only a secular state can properly protect the heart of religion, proper intent (*niyya*).

All of these efforts are designed to contribute to the process, as Imam Abdul Rauf put it, of helping the Muslim community "evolve from 'Muslims in America' to 'American Muslims.'"[112] This is a process every religious community, especially one constituted largely by immigrants, has had to do. Protestant Christians made this transition earlier (although it was not consistently realized until the nineteenth century), and Catholic Christians developed the indigenous theology along these lines by the mid-twentieth century with the work of John Courtney Murray and helped along by Vatican II.[113] Given their recent arrival in critical mass in this country, the Muslim community in America is developing this vernacular quickly. Dr. Abd-Allah of the Nawawi Foundation noted the importance of this cultural work, work that is not fully realized but certainly well on its way:

> I imagine there needs to be a matrix of ideas that would embrace hopefully all of the Muslim community, a master key consisting of things that we could all agree on as essential to our identity. And I would say that what must be a fundamental part of that matrix is to embrace the American Constitutional legacy. Because when you accept the Constitution, then you become American.[114]

This task of developing a "matrix of ideas" that serves as a "master key" for unlocking a sense of shared communal identity that is both American and authentically connected to core beliefs is a task each community must do for itself, and the voices featured here are leading the way.

If they are successful, the soil of American democracy will nourish the Islam that takes root in America, and American Muslims will shape the next generation of American democracy. As Imam Abdul Rauf argued, the best of America and the best of Islam should be quite compatible and the connection of the two should prove mutually beneficial:

> What's right with America and what's right with Islam have a lot in common. At their highest levels, both worldviews reflect an enlightened recognition that all of humankind shares a common Creator— that we are, indeed, brothers and sisters. . . . To hold high the lamp of freedom, hope, and friendship is America's greatest gift to the world—and its sacred responsibility.[115]

Bringing Justice and Beauty to Earth:
New Initiatives by Progressive Muslims

Clearly, in the Muslim community the leading issues of concern are in some ways more basic (i.e., about embracing democracy and pluralism) and the state of institutional development less mature than in the Christian and Jewish communities in America. However, given that two-thirds of the adult Muslim community are first generation, the intellectual coherence and institutional structure that exists is nothing short of remarkable. Dr. Safi's characterization of the current state of development of the Muslim community in America warrants quoting at length.

> I'm a parent, so I always think in terms of parental analogies. I have an adolescent teenager, and I have a child slightly older than a toddler. The Muslim community is somewhere between the two. We have some attributes of the toddler, and we have some of the adolescent—someone in whom you occasionally see all the promise of a grown-up and also the gawkiness and the awkwardness of someone whose body hasn't quite caught up with them. Intellectually, morally, I think we are well ahead of where we are institutionally. And it's a matter of the rest of us catching up with ourselves. Our ability and willingness to organize has to catch up with our political vision, with our religious vision and practice. I think [the goal is] forming viable communities that are not defining one group of Muslims against another but along ethical principles: in opposition to hegemony and to domination and to ugliness, regardless of who is committing those actions, Muslim or non-Muslim. That I will take as the measure of our maturity.[116]

Dr. Safi notes that the intellectual and moral capital in the American Muslim community exceeds the capacity of current institutions, and the nascent institutions that exist are still working out their interrelationships. The crisis of September 11, for example, forced American Muslims to shift from an emphasis on internal community building to an emphasis on external public relations. In that crisis, several organizations emerged to fill the void. As a result of that premature public presentation, tensions developed between several factions in the Muslim community as multiple groups clamored to speak for "American Muslims." In the end, many of the organizations that formed during this period, such as the Progressive Muslim Union, did not find long-term footing.[117]

A variety of efforts, however, are bearing fruit, as the organizations profiled here attest: the courageous group of progressive Muslim voices featured in *Progressive Muslims: On Justice, Gender, and Pluralism*, who continue to work in informal alliance on a variety of issues within the Muslim community; the work by a number of women scholars and activists to bring issues of gender justice to the center of American Muslim identity; the intellectual work by scholar-activists to bring into harmony authentic Muslim belief and practice and an affirmation of the American constitutional legacy; and the work of the largest mainstream Muslim organization, ISNA, to emphasize the twin themes of "upholding faith" and "serving humanity" as the core message of what it means to be Muslim in America.

While the broader web of Muslim organizations is still sorting itself out, there is no shortage of healthy activity in individual organizations. A brief look at two organizations demonstrates the vibrancy of new efforts on the ground.

Promoting Pluralism and Service: Interfaith Youth Core

Interfaith Youth Core (IFYC) was established in 2002 by Dr. Eboo Patel to "build mutual respect and pluralism among young people from different religious traditions by empowering them to work together to serve others."[118] The innovative heart of Patel's approach is that it moves beyond interfaith dialogue to shared values and common causes. Instead of emphasizing theological or political differences—the typical stuff of interfaith dialogue—IFYC asks, "What can we do together?"[119]

In an interview, Patel noted that this work began with a stark realization he himself had in his twenties:

> I realized that every time I turned on the television in the 1990s, somebody was killing somebody else to the soundtrack of prayer, and that person was always nineteen or twenty-six or twenty-nine. I said, "Why is it that so many young people are so involved in religious extremism? How does this happen?"[120]

As Patel began to explore what it would take to build an interfaith youth movement that would be a force for pluralism rather than a force for extremism, he said that he stumbled on another disheartening realization. After attending major international meetings such as the Parliament of the World's Religions, he found that most of the interfaith conferences were "a bunch of people over sixty drafting documents, curating ceremonies, having banquets, and planning the next conference."[121] At that point, Patel knew the call was urgent to do something new. As he explained:

> I was twenty-three years old at the time. My hair was on fire, and I saw the world in relatively stark terms. And I basically thought to myself, "If religious extremism is a movement of young people taking action and interfaith cooperation is a movement of old people talking, we're going to lose; it's just that simple." So I said, "Damn it, I'm going to start this. I am not going to forfeit what it means to be religious, and I'm not going to forfeit the world that I love to religious extremists who are exceptional at identifying, recruiting, and training young people for their murderous causes." So that was the animating spark of the Interfaith Youth Core.[122]

In just five short years, Patel has built an impressive organization that is active on more than fifty college campuses. He was invited to speak at the sixteenth annual Nobel Peace Prize Forum, and Queen Rania of Jordan invited him to set up a U.S.-Jordan youth exchange program. He has also become a sought-after speaker on youth issues and pluralism.

The flagship program of IFYC is "Days of Interfaith Youth Service" (DIYS), a campaign that pairs community service and interfaith dialogue in coordinated projects across the country each April. Begun in 2004 with twelve hundred participants at nineteen sites, DIYS has doubled its reach in just three years, expanding to more than thirty-five hundred participants at thirty-two sites, including six international sites.[123] When Patel speaks with students at these community service projects, he often talks about how his own Muslim religious tradition informs his work. Modeling a kind of dialogue that articulates religious reasons for the work he is doing, he typically begins his talk by citing what he calls one of the "most beautiful" verses of the Qur'an, which says that "God made us different nations and tribes that we may come to know one another."[124]

Patel's opening talk to a group of diverse students gathered in Chicago for a service project illustrates well the blend of dialogue and action around shared values:

> Today you will do something that seems small. But the blanket that you make will warm a refugee child when she goes to sleep, and the things that you say to the people next to you will give them a window into Islam, Judaism, Christianity, Hinduism, or Buddhism that they might not have had before.[125]

Through dozens of projects like these that bring together thousands of diverse young people, Patel is helping a new generation of youth "know one another" and slowly but surely building a new interfaith youth movement. Toward the end of our interview, Patel summarized his aspirations, which are rooted in his own Muslim faith: "My hope is to articulate what I love about your tradition, and to teach you what you might love about mine, and to point to a space where we might work together to serve others. And in my mind, that's the example of the Prophet Muhammad."[126]

Merging Service and Activism:
Inner-City Muslim Action Network (IMAN)

Like Eboo Patel, Rami Nashashibi is young, charismatic, and passionate about his Muslim faith. But it wasn't always so. Nashashibi, raised in a secular Muslim home in Jordan, did not find his interest in Islam awakened until he came to Chicago for college. It was then, as he witnessed gritty urban poverty and inequality, that he recognized parallels between the black struggle for civil rights and the plight of his own Palestinian people. As he explained:

> When I drive down Lake Shore Drive and I see the Gold Coast and I see Cabrini-Green—or what's left of it—which is one of the housing projects here in Chicago, within a mile of that plush oasis, and I realize that there's this serious disparity within my society that I

live in and I benefit from, I have to begin to hold myself accountable. Ultimately, that accountability should drive me to seek fairer ends.[127]

Compelled by his faith, Nashashibi and a group of other Muslim students founded Inner-City Muslim Action Network (IMAN) in 1995. Seeking to respond to "the pervasive symptoms of inner-city poverty and abandonment," IMAN began by offering a few direct services aimed at the needs of its South Side Chicago neighborhood.[128] From its humble beginnings, IMAN has grown into an agency that now provides an impressive array of services, including free primary health care, career advancement classes, food assistance, and youth development programs.

In addition to direct service, Nashashibi sees organizing and advocacy as central to IMAN's work combating poverty. One example of this is Project Restore, an initiative that seeks to reduce mass incarceration and provide alternative sentencing for nonviolent drug offenders. Through Project Restore, IMAN provides transitional housing and other supports for formerly incarcerated men. IMAN also engages in legislative advocacy. Most notably, it played a role in the passage of state legislation allowing judges to divert nonviolent drug offenders into alternative treatments.

Arts and cultural expression, both traditional Muslim and contemporary, have also been dynamic and integral pieces of IMAN's work from its inception. Its premier cultural and community event is called "Takin' It to the Streets," a festival of arts, culture, sports, service, and activism. The initial event in 1997 involved several hundred participants, mostly young Muslims. Ten years later, "Takin' It to the Streets" drew over ten thousand people, making it one of the largest and most unique gatherings of its kind.

Nashashibi's work is deeply grounded in Islam, and his leadership of IMAN was mentioned by several other leaders as an example that has caught the imagination especially of younger Muslims. Nashashibi looks to Islam to find, as the IMAN website summarizes it, "the spiritual ideals of community service, social justice and human compassion."[129] And Nashashibi felt a call not only to serve Muslims but to practice charity and advocacy for all the poor: "I started thinking about this when I studied the prophet Muhammad. I saw that quality in his life—his ability to reach out to all sectors of society, whether they were Muslim or not."[130]

Conclusion:
A Progressive Muslim Movement?

Energetic new organizations such as IFYC, IMAN, and others mentioned in this chapter are solid examples of the way progressive Muslims are beginning to create a real institutional presence in American public life. Dr. Safi emphasized the long-term value of these new initiatives:

> As many of us have said, we do this work not for our own sake but actually for the sake of our grandchildren. I don't think any of us will actually get to live long enough to see the fruits of this labor, and that's irrelevant. All of us eat fruits from trees someone planted a long, long time ago.[131]

While it may be too early to call this work in progress a mature movement, these leaders are clearly constructing a new way of being simultaneously progressive, Muslim, and American. Dr. Safi spoke of the emergence of a new *ummah*, "a spiritual community of the faithful."[132] While the typical use of this term is to refer to the ideal global community of Muslims, Safi argued that this term "can and should be reconstituted in local contexts." Noting that "the *ummah* doesn't just descend from heaven," Safi emphasized that it "must be made in every generation."[133] The progressive Muslim leaders featured here represent a hopeful shape of the emerging *ummah* in America.

The journey on which progressive American Muslims have embarked—to forge the bonds between the American ideals of democracy, pluralism, and religious freedom on the one hand and Islam on the other—is a two-way street. American Muslims will continue to learn from the experiences of those who have traveled this path before them, and contemporary democratic ideals will call forth particular parts of the Islamic tradition. But the Islamic tradition will also call forth particular parts of the American democratic tradition. To return to the musical metaphor, each of these traditions will resonate with parts of the other, highlighting notes that have gone unplayed and creating new harmonies and dissonances. This new combination has the potential to offer different, perhaps unexpected compositions that might contribute not only to a better America but, as Dr. Abou El Fadl put it at the beginning of this chapter, to the fulfillment of God's beauty in the world.

Progressive Muslim engagement with American values has the potential to make several positive contributions: to reinvigorate commitments that have been dormant or taken for granted, to extend principles in new directions, to challenge shortcomings and double standards, and to strengthen existing values. These contributions are especially important, as Dr. Eboo Patel noted, in our current age of "the faith line," where the most prominent divisions in society often run along the lines of religion. Dr. Patel noted, for example, how the commitment to diversity and pluralism in Islam can strengthen our nation's commitment to its core values:

> Now, think about the American achievement for a second here. We are the most religiously diverse nation in human history and the most religiously devout society in the West in a moment of global religious conflict. And Sunnis and Shias don't kill each other here, and liberal Protestants and evangelical conservative Protestants don't kill each other in Boise, and Orthodox Jews and Reform Jews don't throw rocks at each other on Devon Avenue in Chicago. But they do all of that on other sides of the world. We have managed to have a relatively thick religious pluralism in this country that has respect for identity, that nurtures community, that focuses people on the common good. What I think we need to do in America is realize that in the early twenty-first century, in the century of the faith line, this is in fact our most precious internal resource and our most important gift to the rest of the world.[134]

The American Muslim community can offer to the more established religious communities an opportunity to renew their own commitments to core values of democracy, pluralism, and justice. Just as sitting at someone else's wedding affords all the couples in the audience the opportunity to renew their own vows as they witness a new couple creatively embarking on their journey together, witnessing Muslims working out their own tradition in relation to these values are important reminders that these affirmations have to be renewed by all in each generation. And as progressive Muslims perform this work in their own key, the original variations they offer can enrich the wider symphony.

CHAPTER 4

Just Sitting Down
How Progressive Buddhists Are Being Peace and Embodying Justice

Beyond the Abrahamic Faiths:
Progressive Buddhists

In addition to the established Jewish and Christian traditions and the growing Muslim tradition, I also interviewed key leaders from the emerging Buddhist tradition. This movement is often described as "engaged Buddhism" because of its explicit emphasis on social engagement as well as individual enlightenment. While engaged Buddhists are even less integrated and established in the public square than American Muslims, they nonetheless are an important part of the emerging progressive religious movement.[1] As a non-Western religious tradition, they offer a unique perspective, and their diffuse cultural influence, via popular culture such as movies and best-selling books, is larger than their numbers might suggest.

The U.S. Religious Landscape Survey by the Pew Forum on Religion and Public Life showed Buddhism virtually tied with Islam (0.7 percent and 0.6 percent of the general adult population respectively) as the third largest world religion in America after Christianity and Judaism.[2] Estimates vary widely, however, ranging from 2.5 million to 4 million adherents.[3] This wide range is due to both the nascent, fluid institutionalization of Buddhism in America and to some unique features of Buddhism itself. Unlike other religions, which have less permeable boundaries and clearer criteria for membership, Buddhism, especially in its American manifestation, is distinguished by its compatibility with commitments to other religious traditions.

Dr. Robert Thurman is Jey Tsong Kappa Professor of Indo-Tibetan Studies at Columbia University and is serving at the request of the Dalai Lama as cofounder of Tibet House US in New York City, an initiative working to preserve Tibetan culture. Dr. Thurman summarized the difficulty in getting an accurate count of American Buddhists in the following way:

> It's impossible for sociologists of religion to get a good number of how many Buddhists there are in America because when you ask people, "Are you Buddhist?" they'll say, "Well, maybe, maybe yesterday; tomorrow I'm Jewish again." In other words, they're very loose about their identity because it's not a matter of signing up for a credo or a belief system usually. So everybody's a "Jew-Bu" or a "Chri-Bu" or a "Hin-Bu" or any other kind of Bu, and it's hard to get a solid number.[4]

As Dr. Thurman notes, the very existence of slang phrases, such as "Jew-Bu," are themselves testimony to the numbers of Americans who have blended a Western religious identity, such as Judaism, with Buddhism.

Like the other major world religions, which have developed across millennia and multiple cultures, Buddhism has within it several major schools of thought, all of which are represented in the United States: the Theravada tradition from south Asia, the Mahayana tradition of east Asia, and the Vajrayana tradition of Tibet and central Asia.[5] The most prominent schools of thought in America are Zen (within the Mahayana tradition) and, increasingly, because of the high profile of the Dalai Lama, Tibetan Buddhism (within the Vajrayana tradition).

Buddhism in America also shares some of the features of the other major religion constituted by recent immigrants, Islam. Like Islam, Buddhism has thus far been able to be fairly ecumenical in terms of different schools of Buddhist thought; it has largely been successful in leaving behind many of the tensions between Buddhist sects that exist in Buddhist-majority countries. Like Islam, Buddhism in America also has two distinct communities of practitioners who are continuing to get to know one another and learn from one another: immigrant communities from Asia and native-born Euro-American converts or dual-identity practitioners.

Beyond all this, Buddhism, along with other Eastern religions such as Hinduism, Sikhism, Jainism, and others, has managed to become incorporated into American culture in indirect ways. Although many if not most Americans would not be able to name a single Hindu deity out of the possible thousands or know any of the "Four Noble Truths" in Buddhism, the practices of yoga and meditation, which are in actuality ancient spiritual disciplines born out of Eastern religions, have become commonplace, albeit often without their religious trappings. This point was recently driven home to me by my daughter, who put a "Yoga Kids" video on her Christmas list after participating in a yoga after-school club that was offered through her public elementary school in Maryland. As only seven-year-old girls can, she wrote out a list of poses, and as the video started she instructed me, "Darling, we begin the class by saying '*Namaste*' like this (hands folded)," and "Now, sweetheart, this is tree pose; since this is your first time, do it for as long as it is comfortable."

Lama Surya Das also noted the spread of Eastern traditions in America. Lama Surya is founder and director of the Dzogchen Foundation, a Tibetan monk who has been dubbed "the American Lama" by the Dalai Lama.

> There are 20 million people doing meditation and yoga in this country. . . . Everybody's doing yoga for health and spiritual happiness, and it's in every YMCA and some schools. These things are not "New Age." They're ancient. They're older than Christianity and Islam. And yet there's a feeling in this country of freshness and newness about them, so people are very open to this more trans-sectarian or post-denominational spirituality that's not just tied to any one religion or "ism."[6]

Ten years ago, *Time* magazine noted "America's Fascination with Buddhism," which had gone beyond the 1960s counterculture movement into the mainstream.[7] Over the last decade, that trend has if anything intensified;

as Lama Surya indicates, Buddhism in America is clearly "here to stay."[8] A visit to any large commercial bookstore gives an indication of the quiet reach of Buddhism and other Eastern religions. In the DVD section, one finds mainstream American movies about Buddhism, such as *Kundun* and *Seven Years in Tibet*, and stars associated with these films such as Brad Pitt and Richard Gere have worked through the media to promote American awareness of Buddhism, particularly Tibetan Buddhism. The exercise section is virtually overrun with yoga books and videos. In fact, the market for yoga instruction has exploded, with an estimated twenty-eight million Americans practicing yoga in 2002, up from four million in 1990.[9] The health and medicine section has a "mind-body" subsection that is populated by the new synthesis of Eastern and Western medicine, especially in psychology. In the business section, there are books applying meditation techniques for reducing stress and increasing concentration, and major corporations are including such sessions in executive training. In the religion section, the Buddhism shelf is getting longer. To give just one snapshot of the reach of these books, at the end of 1999 the Dalai Lama had two books simultaneously on the *New York Times* bestseller list, *The Art of Happiness* (37 weeks) and *Ethics for a New Millennium* (7 weeks).[10]

Engaged Buddhism in America

Among all of these streams of Buddhist practice, an ecumenical movement has been growing over the last few decades called "Engaged Buddhism." Its origins in America can be traced to Vietnamese monk Thich Nhat Hanh, who first came to the United States at the invitation of the Fellowship of Reconciliation, a multireligious peace movement. Thich Nhat Hanh was an outspoken critic of the war in Vietnam and a staunch advocate for peace; for his work, Martin Luther King Jr. nominated him for the Nobel Peace Prize.[11] Over the last four decades, Thich Nhat Hanh has authored over seventy-five books, helping to coin not only the term "Engaged Buddhism" in the 1950s but also an entire English vocabulary for Buddhist social engagement. For Nhat Hanh, the central concept of Engaged Buddhism is the "interbeing" of all things—he often says that we "inter-are"—and, following from this insight, the necessity of not just working for peace, but of "being peace."[12]

Hozan Alan Senauke noted the extraordinary growth of Engaged Buddhism, which thirty years ago was "a small tendency or vector within the growing Buddhist community" but has now become "one of the marks of Buddhism in America."[13] Senauke is Soto Zen priest and vice abbot of the Berkeley Zen Center as well as a longtime leader in the Buddhist Peace Fellowship (BPF). BPF was established in 1978 to promote democracy and human rights around the globe through Buddhist principles of nonviolence and peace, and it has served as an important hub for the Engaged Buddhist movement. When I asked Senauke about Engaged Buddhism, he described it this way:

> If I wanted to be somewhat provocative, I would say, "Well, it's just Buddhism," because all Buddhism, all mindfulness, is engaged. . . . At Buddhist Peace Fellowship, Engaged Buddhism is inclusive of people from all traditions, and it's about being involved in social action and having a concern that includes notions of suffering, or *dukkha*, that are structural. So racism is a form of structural *dukkha*, structural suffering. All kinds of oppression—gender oppression, class oppression, economic oppression—have structural aspects. The structures are made up of people, and yet the structures get away from us as if they have a seeming illusory separate life. So engaged Buddhists are willing to look at structural change and not solely at a kind of individual transformation or individual liberation.[14]

Most of the leaders I interviewed addressed this stereotype of Buddhism: that the heart of Buddhism is accurately captured by the image of an individual sitting alone in a room. Pushing back against this stereotype was a strong theme among the seven Buddhist leaders I interviewed. On the one hand, this image accurately communicates the calmness and concentration that is an accurate and important part of Buddhist values and practice. On the other hand, many argued that it occludes the important social engagement demonstrated, for example, by the Buddha himself. Bill Aiken, Director of Public Affairs at Soka Gakkai International—USA, a lay Buddhist organization with Japanese roots that does advocacy work on peace and religious liberty issues, noted that one of the earliest representations of the Buddha in Buddhist temples was an image of two footprints encased in concrete. Aiken, one of the few Buddhist lobbyists in Washington, D.C., explained why this image was appropriate:

> The thing about the Buddha was, he walked. He didn't just sit. He walked from village to village to village and he met all kinds of people, and he listened to them, and he talked with them in ways that were meaningful to them. And so he led a movement.[15]

Echoing this theme, Lama Surya Das noted that "the Buddha was a social activist who broke the caste system and educated women."[16] By his own example, therefore, the Buddha demonstrated the vital link between individual and social liberation. This dual emphasis is embodied in the life of a *bodhisattva*, a term used in Mahayana Buddhism to describe an enlightened being who, rather than realizing his or her own enlightenment and achieving nirvana, continues to work altruistically for the liberation of others, affirming the vow: "Sentient beings are numberless; I vow to save them."[17] Among the leaders I interviewed, the importance of helping people find liberation not only from their own ignorance but from structural oppression was a strong theme, and one that connected these Buddhist leaders to the progressive traditions in the Abrahamic religions. Susan Moon, editor of *Not Turning Away: The Practice of Engaged Buddhism* and BPF's *Turning Wheel Magazine*,[18] summarized the heart of Engaged Buddhism in her first editorial in the magazine in 1990: "Engaged Buddhism is about the *bodhisattva*'s understanding that no one is really free until everyone is free."[19]

Letting Go

Alan Senauke and others talked about the centrality of the idea of relinquishment, not only of delusions we hold about ourselves but of our material privilege. In America, Senauke argued, where "the dominant religion is consumerism," the Buddhist emphasis on renunciation is important in two ways. First, it combats the American myth that says "you can have it all" and asks practitioners to relinquish their grasp not only on material things but on their privilege, which has been purchased at the expense of others' well-being.

To me the Buddhist precepts boil down to not living your life at the expense of other beings. In our meal chant we say, "Innumerable labors have brought us this food." When we know how our food comes to us, we have the beginnings of a sense of responsibility. And this is very difficult to sustain in America. Anyone can be a good person, but do you want to live at the expense of the person in Bangladesh or Pakistan who's making your shirt? Do you want to live that way? Until we address those questions, I don't think we'll have a truly progressive religious movement.[20]

For Senauke, an authentic religious consciousness must involve an awareness both of our presence in a web of interdependence with others and of our participation in structures that exploit other human beings. Although Senauke conceded that "we can't step outside of this system," this awareness is the seed of responsibility that forces the question, "Do I really want to live that way?" And that question provides the potential for growth not only in new personal practices for relinquishing our sense of entitlement to goods produced by an unjust system but also for our engagement in social practices to change those systems.[21]

Senauke also talked about a second form of relinquishment that he saw as a unique contribution of Buddhism in America, what he called "a freedom from the righteousness of the prophetic tradition."

One of the gifts that Asian religion, and Buddhism in particular, offers [to American culture] is a kind of freedom from the righteousness of the prophetic tradition. At the same time, I honor that tradition and have to use it and look at it in myself. But not being caught in it creates some space, hopefully, so that you can actually do what Martin Luther King said: to love your enemy and be in strenuous opposition to his or her acts.[22]

Senauke, who grew up Jewish, went on to clarify that at its best, the prophetic tradition in the Abrahamic religions has provided a way to "speak truth to power," to denounce emphatically injustice, and to call for change. The flipside of this tradition, however, is that it can lead to a self-righteousness that too easily divides people into categories of ally and enemy, perpetrator and victim—dualisms that too easily locate the prophet on the side of truth and ultimately undermine the sense of the oneness of all sentient beings. In the face of violence and injustice, avoiding such dualism is certainly a difficult task even for seasoned practitioners. For example, in a talk in Los Angeles in April 1991, Thich Nhat Hanh talked frankly about his struggle to identify both with Rodney King and the misguided, brutal police officers who had beaten him:

> My first reaction [to seeing Rodney King being beaten] was that . . . I was the person who was beaten by the five policemen. I suffered from violence and hatred and fear. But as I continued looking deeply, I saw myself as one of the five policemen. Because the society is filled with violence and hatred and fear. If I were a young man entering into the police training academy, I might easily become one of the five. . . . In the *Majjima Nikaya*, the Buddha said, 'This is like this, because that is like that.' Our society is like this; therefore the policemen are like that. We are coresponsible.[23]

The difficult but central insight here is that even in the midst of clear unjustified violence on the part of a few, there is a real sense in which all of us who live in this society, or *sangha*, are coresponsible. Senauke is not here claiming that the Abrahamic traditions are without resources for similar insights, as his citation of Martin Luther King Jr. makes clear, but he is arguing that the path to this difficult realization is central to Buddhism and as such can provide when needed a helpful correction in the American context.

Truth and Religion without God and the Bible

One of the most unique features of Buddhism, at least from the perspective of a nation where theistic traditions are by far in the majority, is the idea of a religion that exists without God or a sacred text such as the Bible or the Qur'an that contains revelations about or of that God. Lama Surya Das stated a common way of distinguishing Buddhism from Western religions like Christianity: "Buddhism is a wisdom tradition, not a faith. We don't believe; we try to discover and become wise and enlightened ourselves just like Buddha did."[24] Expounding on a similar point that Buddhism is a "practice" leading to insights rather than a "belief system" that demands having faith, Dr. Robert Thurman explained:

> Practice really involves the development of wisdom, which is the primary goal, because wisdom, defined as an accurate knowledge of the nature of reality both of the self and of the world, is what liberates you from suffering. Faith can only be aiming yourself toward liberation, believing there is such a thing, believing that there are beings that have attained it, believing that you can attain it. . . . In that sense, [faith] is important—a sort of starter-upper. But faith by itself cannot lead to that liberation from suffering.[25]

In Buddhism, then, faith can only be a "starter-upper," something that gets one on the path but that cannot ultimately lead to the destination. As Thurman explained, while Buddhists revere the *sutras* that record in various ways the nearly fifty years of the Buddha's teaching, "Buddhists are more aware of human mediation and therefore able, while giving it sacred authority, to consider that that sacred authority tells them to use their own critical faculties to analyze things."[26] As several leaders pointed out, the role of individual, direct experience and critical thinking in Buddhism can hardly be overstated; the Buddha himself urged his followers to follow their own insights and to use his teachings that they found useful and to discard the teachings they found less useful.

Ultimately, truth in Buddhism is understood as seeing reality for what it is, what Buddhists call "mindfulness." Lama Surya Das explained:

> It's very unfortunate that so many people want to see the world change and change the world, but who is ready, willing and able to change oneself? That's a big issue today. . . . What's sorely lacking in our statesmen and in our politics is more reflection, more introspection. Not just personal introspection—which is lacking of course among people who don't read but lead—but communal introspection about how we fit in with others, how we are seen by others, and how our actions affect the world. What's missing in American politics, I'd say, is the sense of self-reflection that might help us slow down a little . . . [beyond] our speedy, modern, technological, short-term fix

mentality. I think Buddhist mind training, energy, and balancing could help us to pay attention better, to see things as they are, not as we would like them to be. And [to see ourselves] as we are.[27]

There are many insights packed into this paragraph. First, there is the intimate connection between individual and social change, with the Buddhist emphasis on the former as a means to the latter. Being "ready, willing, and able" to change oneself is often more difficult, more necessary, and more effective than making a commitment to change the world in the absence of a transformed self. As Lama Surya makes clear, however, American politics also sorely needs more communal introspection that asks the big questions about global interdependence and the long-term implications of current decisions.

Finally, Lama Surya notes the central idea of mindfulness and wisdom: seeing things "as they are, not as we would like them to be." On the one hand, this wisdom would demand that American leaders take into account the real complexities in the world and move us far beyond a dualistic mentality that declares, "Either you are with us, or you are with the terrorists."[28] On the other hand, it would call us to a careful, critical self-reflection that sees our individual selves and our nation, not as we would like to be seen but as we really are, to face up to the gaps between our best ideals and our flawed realities. Moreover, the practice of mindfulness is a means of change that allows the better part of ourselves—what Buddhists call our "Buddha nature"—to guide our actions. This discipline would pay real dividends; as Lama Surya concluded, "Paying attention really pays off; we have not been paying attention, and we're paying the cost."[29]

Engaged Buddhism on the Ground: Zen Meets Community Development

Most of the leaders I interviewed talked passionately about the growing responsibilities of Buddhists as they become more integrated and institutionally established in America. Lama Surya lamented that Buddhists have not been visible enough, especially in the wake of heightened militarism following September 11, and said that he had concluded that "we have to think about future generations, be more engaged, and 'pick up our meditation cushions and walk,' as I like to say, echoing Jesus."[30] Today, there are an increasing number of Buddhist organizations doing just that, becoming more visible and having measurable impacts in their communities and in society at large. There are numerous examples to point to, such as Alan Senauke's work with the Buddhist Peace Fellowship in and on behalf of death row prisoners in San Quentin Prison in San Francisco, and among others such as Joan Halifax Roshe, founder and abbot of the Upaya Institute in Santa Fe, New Mexico, who has dedicated her work to being with dying patients in hospice.

One of the largest and longest-running Buddhist social engagement projects in America is the Greyston project. Zen Master (Roshi) Bernie Glassman is the founder of the Greyston project and Zen Peacemakers, an international group of Buddhists who are dedicated to Zen practice and social action. Because of his work, which brings together the principles of Zen and community development, Glassman has won numerous awards and has become a widely known social entrepreneur.[31] He has an eclectic background, with a PhD in applied mathematics and a previous career as an aeronautical engineer. He has been practicing Zen for over forty years and became a recognized Zen master in 1995.

At the top of Roshi Glassman's many achievements is what has become known as "the Greyston Mandala" of social service companies he began in 1982 in Yonkers, New York, one of New York's most economically depressed areas.[32] In an interview, Glassman described these organizations as a "pathway" to a better life for many disadvantaged people:

> We created a series of organizations that developed a path for people who were homeless and ex-cons to get off of welfare and out of homelessness. That involved creating housing, creating businesses to create jobs, job training, child care, health facilities for people with AIDS, and housing for people with AIDS.[33]

Glassman went on to note that these organizations have become an economic engine for the city of Yonkers, where homelessness has fallen by 75 percent during the period that Greyston has been operating. This networked circle of companies currently employs over two hundred people and serves more than twelve hundred men, women, and children; it has become a case model for study at major business schools including Harvard University and the Wharton School at the University of Pennsylvania.

Greyston achieved these remarkable results with three main components. First, they founded a successful bakery by adopting a "first come, first served" model of hiring and giving opportunities to people other businesses had deemed unemployable. This business alone has grown to over $6 million in revenue and touts customers such as some of New York's trendiest restaurants and Ben & Jerry's Ice Cream, for which it bakes brownies. Second, Greyston leaders realized that homelessness and home insecurity were a major source of instability for many low-income families. They opened the Greyston Family Inn in 1986 to provide hundreds of low-cost apartments for homeless families, complete with child care and after-school programs. Finally, Greyston opened the Maitri Center and Issan House to provide medical treatment and housing to people with AIDS-related illnesses.[34] Currently, Glassman is involved in creating Greyston II in Springfield, Massachusetts, to provide similar support services to homeless families and the formerly incarcerated.

Glassman, who is now in his late sixties, summarized his current work simply as "still teaching Zen and teaching how the basic principle that we're all connected to the one universe can affect political and social action work."[35] For Glassman and his Zen students involved in this work, this principle of interconnectedness grounds a commitment to "loving actions":

> If you really have the experience of interconnectedness, the limited self—which I see as myself and give myself a name like Bernie—falls away and everything becomes Bernie. So it's all me. . . . So once I have that larger experience, I'm not working for the homeless, I'm taking care of the homeless part of myself. . . . So if you have a transformation of seeing everything as your family, your actions do change, and you have the experience of the oneness of life, what we call loving actions.[36]

And as Glassman demonstrates, "loving actions" are not token acts of charity but are concrete works that transform both individuals and communities.

Engaged Buddhism in the Public Square

Most of the leaders I interviewed were modest about the direct impact of Buddhism on American politics, not least because of the fluid religious identity that many Buddhists hold. They noted, however, that Buddhists are increasingly finding their voice amidst the increasingly pluralistic public square, especially as the emphasis on Engaged Buddhism has become established as one of the main streams of American Buddhism. The Dalai Lama is one of the most popular authors and most recognized religious icons in America. The Buddhist Peace Fellowship is a long-standing and respected member of the Fellowship of Reconciliation, an umbrella of religious peacemaking groups. And groups like Zen Peacemakers are blazing an entrepreneurial trail combining community development and Buddhist insights. These combined efforts over the years have developed a network of *kalyana mitra*, or "spiritual friends," who have followed and continue to cultivate and broaden this path.[37]

Progressive Voices in Other Religious Traditions

Although the focus of this book was on the four most prominent world religions in America—Christianity, Judaism, Islam, and Buddhism—there are certainly a number of leaders in other religious traditions making their own contributions to the emerging progressive religious movement. These include members of the Unitarian Universalist Association of Congregations (UUA), historically most closely related to Christianity, and other Eastern religions such as Hinduism, Sikhism, Jainism, Bahá'í, and others.

It is beyond the scope of this book to treat each of these here, but I would be remiss if I did not highlight briefly the important role of the UUA, a self-described "liberal religion with Jewish-Christian roots" that represents about 0.3 percent of the adult population.[38] As its name indicates, the UUA traces its theological roots to religious liberals in the early nineteenth century who rejected the idea of the trinity in Christianity and who believed in universal salvation.[39] The UUA has been the most prominent, long-standing religious tradition staking out the pole of what might be called a religious left or liberal religion in America (for example, the UUA web e-zine is titled "Liberal Religion and Life"). Rev. William Sinkford, president of UUA, characterized the UUA as a group that pitches "a big theological tent" and unapologetically embraces pluralism and liberalism.

> We do pitch a big theological tent. It's absolutely normal [in a UUA congregation] for a person who considers herself a liberal Christian to

be sitting next to a person who is a secular humanist sitting next to a pagan sitting next to a person who follows one of a variety of Buddhist meditative practices. . . . There is a vast difference between faith communities that believe that they have the only revealed truth, that they have the only path to salvation, that they have the only road to the beloved community, and those who like Unitarian Universalism believe that there are twelve gates to the city, to cite the old African American spiritual, that there are many paths to the holy and that all of those paths can be appropriate and rewarding and satisfying. [40]

Referencing the UUA's steadiness amid mainline Protestant numerical decline, he concluded, "It's very clear that there are many, many people out in the wider world who actually yearn for a liberal way of being religious. I believe that we're called to offer that to them."[41]

Although the level of public engagement with these other religious groups is uneven compared with the larger religious traditions featured in this book, these groups, too, are finding their public voice. Like socially engaged Buddhists, established traditions such as the UUA alongside newer religions to America with Eastern roots will increasingly play a vital role in the development of a coherent progressive religious movement in America.

Progressive & Religious
The New Face of Religion in American Public Life

Beyond Left and Right, Secular and Religious:
The Future of Faith in America

Two meta-narratives about religion dominated elite circles in the twentieth century. On the one hand, mainline Protestant Christians were optimistic that the twentieth century would witness the full blossoming of Christian (read "mainline Protestant") principles in "Christian nations" that would elevate human society. In the final 1899 issue of *The Christian Century*, the flagship Protestant magazine that was self-consciously named to capture this idea, the editorial page declared, "We believe that the coming century is to witness greater triumphs in Christianity than any previous century has ever witnessed, and that it is to be more truly Christian than any of its predecessors."[1] On the other hand, other cultural elites, particularly sociologists, predicted the demise of religion in the face of advancing science and reason.

By the end of the twentieth century, both of these grand visions were bankrupt. The mainline Protestant optimism about the Christianizing of the culture was bludgeoned by two world wars, including the horrific experience of the Holocaust in which many Christian churches were complicit, followed by the Cold War standoff between two superpowers often on the brink of destroying the entire planet. And its hegemonic equation of progress with the advance of a white, male-dominated, Protestant culture was run under by the struggles toward realizing greater equality for minorities and women and the rise of multiculturalism. Likewise, the great theorists of secularization were poised to finally claim victory in the midst of the 1960s upheavals and the rise of the "God is dead" movement, only to find religion stubbornly persisting alongside and even challenging science through the last decades of the century.

In the place of these exhausted visions, the two forces with which I began the book arose: a defiant, rejectionist form of religion represented by the religious right and an equally militant condemnation of religion by the angry neoathiests—a standoff that E. J. Dionne insightfully characterized as "an overreaction" and "an overreaction to an overreaction."[2] Caught in the cross fire between these reactionary parties, the vast majority of Americans have begun to look beyond the culture wars for a broader approach that represents their faith and political progress. The multireligious, progressive voices represented here are the vanguard of a new public face of religion in American public life.

For Such a Time as This: We Believe Ohio

> There is a new wind blowing through our land. And God is calling
> us to work and witness for such a time as this.[3]

In December 2006, I had the privilege of hearing Rev. Tim Ahrens read these words, which he had written a month earlier on the day after the 2006 congressional elections, at a gathering of progressive faith leaders in Washington, D.C. Rev. Ahrens, founder of We Believe Ohio and senior minister of the First Congregational Church (United Church of Christ) in Columbus, Ohio, was filled with emotion as he reflected on the new spirit in Ohio and the new organization that had sprung up with literally no money and no staff from a single e-mail. At the time of his speech, We Believe Ohio had grown in just one year into a vibrant, multireligious, grassroots coalition of more than four hundred pastors, priests, rabbis, cantors, imams, and other religious leaders.

As their mission statement declared, these leaders were reclaiming a new public space for religion beyond the narrow agenda and divisive methods of the Religious Right:

YES to justice for all; NO to prosperity for only a few.

YES to diverse religious expression; NO to self-righteous certainty.

YES to the common good; NO to discrimination against any of God's people.

YES to the voice of religious traditions informing public policy; NO to crossing the lines that separate the institutions of religion and government.[4]

Like many of the progressive religious leaders I talked with across the country, Rev. Ahrens and the other religious leaders of We Believe Ohio were catalyzed to organize by the excessive claims of political conservatives to own all of religion and morality and to limit its political relevance to a narrow set of issues. For Ahrens, the breaking point finally came in October 2005. Riding the wave of the "values voters" mythology from the 2004 elections, Pastor Rod Parsley, a fundamentalist, prosperity-gospel megachurch preacher, organized a televised rally on the steps of the Ohio Statehouse in Columbus to launch his new group, Reformation Ohio. With a bused-in crowd of nearly one thousand supporters cheering him on and with Senator Sam Brownback (R-KS) and GOP gubernatorial candidate and Secretary of State Ken Blackwell on the platform, Parsley announced Reformation Ohio's goal to combine proselytizing and voter registration to reach 1 million Ohioans before the 2008 elections.[5] Parsley's words were a call to arms: "A Holy Ghost invasion is taking place! Man your battle stations, ready your weapons, lock and load. Let the Reformation begin!" Parsley went on at some length, calling on a spiritual army of Christians to do battle to defeat "the hordes of hell."[6]

Deeply disturbed by this militant, divisive use of religion in politics, Rev. Ahrens sent out an e-mail to a network of fellow clergy that began with a blunt question, "Is your faith driven by militaristic imagery or by the Prince of Peace?"[7] Ahrens was also incredulous that the major issues that affected so many Ohioans—poverty, high job losses, and broken health care and education systems (declared unconstitutional three times by the Ohio Supreme Court)—were completely absent from Parsley's agenda, which focused mainly on the divisive issues of abortion and same-sex marriage. Within a few weeks, Ahrens had gathered fifty church pastors to pray and discern what God might be calling them to do. Over the winter of 2006 they continued to pray, talk, and organize, expanding the initial network to include Jewish, Muslim, Sikh, and other religious leaders across the state, and establishing official chapters in Columbus and Cleveland. As the conversations continued, Cantor Jack Chomsky noticed that their conversations were filled with statements that began with "we believe," and the name "We Believe Ohio" was born.

The moment was right. Ahrens explained that support flooded in: "It was like [the Dr. Seuss book] *Horton Hears a Who*. There were people saying, 'We are here, we are here, we are here' and 'Oh my gosh, thank goodness somebody else thinks this is crazy.'"[8] In the reflections he recorded the day after the 2006 election, Ahrens articulated proudly the return of "a prophetic imagination" that We Believe Ohio had articulated across the year:

> Today, I am proud of those in all faith traditions with whom I stand to make a brighter and more beautiful future. We love God with our whole hearts, minds, and souls. We love our neighbors as ourselves. We are multicultural and multiracial. We are bridge builders. We love humanity and don't seek to demonize others. We are faithful and moral to the core of our souls, but we will not impose our faith and morality on others. We are uniting people everywhere and we are united in this effort. We are and will continue to be ones who seek to heal the world. We will not be silent. We will listen to the voice of God guiding us forward in faith and action.[9]

We Believe Ohio's work paid off. The right-wing candidates who were supported by Parsley and Reformation Ohio, particularly Kenneth Blackwell, were defeated. Governor-elect Ted Strickland, himself a Methodist minister who stumped as a "Golden Rule Democrat" and as a senator insisted on paying for his own health coverage as long as his constituents were not covered,[10] gained fourteen points among voters who attended religious services once a week or more, compared to support these voters gave Senator John Kerry in 2004.[11] And voters, including a majority (51 percent) of weekly church attenders, supported a long-overdue ballot measure to increase the minimum wage.

Most significantly, lawmakers began hearing from progressive religious leaders on a broader range of issues, such as poverty, the environment, and education. And lawmakers began to express their gratitude for a new spirit these leaders introduced in the public square. During our interview, Ahrens quoted a legislative aide who said the following to him during a visit to advocate for increased educational support, "You know, I've got to tell you, I've been an aide for some time. You're the first group to come in and just say thank you from a religious perspective and pray with us very gently. I just want to say thank you to you for not bashing us and banging us."[12]

Ohio, the heart of the heartland, is often thought of as a bellwether for national politics. The shift in the public role of religion in Ohio, from divisive culture warriors locking and loading to bridge builders who are embracing social justice and the common good, is a hopeful sign. In thinking about the significance of We Believe Ohio, Rev. Ahrens was drawn to a story in the Bible, where Queen Esther's Uncle Mordecai admonishes her to speak out to save her fellow Jews from the King's death edict, saying, "Who knows? Maybe you were made to be a leader for such a time as this (Esther 4:13–14)."[13] Ahrens summarized We Believe Ohio's own feeling of responsibility to speak out and their sense of a providential new spirit blowing across the state: "Across twenty-five hundred years, this story has spoken to me and many other key religious leaders in central Ohio. We have formed We Believe Ohio for such a time as this!"[14]

Progressive and Religious:
Shared Principles and Values

The nearly one hundred religious leaders I have had the privilege to meet on this three-year journey across America have provided an inspiring composite portrait of the emerging face of religion in this new era, which E. J. Dionne and others have dubbed "a post–religious right America."[15] As I noted at the beginning of the book, however, these leaders are not building an equally politicized religious left that is the mirror image of the religious right. Neither are they conceding the religious ground to the angry, reactionary secularists who are announcing, in knee-jerk response to the misguided excesses of the religious right, that religion "poisons every-thing."[16] Instead, they are building a progressive religious movement that represents a broad kind of left-center coalition that defies easy political categorization.

What exactly do these voices have in common? It is certainly a daunting—and potentially hazardous—task to try to generalize from nearly one hundred interviews spanning four religious traditions. Stepping back, however, five common characteristics of a progressive religious orientation emerged: an emphasis on social injustice, a relational approach to truth, a rigorous and critical engagement with tradition, a profound belief in the unity of all humanity, and a new vision of America that emphasizes generosity and interdependence as the foundation of prophetic patriotism.

An Emphasis on Social Injustice

Perhaps the most fundamental feature of a progressive religious orientation is a social vision, which sees the heart of the religious life not only in developing personal piety but also in addressing structural injustice. I heard this theme consistently through my interviews across religious traditions. Dr. Ron Sider of Evangelicals for Social Action captured this emphasis well: "The New Testament understanding of salvation is not just me and Jesus walking in the garden alone—it's partly that—but it's also this new community where there's economic sharing and slaves and Gentiles and women receive a new dignity."[17] Alan Senauke of the Buddhist Peace Fellowship talked about the importance, for engaged Buddhists, of addressing what he called "structural dukkha," or structural suffering, which must be addressed not only with individual trans-formation but with social change and institutional reform.[18] For progressive religious leaders, religious responsibility goes beyond taking, as the old Christian gospel song goes, "just a closer walk with thee." It involves "picking up the meditation cushions and walking" in ways that create new, more just communities.[19] As these progressive religious voices remind us, working for social justice is not optional; rather, it is central to salvation and enlightenment.

The Jewish concept of *tikkun olam*, healing the world, is a prominent way of expressing this social vision that resonated across religious traditions. This rich concept provides a much-needed corrective to the obsession with individual salvation and "other-worldliness" that the dominant strain of American Protestantism has too often emphasized to the detriment not only of the poor but of the earth itself. As Rabbi Eric Yoffie of the Union for Reform Judaism emphasized, *tikkun olam* "is not simply a matter of dealing with particular symptoms by extending kindness to a person in trouble, but it means repairing the world in order to establish conditions of justice."[20] Citing a mystical sensibility that "we are perpetually returning to God"—an idea that Sufi Muslims and Kabbalistic Jews share—Dr. Omid Safi concluded his introduction to *Progressive Muslims* by calling on his fellow Muslims to "have the courage, the vision, and the compassion to heal this fractured world" on their journey back to God.[21] Finally, Rev. Dr. Susan Thistlethwaite of Chicago Theological Seminary summarized her own theological approach by appealing to this rich concept: "That's the divine-human project, to heal the world."[22]

A Relational Approach to Truth

The second distinctive characteristic of a progressive religious orientation is what I call a relational approach to truth. Truth, from this perspective, has a number of attributes. It is experiential versus propositional, inductive versus deductive, and internal to a community versus external to individuals. Given this strong emphasis on experience in community, it is not surprising that, among these leaders, the critical human faculty for understanding truth was not reasoning but hearing.

When asked about truth, leaders in the Abrahamic traditions emphasized the importance of hearing God's voice in a wide range of human experiences. For example, Dr. Omid Safi talked about a "holy triangle" formed by the religious person, the text, and God as the space in which truth can be heard. Within this space, Safi advocated for a "symphonic approach" where religious people listen together for the "resonance" between traditional norms and the demands of the present.[23] Rabbi Jonah Pesner of the Reform movement's Just Congregations initiative emphasized that "we should be less worried about truth and more worried about hearing God."[24] And hearing God, he continued, requires listening to the full range of human experience, from stories of congregants who lack adequate health insurance and are recycling insulin needles to save money, to the intimate experience of hearing his wife's cries while delivering a child. Likewise, Rev. Harry Knox of the Human Rights Campaign noted that one of the main reasons we revere the great religious leaders of the past is that they "listened to God first," and when they found that the tradition was not "big enough" to hold what they were hearing from God, they remained faithful to the truth they were hearing from God, even when it meant disrupting current understandings and practices.[25]

In addition to acknowledging a wide range of human experiences in discerning truth, these religious leaders remind us, we must also acknowledge the human faculties involved in evaluating these sources. This insight is perhaps most prominent in the Buddhist tradition, where, as Dr. Robert Thurman of Columbia University and Tibet House US explained, the Buddhist sacred texts themselves emphasize the need for people to "use their own critical faculties" to discern the truth about reality.[26] But this emphasis on using human discernment was also prominent in the "religions of the book." Dr. Muqtedar Khan of the University of Delaware emphasized the centrality of the notion of *ijtihad*, or independent thinking, in Islam, which he characterized as "a license to think and to rethink."[27] According to tradition attributed to the Prophet Muhammad, God even has a reward for those who engage in *ijtihad* and "get it wrong," a clear indication that the risks of not using the God-given human abilities in discerning the truth are clearly greater than the risks of using them incorrectly. In other words, for these leaders, the biggest concern is not illegitimate innovation but ossified irrelevance.

Finally, progressive leaders emphasized the importance of humility in discerning truth, both because of human limitations and because of the complexity of the world. As Rev. James Forbes, retired senior minister of the Riverside Church in New York, summarized it, "*God* knows the truth, but we human beings . . . what we get is a peek through the window of truth."[28] Embedded in this sentiment is a serious recognition of human finitude. As Rabbi Yoffie noted, "truly religious people . . . don't overstate their own knowledge or certainty about God's will."[29] And, as several leaders noted, this humility is not some modern product of relativism but a deeply religious sentiment, a core virtue of true piety. For example, noting that "Islam is a religion of submission," Dr. Khaled Abou El Fadl of the UCLA School of Law noted that "if you don't have humility, you can't even begin to understand mercy or beauty or anything else."[30] As Rev. Thistlethwaite noted, the belief that "God hath more light and truth yet to break forth from his holy word"—that God is still speaking—is a belief that came to America nearly four hundred years ago with the Pilgrims.[31] And for Buddhists, the willingness to relinquish one's preconceptions about reality is the fundamental beginning of the possibility of enlightenment.

The sense of humility that these leaders talked about was also rooted in a view of the world as a complex, changing place. As Rev. Forbes put it, a progressive religious orientation understands that "to be invited into the mechanisms of relativity is God's inviting us into the complexity of the way God sees the world."[32] Rabbi Roly Matalon of B'nai Jeshurun in New York also noted this complexity: "God created a world that is messy, and we have to find our way in a world that is messy—and there are no certainties."[33] Like the notion of *ijtihad* above, the assumptions behind this worldview are that the biggest dangers lie not in adapting tradition wrongly—something from which we learn—but in failing to live out our shared responsibility to discern truth in a complex world.

A Rigorous and Critical Engagement with Tradition

Across the board, the progressive religious leaders I interviewed were emphatic that a progressive religious orientation requires a rigorous engagement with tradition rather than a break with tradition.[34] One of the most frequently mentioned ways of understanding this complex relationship with tradition—mentioned by a number of religious leaders across the Abrahamic traditions—was the late Rabbi Mordecai Kaplan's well-known declaration that "the past has a vote but not a veto." From this perspective, the past should be revered and respected, but it cannot be allowed to trump the present. Just as our ancestors and great religious saints and heroes struggled to find the best of the tradition in their own time, so we have a responsibility to critically engage what we have received from them in the context of our own present challenges. Rabbi Or Rose of the Rabbinical School of Hebrew College, citing his teacher Rabbi Zalman Schachter-Shalomi, offered an explication of this approach; he noted the difference between being on "the cutting edge" of tradition, where the old is too easily shorn off by the winds of change, and "the growing edge" of tradition, where more careful pruning happens.[35] The growing edge is the place of critical engagement.

Dr. Omid Safi summarized this approach in the Muslim context eloquently:

The progressive Muslim project is not so much an epistemological rupture from what has come before as a fine-tuning, a polishing, a grooming, an editing, a re-emphasizing of this and a correction of that. In short, it is a critical engagement with the heritage of Islamic thought, rather than a casual bypassing of its accomplishments.[36]

As Saleema Abdul-Ghafur, author of *Living Islam Out Loud*, pointed out, this way of engaging tradition is especially important for women and other minority groups not represented in the texts, allowing them to find an authentic Islam that could be "expressed through" their experiences rather than an Islam that was artificially imposed on them from without.[37]

Progressive religious leaders also talked passionately about the ways in which a rigorous and critical engagement with tradition sustained activism. Alan Senauke of the Buddhist Peace Fellowship described how the discipline of meditation provides the courage, fortitude, and stamina not only to visit violent offenders and offer services at San Quentin State Prison but to sit in vigil in the rain on a cold night to protest an execution.[38] And Daniel Sokatch of Progressive Jewish Alliance spoke of the importance of studying Talmud in the park prior to standing in solidarity with hotel workers.[39] Rev. Tracy Lind of Trinity Episcopal Cathedral in Cleveland and Rabbi Sharon Brous of IKAR Congregation in Los Angeles both spoke in different ways of the importance of the theological vision that the concept of the reign of God and the practice of *Shabbat* supply.[40] These visions of justice juxtapose God's "dream" with the current reality and inspire us, even in the midst of disheartening circumstances, to "lift the line of history until it matches the dream."[41]

A Belief in the Unity of All Humanity

The fourth feature of a progressive religious orientation was a profound belief in the unity of all humanity. In the Abrahamic traditions, this conviction follows from the belief that all are created in the image of God, that all have the divine breath within them. Rev. Steven Baines of the Faith Action Network at People for the American Way Foundation claimed Genesis 1, which depicts humanity being created in God's image, as the foundation of his theology. He explained the impact of that belief on his own perspective as follows: "If humanity is made in God's image, then every act that I do to another living person, I'm doing to the image of God."[42] Likewise, Dr. Kecia Ali noted the centrality of an egalitarian understanding of creation for feminist and progressive Muslim scholarship. She noted that the fourth chapter of the Qur'an declares: "Oh people, be conscious of your Lord who created you from a single soul and created from her, her mate; and from them, many men and women scattered far and wide."[43] From this perspective, the unity of humanity is deep indeed; all people, men and women, are not only created by God but are descended from a single soul.

In the Buddhist tradition, this sense of oneness goes beyond human beings to all sentient beings. Bill Aiken of Soka Gakkai International—USA explained that individual beings are like waves on the ocean. Although each wave has a sense of its own separateness (its "lesser self"), it is better understood as part of the ocean (its "greater self"). "Buddhism," Aiken explained, "is about awakening to the larger truth that you're part of the ocean—not just part, you are the ocean."[44] Similarly, Dr. Bernie Glassman of Zen Peacemakers noted the importance of the foundational truth that "we're all connected to the one universe," and explained that when the truth of that insight is in full bloom, we can truly engage in "loving actions." Loving actions flow from us naturally when we realize, for example, that in working for the homeless, we're "taking care of the homeless part" of ourselves.[45]

The implications of this basic insight about the unity of all humanity are fairly radical. As many leaders emphasized, God created human beings to share not only a common origin but also a shared fate. Susan Moon of *Turning Wheel Magazine* noted that this belief in the oneness of all sentient beings is the essence of the *bodhisattva* understanding that "no one is really free until everyone is free."[46] Dr. Rosemary Radford Ruether of Claremont Graduate School noted a similar conviction rooted in her work on liberation theology from a Catholic perspective, that "any liberation which is somebody's else's disaster is false liberation."[47] And Rev. Dr. Kenneth L. Samuel of Victory Church in Stone Mountain, Georgia, eloquently noted that when we pursue policies that are not aimed at the good and inclusion of all, it will ultimately "lead to our detriment" because "in God's providential design, we are one human family."[48]

This vision of human unity and commitment to solidarity not surprisingly leads to an "image of God" agenda that, as Simon Greer of Jewish Funds for Justice explained, represents a courageous and "prophetic calling beyond the winnable issues."[49] These issues include the triad of common good issues that Rev. Bob Edgar of the National Council of Churches memorably called "peace, poverty, and planet earth."[50] For many, this prophetic calling—rooted in a rigorous engagement with tradition and an attentive listening for God's voice for our day—also led their communities to support full inclusion and justice for LGBT persons and to say unequivocally to all people, "we will welcome you and embrace you."[51] And even among the minority of leaders I interviewed who have concluded that sexual acts between adults of the same sex run contrary to their best understanding of their religious tradition or who are still listening for God's voice on LGBT issues, the belief in the oneness of humanity leads them to clearly reject the politicization of these issues and the demonization of people, which has done so much damage not only to the country but to religion itself.

A New Vision of America: From Empire to Interdependence and Generosity

The fifth mark of a progressive religious orientation was a new vision of America that emphasized interdependence, generosity, and prophetic critique. As many leaders noted, this new vision is a direct response to the troubling shifts in American foreign policy toward unilateralism and a security state that has embraced preemptive war and even sanctioned torture. The heart of this new vision, as Rev. Jim Wallis of Sojourners noted, is a call to religious people to reevaluate their relationship to America. He bluntly declared that the post–September 11 brand of hypernationalism, with its "pretentious claims and demands for ultimate allegiances" is "a lethal disease" for people of faith and is, from a Biblical perspective, "heresy."[52] Importantly, every leader who offered such a critique also emphasized that this call to repentance for misplaced loyalties is not counter to a love for America but in service of it. Dr. Ruether put it his way: "To critique the follies, the oppressiveness, the mistakes of your country and your church is patriotism. . . . Any serious concern for a better America and better world has to grapple with the way the national security state promotes continual patterns of violence."[53]

An essential part of this shift to a new vision for America is a shift from unilateralism to interdependence, to see American not as "the indispensable nation" but as an important leader in a family of nations.[54] As Lama Surya Das of the Dzogchen Foundation emphasized, a real understanding of interdependence requires more "mindfulness" to the interconnectedness of all things, from individual beings to nations. We're "paying the price," he argued—both in terms of the condition of the world and America's reputation in the world—for "not paying attention" to this fundamental truth.[55]

One of the most concrete proposals on this front is what Rabbi Michael Lerner and the Network of Spiritual Progressives call a "Global Marshall Plan." This plan focuses on ending global poverty in our lifetime and saving the global environment from its current precarious state. Such a sweeping aspiration obviously demands working together beyond the paradigm of "national interest," and this plan adopts "a 'strategy of generosity' to replace the 'strategy of domination' that currently informs our foreign policy."[56] According to Lerner, this approach is based on "the central realization, which is where twenty-first-century politics has to start, that our well-being depends on the well-being of every other person on this planet and the well-being of the planet itself."[57]

Several others also cited generosity as the cardinal virtue of this new vision of America in the world. Alan Senauke explained that generosity is the "first of the *bodhisattva* practices," and it is rooted in an understanding that "human beings have the same wishes: they all want to be happy, they all want to be safe, they all want to be well."[58] Dr. Umar Faruq Abd-Allah of the Nawawi Foundation emphasized a related teaching by the namesake of his foundation, the great thirteenth-century Sufi teacher Nawawi, who declared that "None of you believes until he loves for his brother what he loves for himself."[59] These leaders were clear that such a policy of generosity would also entail a willingness on the part of relatively privileged Americans to give up the elusive—what Wallis called "idolatrous"—pursuit of absolute security. Sr. Simone Campbell of the Network talked of the need for a "theology of insecurity," and Dr. Ruether explained the need to develop a "theology of letting go" for the privileged as the flipside of liberation theology for the disadvantaged.[60]

The identification of these five shared characteristics of a progressive religious orientation does not imply that these leaders are speaking with one voice. Disagreements remain, especially over complex issues such as the Israeli-Palestinian conflict and gay and lesbian issues, and there are unique contributions. Yet, as these shared attributes make clear, these leaders are echoing, borrowing from, learning from, and amplifying each other in significant—and hopeful—ways. If these leaders have not yet birthed a mature progressive religious movement, they have nonetheless found a *hevre,* a *koinonia,* an *ummah,* a *kalyana mitra*: fellow travelers, a fellowship, a community, spiritual friends.

Why Political Progressives Should Welcome the Emerging Progressive Religious Movement

I want to close the book by addressing the question of why this emerging progressive religious movement is important to the broader progressive political movement.[61] One way of answering this question is by addressing head-on the concerns often voiced by the influential minority of nonreligious political progressives who are wary of a strong role for religion in the public sphere. This group may not all be as jaded as Sam Harris and the other neoathiests who flatly believe that things would be better if religion joined other relics of our evolutionary past, but what this group has in common is a judgment that religion is primarily a problem rather than a resource in modern democratic society.[62] Given especially the divisive, intolerant, and uncivil turn that religion has taken over the last few decades in America, these concerns are real and legitimate. To judge all of religion by the behavior of the far Christian right, however, is to mistake the part for the whole. As I hope this book makes clear, these voices do not represent all Christians, much less all religious people.

The worries of "religion as problem" progressives typically center around three concerns: that religious people ultimately prefer a theocracy of their own religion to democratic pluralism; that religion tends toward an uncritical ideology that breeds incivility and intolerance; and that religious passion is dangerously irrational and makes people of faith unreliable partners. Most of those who carry these worries do not think that these problematic tendencies are inevitable, but they often believe that positive religious contributions are cutting against the grain rather than naturally expressing the deep structure of religion. Again, these fears are not without basis, especially from the perspective of the last few decades of American politics, but a longer view back and the vista opening ahead promise an authentic progressive expression of religion that, as these pages attest, is once again finding its voice.

Theocratic Tendencies

The most direct response to the worries about theocracy is to point out that the emerging progressive religious movement is—unlike the homogeneous religious right—itself pluralistic. This feature of the movement brings it much closer to James Madison's early vision that the proliferation and flourishing of many different religious groups would itself be a healthy check on the theocratic ambitions of any.[63] Rather than being constituted by a single group of white evangelical Protestant Christians, the emerging progressive religious movement is made up of a variety of Protestant and Catholic Christians, Jews, Muslims, Buddhists, and other religious groups who share not only a self-interested commitment to religious freedom for themselves, but also principled positive support for religious pluralism and freedom grounded in their own traditions. For example, Eboo Patel of the Interfaith Youth Core emphasizes moving beyond mere tolerance for diversity to affirmation of it as a core positive value. He and several other Muslims I interviewed grounded this commitment to pluralism in a passage in the Qur'an that declares that God created humans in diverse cultural groups so that humans might "come to know one another," and presumably themselves, through encounters with others.

In addition to supporting pluralism, religious progressives are positioned to make a vital contribution to the related, broader debates around "separation of church and state." Most important, religious progressives expose the false stereotype, hyped by the religious right, that these battles are being waged between people of faith (who are being persecuted) on the one hand and secularists on the other. By grounding a strong religious defense of both nonestablishment and freedom of religious expression, the progressive religious movement is poised to turn down the flame on this debate and remind us that some of the staunchest early defenders of religious liberty were people of faith such as John Leland, a Virginia Baptist. Because of their multireligious makeup, progressive religious leaders can also help move the vocabulary beyond the clumsy "separation of church and state" language, which is so easily misconstrued, to more accurate descriptions about the dangers of excessive entanglement between government and religious institutions of all kinds, whether church, synagogue, mosque, meditation hall, or others.

Incivility and Intolerance

The second major concern of "religion as problem" progressives is a fear that all religions demand an absolute adherence to an uncritical ideology that in turn leads to incivility and intolerance. It is certainly not difficult to look through religious history both far and near for evidence that fuels this worry. A fundamental blind spot that so many of the neoatheist critics of religion share is that they have been unable to imagine an authentic religion that does not operate with certainty as its only common coin; as Rabbi David Saperstein of the Religious Action Center for Reform Judaism noted, they begin with the mistaken assumption that "the more fundamentalist people are, the more authentic they are."[64] In his best-selling *The End of Faith*, for example, Sam Harris bases his entire argument on this mistake. Harris declares that there are only two categories of religious people, "religious extremists" and "religious moderates." He then goes on to disqualify religious moderates as authentically religious by declaring that "religious moderation is the product of *secular* knowledge and scriptural *ignorance*—it has no bona fides, in religious terms."[65] Those who take scripture seriously or "really believe," declares Harris, must in the end be intolerant fundamentalists if they also want to be honest.

This view creates a straw man by denying that authentically religious people might understand religion as the product of human culture, a view that the overwhelming majority of progressive religious voices featured here embrace.[66] One of the basic tenets of progressive religion (which is decidedly *not* Harris's watered-down moderate religion) is its explicit acknowledgment of the interplay between contemporary experience and ancient traditions, an approach Rabbi Mordecai Kaplan famously described as giving the past "a vote but not a veto." From a progressive religious perspective, the act of "hearing God's voice" is not a wooden act of passive obedience that results in certainty but a process of active and ongoing discernment.

Rev. James Forbes summarized it as follows, "There's a humility that more truth can break out, but also that all the different people who are in the world are accessing [truth] as their limited perceiving makes possible. . . . We are not the receivers of the truth just because we hold a Bible in our hands."[67] This commitment to humility and civility is also supported by the evangelical leaders featured here; Dr. Ron Sider of Evangelicals for Social Action worked with the National Association of Evangelicals to approve a historic document on civic engagement that put it this way:

> We must practice humility and cooperation to achieve modest and attainable goals for the good of society. We must take care to employ the language of civility and to avoid denigrating those with whom we disagree. Because political work requires persuasion and cooperation with those who do not share our Christian commitment, we must offer a reasoned and easy-to-grasp defense of our goals.[68]

This more humble and complex religious posture, with its affirmation of multiple perspectives and appeal to reason, is an invitation to dialogue in service of common purpose rather than, as many "religion as problem" progressives fear, "a conversation stopper."[69]

Passion

The third major concern that "religion as problem" progressives hold is that religious passion is dangerously irrational and makes people of faith unpredictable and unreliable partners. Rev. Alexia Salvatierra of Clergy and Laity United for Economic Justice (CLUE) told me about the surprising anxiety that she encountered after organizing a panel of progressive faith leaders for a statewide meeting of the California Democratic Party following the 2004 elections:

> The passion [expressed by the panelists] looked [to many Democrats at the meeting] like it was dangerous, which is true. They were saying, "If you can be passionate today about people having a living wage, tomorrow you might be passionate about getting rid of me as a homosexual. How do I know you're not going to be? How do I know you're not going to tell me as a woman what to do with my body?"[70]

The most straightforward reply to this concern is to note that passion is not without content; it is rooted in a particular view of the world and governed by particular, articulatable convictions. These passions and convictions are not random but are connected in coherent, recognizable ways. Revolutionary colonists fighting for freedom, abolitionists working to end slavery, the struggle to give women the vote, the labor movement's organizing for workers rights, the movements to provide a social safety net in the wake of the Great Depression, and the civil rights movement—each of these were driven by passion to overthrow particular injustices, to create solidarity, and to move toward a freer and more egalitarian society. These passions were certainly not exclusively religious, but in all cases, progressive religious leaders and groups played significant, often leading roles in bringing about these important changes in American society. The progressive religious leaders featured here represent precisely those kinds of voices. As liberal political theorist Michael Walzer put it, such voices have "conviction energized by passion and passion restrained by conviction."[71]

In his insightful book *Politics and Passion*, Walzer directly tackled this liberal discomfort with passion, what he called a "hidden issue" that is contributing to the inadequacy of contemporary progressive politics. Walzer acknowledges the danger of unbridled passion in the political sphere, the worst of which "knows no limits, sweeps all before it . . . [pressing] inexorably toward violent resolutions."[72] But Walzer also notes that the liberal aversion to passion carries its own serious risks.[73]

As I noted in the introduction, analysts ranging from sociologist Stephen Hart to linguist George Lakoff have noted that an aversion to passion has resulted in an anemia that has plagued recent progressive politics.[74] Hart noted that political progressives too often engaged in constrained discourse that seemed to intentionally eschew people's deepest values, religious or otherwise. Walzer concluded that this strategy was ultimately a peculiar "ideology of risk-avoidance" that "can't, almost by definition, provide much inspiration; it can't move men and women to action. . . . [It] is more an excuse for failure than a program for success."[75]

For Walzer, this anemic politics of playing it safe is linked to a misunderstanding of the nature of everyday politics. While political liberals like to imagine ideal "speech situations" or hyper-rational, cool-headed deliberations where evidence is carefully considered in turn, Walzer notes that these constructions little resemble the messier world of real politics. "Opposition and conflict, disagreement and struggle where the stakes are high," Walzer argues, "that's what politics is." The recent past has too often consisted of an uneven playing field. Those opposed to progressive politics have been actively marshaling religious and other strong views of the world to recruit people to their causes, while progressives have been shaping their politics to fit abstract theoretical ideals, mounting rational appeals buttressed by statistics and complicated policy talking points. Walzer bluntly concludes that if progressive political activists do not become more passionately engaged, "they will lose every struggle for political power."[76]

In our own time, with so much at stake, it is time to move past a risk-avoidance strategy to realize that the real risks of engaging passionately are outweighed by the equally real, larger risks of a politics that is too small to make a real difference and too meager to motivate. The forces that support the status quo with its imbedded injustices are making no qualms about fortifying their ranks with impassioned appeals. If these forces are to be opposed, progressives must be willing to risk engaging real enthusiasm and even righteous indignation, and such a movement will need all the allies it can muster. As Walzer put it, "There is no way to join the parties and movements that are struggling for greater equality, and to support the good passions and convictions against the bad ones, except to do so . . . passionately."[77]

From Religion as Problem to Religion as Resource

E. J. Dionne has persuasively argued that the national elections of 2006 marked the emergence of a new religious landscape in America, one he described as the end of the era of the religious right.[78] As these pages have demonstrated, the retreat of the religious right has not left the political field devoid of religion. On the contrary, many observers are noting the significant new energy and organizing among progressive religious voices. Rev. Jim Wallis has characterized these shifts as a new "great awakening."[79] Rev. Susan Thistlethwaite has argued that they represent nothing less than a "second reformation."[80] The contribution of this book has been to begin to demonstrate the breadth and depth of this new movement. This new religious landscape includes an emerging left-center coalition of authentically religious voices that are working for social justice and for the healing of the world, including healing the wounds caused by the acrimonious tone and divisive agenda of the Christian right.

As my arguments addressing the concerns of "religion as problem" progressives have demonstrated, political progressives should celebrate this emerging movement and welcome these voices as important allies. Progressive religion, as I have noted, is a large, authentic, enduring strain in American religion. And even skeptical political progressives must remember, however hard it may be against the recent culture wars backdrop, that progressive religion has been a powerful force for good. To take just one prominent example, few would dispute that the civil rights movement would have been a shadow of itself were it not for the churches and synagogues that served as much of the infrastructure of the movement. Churches and synagogues supplied not only many of its key leaders, but the buses, the meeting places, the financial resources, and the passionate activists that made this movement work. And it is worth remembering that Martin Luther King Jr.—the single most-mentioned person in my interviews across all traditions—was not just a gifted organizer, orator, and writer. He was first of all Rev. King, a Baptist minister who skillfully wove biblical lines about "justice rolling down like waters" and "righteousness as a mighty stream" into a new American dream that moved huge segments of our nation to action.

There is solid evidence that we are once again in our own time looking out over a land of new possibilities. The words of King's last sermon, given the night before he was assassinated, ring true again today, calling us to unfinished work:

> The nation is sick. Trouble is in the land. Confusion all around. . . . But I know, somehow, that only when it is dark enough, can you see the stars. And I see God working in this period of the twentieth century in a way that men, in some strange way, are responding—something is happening in our world. . . . And we've got to say to the nation: we know how it's coming out. For when people get caught up with that which is right and they are willing to sacrifice for it, there is no stopping point short of victory. . . . And let us move on in these powerful days, these days of challenge to make America what it ought to be. We have an opportunity to make America a better nation.[81]

Together, these new voices represent a hopeful turning of the page from our current national posture of fear and self-interest, one that fuels policies of domination more reminiscent of empire than a free democratic people. These leaders were clear that neither America nor any other human state will ever usher in the full realization of *shalom*, God's beauty in the world, or the reign of God where the lion lies down with the lamb. And their prophetic voices will certainly prove to be inconvenient to any political movement, progressive or otherwise, that compromises its convictions or opts for ideology over principle. But the amalgam of passion and conviction in these voices that are at once progressive and religious will be faithful reminders that we can and must do better for our world, our country, and ourselves.

Interviewees

Judaism

Rabbi Richard Block
Senior rabbi, The Temple—Tifereth Israel, Cleveland, Ohio; executive committee, We Believe Ohio

Rabbi Sharon Brous
IKAR Congregation, Los Angeles, California

Cantor Jack Chomsky
Congregation Tifereth Israel, Columbus, Ohio; executive committee, We Believe Ohio

Dr. Leonard Fein
Founder, *Moment* magazine, MAZON: A Jewish Response to Hunger

Rabbi Marla Feldman
Director, Commission on Social Action, Union for Reform Judaism

Simon Greer
President, Jewish Funds for Justice

Rabbi Steve Gutow
President, Jewish Council for Public Affairs

Rabbi Jill Jacobs
Director of education, Jewish Funds for Justice

Rabbi Michael Lerner
Editor, *Tikkun* magazine

Dr. David Luchins
Vice president, The Orthodox Union; former senior policy advisor to Sen.
  Patrick Moynihan

Rabbi Rolando Matalon
Rabbi, Congregation B'nai Jeshurun

Ruth Messinger
President, American Jewish World Service

Rabbi Jonah Pesner
Director, Just Congregations, Union for Reform Judaism

Rabbi Or Rose
Associate dean, The Rabbinical School of Hebrew College

Rabbi David Rosenn
Founding director, AVODAH, The Jewish Service Corps

Rabbi Jennie Rosenn
Program director, Jewish Life and Values, Nathan Cummings Foundation

Rabbi David Saperstein
Director, Religious Action Center for Reform Judaism

Daniel Sokatch
Director, Progressive Jewish Alliance

Al Vorspan
Civil rights leader; director emeritus of the Commission on Social Action
and vice president emeritus of the Union for Reform Judaism; founding director of Religious Action Center for Reform Judaism

Rabbi Arthur Waskow
Director, The Shalom Center

Rabbi Eric Yoffie
President, Union for Reform Judaism

Christianity

Rev. Tim Ahrens
Senior minister, First Congregational Church, Columbus, Ohio; director,
We Believe Ohio

Rev. Steven Baines
Director, Faith Action Network, People for the American Way Foundation

Kim Bobo
Director, National Interfaith Committee for Worker Justice

Dr. Rita Nakashima Brock
Director, Faith Voices for the Common Good

Dr. Delwin Brown
Coordinator, Progressive Christian Witness

Rev. Eric Brown
Pastor, Woodland Christian Church, Columbus, Ohio; executive committee, We Believe Ohio

Rev. Jennifer Butler
Director, Faith in Public Life

Sr. Simone Campbell
Director, Network, a National Catholic Social Justice Lobby

Dr. Tony Campolo
Evangelical leader; author of thirty books; professor of sociology, Eastern
    University

Rev. Jeff Carr
CEO, Sojourners/Call to Renewal (at time of interview); currently direc-
    tor of gang reduction and youth development, Los Angeles

Rev. Felix Carrion
Senior minister, Euclid Avenue Congregational Church, Cleveland, Ohio;
    executive committee, We Believe Ohio

Dr. Shaun Casey
Associate professor of theology, Wesley Theological Seminary; senior fel-
    low in religion, Center for American Progress, 2007

Sr. Joan Chittister
Cochair, Global Peace Initiative for Women; Network of Spiritual Progressives

Dr. John Cobb Jr.
Author, scholar, and cofounder of Progressive Christians Uniting

Judy Coode
Council chair, Pax Christi USA

Rev. Joseph Darby
Civil rights leader; pastor, Morris Avenue Baptist Church, Charleston,
    South Carolina

Fr. John Dear, SJ
Author and peace activist

Marie Dennis
Director, Maryknoll Office for Global Concerns; vice president, Pax Christi
    International

Rev. Mark Diemer
Pastor, Grace of God Lutheran Church, Columbus, Ohio; executive committee, We Believe Ohio

Rev. Robert Edgar
General secretary, National Council of Churches (at time of interview); currently president and CEO, Common Cause

Rev. Dr. James Forbes
Senior minister, The Riverside Church, New York; founder, The Healing of the Nations Foundation

Rev. Vincent Frosh
Pastor, First A.M.E. Zion Church, Columbus, Ohio; executive committee, We Believe Ohio

Rev. Welton Gaddy
Director, The Interfaith Alliance

Brenda Girton-Mitchell
Associate general secretary for justice and advocacy, National Council of Churches

Fr. James E. Hug, SJ
President, Center of Concern

Rev. Vince Isner
Director, Faithful America (at time of interview); currently president, Vince Isner Productions

Alexia Kelley
CEO, Catholics in Alliance for the Common Good

Rev. Harry Knox
Director, Religion and Faith Program, Human Rights Campaign

Rev. Jennifer Kottler
Associate director, Protestants for the Common Good (at time of interview); currently director, Let Justice Roll Living Wage Campaign

Rev. Peter Laarman
Director, Progressive Christians Uniting

Rev. Dr. John Lentz Jr.
Senior pastor, Forest Hill Church, Cleveland, Ohio; executive committee, We Believe Ohio

The Very Rev. Tracey Lind
Dean, Trinity Episcopal Cathedral, Cleveland, Ohio; executive committee, We Believe Ohio

Rev. Timothy McDonald III
Senior pastor, First Iconium Baptist Church, Atlanta, Georgia; chair, African American Ministers in Action, People for the American Way Foundation

Rev. Brian McLaren
Author, speaker, pastor; leader in the Emerging Church movement

Dr. Rosemary Radford Ruether
Professor of theology, Claremont Graduate School

Rev. Alexia Salvatierra
Director, Clergy and Laity United for Economic Justice

Rev. Dr. Kenneth L. Samuel
Civil rights leader and senior pastor, Victory Church, Stone Mountain, Georgia

Rev. Daniel Schultz
Founder, Streetprophets.org; pastor, Salem United Church of Christ

Maureen Shea
Director of government relations, The Episcopal Church; former liaison to religious communities for President Bill Clinton, 1997–2000

Dr. Ron Sider
President, Evangelicals for Social Action; author of numerous books; professor of theology, holistic ministry, and public policy at Palmer Seminary at Eastern University

Rev. Ron Stief
Director of the Office of Public Life and Social Policy, United Church of Christ (at time of interview); currently director of organizing strategy, Faith in Public Life

Rev. Dr. Susan Thistlethwaite
President, Chicago Theological Seminary; visiting senior fellow in religion, Center for American Progress

Rev. Jim Wallis
President, Sojourners/Call to Renewal

Islam

Dr. Umar Faruq Abd-Allah
Chairman and scholar in residence, Nawawi Foundation

Saleemah Abdul-Ghafur
Author of *Living Islam Out Loud*, second-generation African American Muslim activist for women's equality in Islam

Imam Feisal Abdul Rauf
Imam of Masjid al-Farah, New York City; founder of American Society for Muslim Advancement (ASMA)

Dr. Khaled Abou El Fadl
Omar and Azmeralda Alfi Distinguished Fellow in Islamic Law, UCLA
    School of Law

Dr. Kecia Ali
Assistant professor of religion, Boston University

Dr. Abdullahi Ahmed An-Na'im
Professor of law, Emory University; human rights activist

Sarah Eltantawi
Former communications director, Progressive Muslim Union

Rabia Terri Harris
Coordinator, Muslim Peace Fellowship

Gray Henry
Director, Fons Vitae Press

Dr. Nazir Khaja
Chairman, Islamic Information Service

Dr. M. A. Muqtedar Khan
Associate professor of political science, director of Islamic Studies Program,
    University of Delaware

Dr. Eboo Patel
Founder and director, Interfaith Youth Core

Dr. Omid Safi
Professor of religion, University of North Carolina

A'isha Samad
Executive committee, We Believe Ohio, Cleveland, Ohio

Buddhism

Bill Aiken
Director of public affairs, Soka Gakkai International

Lama Surya Das
Founder, Dzogchen Foundation

Bernard Glassman
Founder, Zen Peacemakers

Rev. Masao Kodani
Senshin Buddhist Temple, Los Angeles, CA

Bhante Yogavacara Rahula
Vice-abbot, Bhavana Society

Alan Senauke
Head of practice, Berkeley Zen Center; director of programs and peacework coordinator, Buddhist Peace Fellowship

Robert Thurman
Professor of Buddhist studies, Columbia University; president, American
Institute of Buddhist Studies

Unitarian Universalism

Rev. Dr. Bill Schulz
Director, Amnesty International USA; former president, Unitarian Universalist Association of Congregations

Rev. William Sinkford
President, Unitarian Universalist Association of Congregations

Religiously Engaged Progressive
Political Leaders and Public Intellectuals

Melody Barnes
Executive vice president for policy, Center for American Progress

Leah Daughtry
Chief of staff, Democratic National Committee

E. J. Dionne
Senior fellow, Governance Studies, Brookings Institution; columnist for
Washington Post

Dr. Diana Eck
Director, The Pluralism Project, Harvard University

Mike McCurry
Former press secretary, President Bill Clinton

Ted Strickland
Governor, State of Ohio

Amy Sullivan
Editor, *Washington Monthly* (at time of interview); currently nation editor,
Time magazine

Mara Vanderslice
President, Common Good Strategies; director of religious outreach for Sen.
John Kerry's 2004 presidential campaign

Notes

Introduction:
Moving Beyond the Culture Wars:
Finding Progressive Religion in America

1. Robert P. Jones, *The American Values Survey* (Washington, DC: Center for American Values in Public Life, People for the American Way Foundation, 2006).

2. Source: People for the American Way, www.pfaw.org/pfaw/general/default .aspx?oid=3147 (accessed August 5, 2007). Revenue taken from IRS Form 990 for tax year 2005.

3. Dan Gilgoff, *The Jesus Machine: How James Dobson, Focus on the Family, and Evangelical America Are Winning the Culture War* (New York: St. Martin's Press, 2007).

4. Because NPR serves large city media markets, its weekly listener base is much larger than Dobson's: 26 million weekly listeners (www.npr.org/about/, accessed September 7, 2007) vs. Dobson's 3.4 million weekly listeners. Dobson's greater geographic spread in smaller markets, however, is significant for reaching a broad swath of listeners who can be mobilized at the grassroots level. See CNN, "Christian Right Leader Writes Off Giuliani," CNN, www.cnn.com/2007/POLITICS/ 05/17/giuliani.dobson/index.html.

5. Earl Black and Merle Black, *The Rise of Southern Republicans* (Cambridge, Mass.: Harvard University Press, 2002), 160.

6. Black and Black identify the main source of "the Great White Switch" as a backlash against civil rights legislation. Since the passage of the Civil Rights Act in

1964, despite the fact that no Deep South Democrat supported it, more whites have voted Republican than Democratic in every presidential election; by the time of Reagan's presidency in 1984, more Southern whites began to think of themselves as Republicans than Democrats. See Black and Black, *Rise of Southern Republicans*, 160, 205. See also "The Unintended Consequences of Dixieland Postliberalism" for a more thorough analysis of the influence of federal interventionism on Evangelical theology. Robert P. Jones and Melissa C. Stewart, "The Unintended Consequences of Dixieland Postliberalism," *Cross Currents*, Winter 2006.

7. John Green, *Fourth National Survey of Religion and Politics* (Akron, OH: Bliss Institute, University of Akron, 2004).

8. "National Election Pool Exit Poll," 2004.

9. See Rozell and Das Gupta for an analysis of the impact of the "values campaign" on Bush's 2004 victory. See Mark J. Rozell and Debasree Das Gupta, "'The Values Vote'? Moral Issues and the 2004 Elections," in *The Values Campaign? The Christian Right and the 2004 Elections*, ed. John Green, Mark J. Rozell, and Clyde Wilcox (Washington, DC: Georgetown University Press, 2007).

10. See Randall Balmer's *Thy Kingdom Come* for an excellent account of how the choice of abortion as a litmus-test issue was driven by strategic political reasons. See Randall Herbert Balmer, *Thy Kingdom Come: How the Religious Right Distorts the Faith and Threatens America; An Evangelical's Lament* (New York: Basic, 2006).

11. Interestingly, the "I Vote Values" rig was a transformed a semi-truck that previously belonged to the Charlie Daniels band. See Hanna Rosin, "Redeem the Vote Spreads the Election-Year Gospel," *Washington Post*, October 29, 2004.

12. Alan Cooperman and Thomas B. Edsall, "Evangelicals Say They Led Charge for the GOP," *Washington Post*, November 8, 2004.

13. The values language was ubiquitous on multiple levels for Republicans. For example, even Roy Blunt's (R-MO) PAC was called "Rely on Your Beliefs." Also, the Bush campaign dispatched Ralph Reed to the summer 2004 SBC Convention to host a "pastors reception" paid for by the campaign, where an aide collected signatures from ministers pledging to endorse Bush's reelection publicly. See David D. Kirkpatrick, "Bush Allies Till Fertile Soil, among Baptists, for Votes," *New York Times*, June 18, 2004.

14. Tom Strode, "President Bush Wins Re-Election; Exit Polls Show Values Voters Made the Difference," *Baptist Press News*, November 3, 2004.

15. The *Washington Post's* Dick Meyer, one of the more vocal debunkers of what he mockingly called the "Unified Theory of Election 2004," provided an illustrative list of headlines from television and newspapers in his "Anatomy of a Myth" column. See David Meyer, "Moral Values Malarkey," CBS News, November 5, 2004. CBS News, www.cbsnews.com/stories/2004/11/05/opinion/meyer/main653931.shtml.

16. David R. Jones, "Why Bush Won," CBS News, November 3, 2004.

17. Katharine Q. Seelye, "Moral Values Cited as a Defining Issue of the Election," *New York Times*, November 4, 2004.

18. Astonishingly, Republican pollster Bill McInturff admitted that the term had become a partisan brand with peculiar content, and then used that fact to defend its use. He argued, "The people who picked moral values as an issue know what that means. It's a code word in surveys for a cluster of issues like gay marriage and abortion." See Jim Rutenberg, "Emphasis on 'Moral Values' in Exit Poll Sparks Debate," *New York Times*, November 6, 2004.

19. Meyer, "Moral Values Malarkey."

20. Gary Langer, "A Question of Values," *New York Times*, November 6, 2004.

21. "National Election Pool Exit Poll," 2004.

22. Pew Research Center for the People and the Press, *Moral Values: How Important?* (Washington, DC: Pew Research Center for the People and the Press, 2004). Moreover, the term "moral values" has little history or comparative context in the polling universe. Neither the 2000 exit poll nor any other major national poll contained a question about moral values as an issue. The closest question on a recent exit poll was a question about "priorities for the new administration" in 1996, where an equally fuzzy "family values" was the top concern of 17 percent, second to "health of the economy." Although this "family values" group largely went for Bob Dole, Bill Clinton handily won that election.

23. For example, as recently as January 2008, a *USA Today* story twice referred to Republican candidate Mike Huckabee's supporters as "values voters." See Media Matters, "*USA Today* Labeled Conservative Evangelical Huckabee Supporters as 'Value Voters,'" Media Matters, mediamatters.org/items/200801250016.

24. www.amazon.com (accessed August 3, 2007).

25. Christopher Hitchens, *God Is Not Great: How Religion Poisons Everything* (New York: Twelve, 2007).

26. Richard Dawkins, *The God Delusion* (Boston: Houghton Mifflin, 2006).

27. Sam Harris, *The End of Faith: Religion, Terror, and the Future of Reason* (New York: Norton, 2004); Sam Harris, *Letter to a Christian Nation* (New York: Knopf, 2006).

28. Hitchens, *God Is Not Great.*

29. Jones, *American Values Survey*; Michael Hout and Claude S. Fischer, "Why More Americans Have No Religious Preference: Politics and Generations," *American Sociological Review* 67, April 2002.

30. Barna and Kinnaman's definitions of "born again" and "outsider" are highly subjective. First, Barna's definition of "born again" does not allow respondents to self-identify (the practice followed by most public opinion experts) but depends

on a range of specific theological criteria that represent a distinctively evangelical perspective. Kinnaman compounds this difficulty by employing a double standard in his definition of "insider" and "outsider." Kinnaman includes *all* "born again" Christians as insiders, but only includes non-born-again Christians (that is, non-evangelical Christians such as Catholics and mainline Protestants) as insiders if they attend church frequently. As a result, his category of Christian "insiders" is vastly overpopulated by evangelicals, and many Catholics and mainline Protestants are included in the "outsiders" category. His results should be read in this light. See David Kinnaman, *Unchristian: What a New Generation Really Thinks about Christianity . . . and Why It Matters* (Grand Rapids, MI: Baker, 2007), 17.

31. In fact, seven out of the top ten attributes young outsiders used to describe Christianity were negative, including "old-fashioned" (78 percent), "too involved with politics" (75 percent), "out of touch with reality" (72 percent), and "insensitive to others" (70 percent). The only three positive attributes mentioned were "teaches same basic idea as other religions" (82 percent), "has good values and principles" (76 percent), and "friendly" (71 percent). It is also worth noting that there is nothing distinctively Christian in the top positive attribute. See Kinnaman, *Unchristian*, 28.

32. Kinnaman, *Unchristian*, 15.

33. Kinnaman, *Unchristian*, 33–34.

34. John Green and Steve Waldman, "The Twelve Tribes of American Politics," Beliefnet, www.beliefnet.com/story/167/story_16763_1.html.

35. The majority (50 percent) of Americans are "religious centrists." I was the principal researcher for the American Values Survey during my tenure as the director and senior fellow at the Center for American Values in Public Life at People for the American Way Foundation.

36. Jones, *American Values Survey*.

37. Scott Keeter, "Will White Evangelicals Desert the GOP?" Pew Research Center for the People and the Press, May 2, 2006, Pew Research Center for the People and the Press, pewresearch.org/pubs/22/will-white—evangelicals—desert-the-gop. In 1992, evangelicals represented 24 percent of the population, and in 2004 they represented 26 percent of the population. See Andrew Kohut and Scott Keeter, "Religion and the Presidential Vote," Commentary, Pew Research Center for the People and the Press, December 6, 2004, Pew Research Center for the People and the Press, people-press.org/commentary/display.php3?Analysis ID=103. Also see Green, *Fourth National Survey of Religion and Politics*.

38. Will Herberg, *Protestant, Catholic, Jew: An Essay in American Religious Sociology* (Garden City, NY: Doubleday, 1955).

39. Diana L. Eck, *A New Religious America: How a "Christian Country" Has Become the World's Most Religiously Diverse Nation* (San Francisco: HarperSanFrancisco, 2001).

40. Green and Waldman, "Twelve Tribes of American Politics."

41. Jones, *American Values Survey*.

42. David Saperstein, director, Religious Action Center for Reform Judaism; interview, July 10, 2007.

43. Stephen Hart, *Cultural Dilemmas of Progressive Politics: Styles of Engagement among Grassroots Activists* (Chicago: University of Chicago Press, 2001), 20.

44. Hart, *Cultural Dilemmas*, 15.

45. Mainline Protestants, one of the key groups constituting the religious left, consist of more than twenty-two million members in seven major denominations including the United Methodist Church (UMC), the Evangelical Lutheran Church in America (ELCA), the Presbyterian Church USA (PCUSA), the Episcopal Church, the American Baptist Churches (ABC), the United Church of Christ (UCC), and the Disciples of Christ (DOC).

46. Robert Wuthnow and John Hyde Evans, *The Quiet Hand of God: Faith-Based Activism and the Public Role of Mainline Protestantism* (Berkeley: University of California Press, 2002), 399.

47. Wuthnow and Evans, *Quiet Hand of God*, 399.

48. Media Matters, "Left Behind: The Skewed Representation of Religion in Major News Media," (Washington, DC: Media Matters, 2007).

49. Media Matters, "Left Behind."

50. Caryle Murphy and Alan Cooperman, "Religious Liberals Gain New Visibility: A Different List of Moral Issues," *Washington Post*, May 20, 2006.

51. Jim Wallis, president, Sojourners/Call to Renewal; interview, September 11, 2007.

52. Joan Chittister, cochair, Global Peace Initiative for Women; Network of Spiritual Progressives; interview, November 30, 2007.

53. Jennifer Kottler, associate director, Protestants for the Common Good; interview, April 1, 2007.

54. Arthur Waskow, director, The Shalom Center; interview, May 16, 2007.

55. Eboo Patel, founder and director, Interfaith Youth Core; interview, August 31, 2007.

56. Tracy Lind, dean, Trinity Episcopal Cathedral, Cleveland, Ohio; executive committee, We Believe Ohio; interview, May 25, 2007.

57. Saleemah Abdul-Ghafur, second-generation African American Muslim activist for women's equality in Islam; interview, March 2, 2007.

58. John B. Cobb, *Progressive Christians Speak: A Different Voice on Faith and Politics* (Louisville, KY: Westminster John Knox Press, 2003).

59. Abdul-Ghafur, interview, March 2, 2007.

60. Omid Safi, professor of religion, University of North Carolina; interview, September 14, 2007.

61. Wallis, interview, September 11, 2007.

62. Cobb, *Progressive Christians Speak.*

63. Or N. Rose, Jo Ellen Kaiser, and Margie Klein, eds., *Righteous Indignation: A Jewish Call for Justice* (Woodstock, VT: Jewish Lights Publishing, 2007).

64. Omid Safi, ed., *Progressive Muslims: On Justice, Gender and Pluralism* (Oxford: Oneworld, 2003).

65. Melvin McLeod, *Mindful Politics: A Buddhist Guide to Making the World a Better Place* (Boston: Wisdom, 2006).

66. Identifying the common threads both within and across these diverse religious traditions is a daunting task, and a brief description of my approach will be helpful in reading the following chapters. In order to help give the research some coherent shape, I started with a common set of questions, and I privileged this interview material over other existing writings by these leaders. My questions concentrated less on official doctrines and more on what might be called the imaginative and institutional infrastructure of progressive religion in America—broad themes such as understandings of religious authority and truth, relationships and approaches to sacred texts, metaphors, distinctive sensibilities, worldviews, and religious practices. Finally, I analyzed how these broad themes connected to specific issues and how they were being embodied in new institutions and movements.

67. One need look no further for evidence of power corrupting principle than former Christian Coalition head Pat Robertson's endorsement of three-time-divorced, pro-choice, New York Mayor Rudy Giuliani over Governor Mike Huckabee, a pro-life Southern Baptist minister.

68. The exact meaning of the Latin root is in dispute. Cicero, for example, thought that *religio* derived from the verb *relegere*, which means "to reread or go over a text," but the fourth-century Christian writer Lactantius argued that it derived from *religare*, which means "to fasten or bind." See Jorunn Jacobsen Buckley et al., *The HarperCollins Dictionary of Religion* (San Francisco: HarperSanFrancisco, 1995).

69. Émile Durkheim, *The Elementary Forms of Religious Life* (1912; New York: Free Press, 1995).

70. Abraham Lincoln, "Second Inaugural Address." Yale University, www.yale.edu/lawweb/avalon/presiden/inaug/lincoln2.htm.

71. Even before the war, Lincoln consistently tempered any identification of human action with divine purpose. For example, in a speech Lincoln gave in 1861 on the brink of war in Trenton, New Jersey, he referred to Americans as an "almost chosen people." See Richard Carwardine, *Lincoln: A Life of Purpose and Power* (New York: Knopf, 2006).

72. There is a growing awareness of the need to understand religion better not only as a source of conflict but also as a resource for resolving it. American politicians and analysts, however, have been more open to this approach in assessing international conflicts than in understanding domestic clashes over policy. See Douglas Johnston and Cynthia Sampson, eds., *Religion: The Missing Dimension of Statecraft* (New York: Oxford University Press, 1994).

73. Patel, interview, May 25, 2007.

74. Patel, interview, May 25, 2007.

75. Patel, interview, May 25, 2007.

76. Tim Ahrens, senior minister, First Congregational Church, Columbus, Ohio; director, We Believe Ohio; interview, May 23, 2007.

Chapter 1.
Lifting the Line of History:
How Progressive Jews Are Healing the World

1. Arthur Waskow, director, The Shalom Center; interview, May 16, 2007.

2. Waskow, interview, May 16, 2007.

3. David Saperstein, founding director, AVODAH, The Jewish Service Corps; interview, July 10, 2007.

4. This consistency is attributable to at least two factors: (1) unlike the other major American religious traditions, Judaism combines religious belief and practice with a single ethnic identity; and (2) unlike Islam and Buddhism, Judaism has a long history of institutional establishment in America, and these institutions channel Jewish public engagement in generally progressive directions.

5. Al Vorspan, civil rights leader; director emeritus of the Commission on Social Action and vice president emeritus of the Union for Reform Judaism; founding director of Religious Action Center for Reform Judaism; interview, March 15, 2007.

6. Saperstein, interview, July 10, 2007. Vorspan clarified that, contrary to the rosy view many Jews have of Jewish involvement in the civil rights struggles, the movement was not unanimous about its prominent involvement; there were painful internal struggles along the path.

7. Steve Gutow, president, Jewish Council for Public Affairs; interview, June 21, 2007.

8. Jill Jacobs, director of education, Jewish Funds for Justice; interview, June 20, 2007.

9. David Luchins, vice president, The Orthodox Union; interview, March 14, 2007.

10. "National Election Pool Exit Poll," 2006.

11. The three Jewish Republican members of Congress are Senator Arlen Specter (PA), Senator Norm Coleman (MN), and Representative Eric Cantor (VA). See Elizabeth Williamson, "Jewish Membership in Congress at All-Time High," *Washington Post*, January 12, 2007.

12. Michael Lerner, editor, *Tikkun* magazine; interview, August 23, 2007.

13. D. Rosenn, interview, March 15, 2007.

14.. Leonard Fein, founder, *Moment* magazine, MAZON: A Jewish Response to Hunger; interview, July 24, 2007.

15. Because of its relatively small size, accurate counts of the Jewish population have been difficult to attain. The Pew Survey is one of the few studies with a large enough sample size to get statistically significant results. Using different methodology, a recently released survey by the Steinhardt Social Research Institute at Brandeis University put the total Jewish population in America at about 6 million. See The Pew Forum on Religion and Public Life, "The U.S. Religious Landscape Survey," 2008, Pew Forum on Religion and Public Life, religions.pewforum.org/reports; Bethamie Horowitz, "Finally, a Jewish Population Study Worth Studying," *Jewish Daily Forward*, March 9, 2007.

16. Pew Forum, "Religious Landscape Survey."

17. Daniel Sokatch, director, Progressive Jewish Alliance; interview, September 20, 2007.

18. *Time* magazine, "The *Time* 100 Most Influential People of the Century," 1998–1999.

19. Jerome Karabel, *The Chosen: The Hidden History of Admission and Exclusion at Harvard, Yale, and Princeton* (Boston: Houghton Mifflin, 2005).

20. Ethan Bronner, "Brandeis at 50 Is Still Searching, Still Jewish and Still Not Harvard," *New York Times*, October 17, 1998.

21. Karabel, *The Chosen*; Harvard Hillel, "Harvard University and Radcliffe College Campus Information," Hillel, www.hillel.org/HillelApps/JLOC/Campus.aspx?AgencyId=17431.

22. Pew Forum, "Religious Landscape Survey."

23. Pew Forum, "Religious Landscape Survey."

24. Pew Forum on Religion and Public Life, "Public Expresses Mixed Views of Islam, Mormonism," September 25, 2007, Pew Forum on Religion and Public Life, perforum.org/surveys/religionviews07.

25. Joe Lieberman, "Lieberman Renews Call for Larger, Lawful Space for Religion in American Public Life," Joe Lieberman, United States Senator, lieberman.senate.gov/newsroom/release.cfm?id=208625.

26. Sokatch, interview, September 20, 2007.

27. Jacobs, interview, June 20, 2007.

28. Eric Yoffie, president, Union for Reform Judaism; interview, March 14, 2007.

29. Slingshot Fund, "Slingshot: A Resource Guide for Jewish Innovation 07–08," Slingshot Fund, www.slingshotfund.org.

30. Sharon Brous, IKAR Congregation, Los Angeles, California; interview, August 21, 2007.

31. Jacobs, interview, June 20, 2007.

32. Fein, interview, July 24, 2007.

33. Luchins, interview, March 14, 2007.

34. Or N. Rose, associate dean, The Rabbinical School of Hebrew College; interview, November 17, 2007.

35. Rabbi Or Rose noted that this more universal focus presents some challenges in engaging the tradition, for two reasons. First, most of the classical texts are focused primarily on justice issues internal to the Jewish community; and second, as Rabbi Rose explained, "Our experience of exile and oppression also led many of our most brilliant sages to adopt extremely negative views of non-Jews (often mirroring the chauvinistic attitudes of our oppressors)." Rabbi Rose concluded, "Religious progressives *must* address these issues honestly as we seek to move forward and create a more just vision of religion and pubic life." Rose, interview, November 17, 2007.

36. Fein, interview, July 24, 2007.

37. Simon Greer, president, Jewish Funds for Justice; interview, March 16, 2007.

38. Ruth Messinger, president, American Jewish World Service; interview, June 22, 2007.

39. Sokatch, interview, September 20, 2007.

40. Rose, interview, November 17, 2007.

41. Luchins, interview, March 14, 2007.

42. Arthur Green, *These Are the Words: A Vocabulary of Jewish Spiritual Life* (Woodstock, VT: Jewish Lights, 1999).

43. Saperstein, interview, July 10, 2007.

44. Brous, interview, August 21, 2007.

45. Lerner, interview, August 23, 2007.

46. Gutow, interview, June 21, 2007.

47. Messinger, interview, June 22, 2007.

48. Yoffie, interview, March 14, 2007.

49. Saperstein, interview, July 10, 2007.

50. Luchins, interview, March 14, 2007. A *midrash* is an exegesis of a biblical passage, often through the creative use of metaphor. Rabbi Arthur Waskow, one

of the more gifted contemporary practitioners of *midrash*, said that he "fell in love" with this method of interpretation when he first encountered it. He described it vividly this way: "The idea that you could take a 3,000-year-old text and give it a twirl and come out somewhere really new, and that the rabbis already 2,000 years ago were doing this with their old text and giving it a new meaning, that was so delicious." Waskow, interview, May 16, 2007.

51. Jonah Pesner, director, Just Congregations, Union for Reform Judaism; interview, July 26, 2007.

52. Rolando Matalon, Congregation B'nai Jeshurun; interview, June 22, 2007.

53. Matalon, interview, June 22, 2007.

54. Yoffie, interview, March 14, 2007.

55. Marla Feldman, director, Commission on Social Action, Union for Reform Judaism; interview, March 15, 2007.

56. Saperstein, interview, July 10, 2007.

57. Feldman, interview, March 15, 2007.

58. Yoffie, interview, March 14, 2007.

59. Brous, interview, August 21, 2007.

60. Sokatch, interview, September 20, 2007.

61. Saperstein, interview, July 10, 2007.

62. J. Rosenn, interview, November 2, 2007.

63. D. Rosenn, interview, March 15, 2007.

64. Sokatch, interview, September 20, 2007.

65. Rose, interview, November 17, 2007.

66. Matalon, interview, June 22, 2007.

67. Pesner, interview, July 26, 2007.

68. Yoffie, interview, March 14, 2007.

69. Saperstein, interview, July 10, 2007.

70. J. Rosenn, interview, November 2, 2007.

71. Jack Chomsky, Congregation Tifereth Israel, Columbus, Ohio; executive committee, We Believe Ohio; interview, June 15, 2007.

72. Abraham Joshua Heschel, *The Sabbath: Its Meaning for Modern Man* (New York: Farrar, 1951), 8.

73. Heschel, *Sabbath*, 3, 13.

74. J. Rosenn, interview, November 2, 2007.

75. Matalon, interview, June 22, 2007.

76. Abraham Joshua Heschel, *Between God and Man: An Interpretation of Judaism* (New York: Free Press, 1997), 217.

77. Brous, interview, August 21, 2007.

78. Rabbi Brous noted that her thinking about *Shabbat* had been deeply influenced by Orthodox Rabbi Irving (Yitz) Greenberg. See Irving Greenberg, *The Jewish Way: Living the Holidays* (New York: Summit Books, 1988).

79. Brous, interview, August 21, 2007.

80. Brous, interview, August 21, 2007.

81. Franz Kafka, *Parables and Paradoxes: In German and English*, bilingual ed. (New York: Schocken Books, 1975).

82. Waskow, interview, May 16, 2007.

83. Waskow, interview, May 16, 2007.

84. René Girard, for example, has argued that ritual acts as a kind of social safety valve to manage communal experiences of violence and violent impulses. See René Girard, *Violence and the Sacred* (Baltimore: Johns Hopkins University Press, 1979).

85. Note that this is the basic idea captured in Émile Durkheim's concept of "collective effervescence," when the community comes together to reconstitute itself around a new set of rituals and symbols. See Émile Durkheim, *The Elementary Forms of Religious Life* (1912; New York: Free Press, 1995).

86. Waskow, interview, May 16, 2007.

87. Waskow, interview, May 16, 2007.

88. Greer, interview, March 16, 2007.

89. Gutow, interview, June 21, 2007.

90. Brous, interview, August 21, 2007.

91. This ruling by a set of legal experts within the Conservative denomination reversed a 1992 affirmation of a ban on gay and lesbian rabbis and same-sex unions. The repeal of the ban also gave individual congregations and institutions the latitude to make their own decisions on these matters. See Neela Banerjee, "Conservative Jewish Seminary Will Accept Gay Students," *New York Times*, March 27, 2007.

92. Banerjee, "Jewish Seminary Will Accept Gay Students," March 27, 2007.

93. Luchins, interview, March 14, 2007.

94. Matalon, interview, June 22, 2007. This welcoming stance toward gays and lesbians ultimately caused enough tension between the congregation and the Conservative movement that the congregation disaffiliated itself from the movement and discontinued its support of Jewish Theological Seminary in the early 1990s.

95. Matalon, interview, June 22, 2007.

96. Brous, interview, August 21, 2007.

97. Rose, interview, November 17, 2007.

98. Messinger, interview, June 22, 2007.

99. Michael Lerner, *The Left Hand of God: Taking Back Our Country from the Religious Right* (San Francisco: HarperSanFrancisco, 2006).

100. Lerner, *Left Hand of God.*

101. *Tikkun* magazine, "2007 Rate Card," www.tikkun.org/magazine/2007ratecard.pdf.

102. *Tikkun* magazine, "2007 Rate Card."

103. Network of Spiritual Progressives, "Join a Local Chapter," Network of Spiritual Progressives, www.spiritualprogressives.org/article.php?story=localchapters. The NSP headquarters does not keep individual membership lists of the local chapters, so estimating the size of the network in terms of individuals is not possible.

104. Network of Spiritual Progressives, "What Is an NSP Chapter?" Network of Spiritual Progressives, www.spiritualprogressives.org/article.php?story=20071031174507751.

105. Network of Spiritual Progressives, "Basic Tenets," Network of Spiritual Progressives, www.spiritualprogressives.org/.

106. Network of Spiritual Progressives, "The Global Marshall Plan," Network of Spiritual Progressives, www.spiritualprogressives.org/article.php?story=20070228183252814.

107. Lerner, interview, August 23, 2007.

108. Peter Dreier and Daniel May, "Progressive Jews Organize," *The Nation*, October 1, 2007. The central leaders the article featured are leaders I interviewed for this book using an independent methodology: Simon Greer of Jewish Funds for Justice, Rabbi Jonah Pesner of Temple Israel in Boston on the Reform Movement's new Just Congregations initiative, Rabbi David Saperstein of the Religious Action Center for Reform Judaism, and Daniel Sokatch of the Progressive Jewish Alliance. It is worth noting here that two of these leaders are rabbis and two come more directly from the legal advocacy and organizing worlds.

109. Richard Wood and Mark R. Warren, "A Different Face of Faith-Based Politics: Social Capital and Community Organizing in the Public Arena," *International Journal of Sociology and Social Policy* 22, no. 11/12, 2002.

110. Dreier and May, "Progressive Jews Organize." Note that Alinsky is another example of the model many leaders cited of Jews doing cutting-edge social justice work but not doing it overtly as Jews or within the context of the Jewish community.

111. Dreier and May, "Progressive Jews Organize."

112. Nancy T. Ammerman, Mark Chaves, and Richard L. Wood, "Synagogues and Social Justice: Creating Sustainable Change within and beyond the Congregation," *S3K Report* no. 3, Fall 2007.

113. Pesner, interview, July 26, 2007.

114. Pesner, interview, July 26, 2007.

115. Pesner, interview, July 26, 2007.

116. Fein, interview, July 24, 2007.

117. Brous, interview, August 21, 2007.

118. Or N. Rose, Jo Ellen Kaiser, and Margie Klein, eds., *Righteous Indignation: A Jewish Call for Justice* (Woodstock, VT: Jewish Lights Publishing, 2007).

119. Rose, interview, November 17, 2007.

Chapter 2.
More Truth Breaking Out
How Progressive Christians Are Seeking the
Reign of God on Earth

1. James A. Forbes, "The Healing of the Nations Foundation," Healing of the Nations Foundation, www.healingofthenations.com/index.shtml.

2. James A. Forbes, senior minister, The Riverside Church, New York; founder, The Healing of the Nations Foundation; interview, March 17, 2007.

3. Pew Forum on Religion and Public Life, "The U.S. Religious Landscape Survey," Pew Forum on Religion and Public Life, religions.pewforum.org/reports.

4. The third major historic branch of Christianity is the Eastern Orthodox churches. In the United States, this historic branch is relatively small—approximately the same size as a midsize single Protestant denomination, such as Presbyterians.

5. In this analysis, I have included Latinos largely within the Roman Catholic denominational family. Two-thirds (65 percent) of Latinos are Roman Catholic; while Latino Catholics are more progressive across a number of measures than white Catholics, they share a common religious orientation that justifies grouping these groups together. While a growing number of Latinos are Protestant (25 percent), this number remains small, and Latino Protestants tend to be Pentecostal and are politically conservative, holding views that are typically closer to white evangelicals. See Robert P. Jones, *The American Values Survey* (Washington, DC: Center for American Values in Public Life, People for the American Way Foundation, 2006).

6. Andrew M. Greeley, *The Catholic Imagination* (Berkeley: University of California Press, 2000), 1.

7. Joan Chittister, cochair, Global Peace Initiative for Women; Network of Spiritual Progressives; interview, November 30, 2007.

8. Greeley, *Catholic Imagination.*

9. These insights follow David Tracy's analysis in his classic work, *The Analogical Imagination.* Tracy calls the Catholic imagination "analogical" and the Protestant imagination "dialectical." See David Tracy, *The Analogical Imagination* (New York: Crossroad, 1981).

10. Louis Dumont, "A Modified View of Our Origins: The Christian Beginnings of Modern Individualism, " *Religion* 12, 1982.

11. Tracy, *Analogical Imagination*.

12. Chittister, interview, November 30, 2007.

13. Robert Wuthnow, *The Restructuring of American Religion: Society and Faith since World War II*, Studies on Church and State (Princeton, NJ: Princeton University Press, 1988), 11. It is important to note that Wuthnow's analysis did not include black Protestant denominations, which have been less affected by the influences of SPGs.

14. Wuthnow, *Restructuring of American Religion*.

15. "National Election Pool Exit Poll," 2006.

16. This approach constructs a composite measure of religiosity based on five measures of belief (belief in God, view of the Bible), practice (frequency of attendance and prayer), and the self-reported importance of religion to the respondent.

17. In other measures of religious ideology, the American Values Survey showed that Christians who consider themselves "traditional" (41 percent) also outnumbered those who considered themselves "liberal or progressive" (28 percent), but by a smaller margin. It is worth noting that the word "liberal" has come to have considerable baggage. One intriguing piece of evidence for this is that the American Values Survey found that 45 percent of Christians said they considered themselves politically "progressive," more than twice the number that self-identified as politically "liberal" (19 percent) in that survey. See Jones, *American Values Survey*.

18. A recent study that I coauthored at Third Way, a progressive think tank, found that despite stereotypes that all evangelicals are conservative, one-fifth of evangelicals are progressive, one-third are moderate, and one-half are conservative. These measures hold true even on so-called cultural issues. See Rachel Laser et al., *Come Let Us Reason Together: A Fresh Look at Shared Cultural Values between Evangelicals and Progressives* (Washington, DC: Third Way, 2007).

19. David Kinnaman, *Unchristian: What a New Generation Really Thinks about Christianity . . . and Why It Matters* (Grand Rapids, MI: Baker, 2007).

20. Jim Wallis, president, Sojourners/Call to Renewal; interview, September 11, 2007.

21. John Dominic Crossan, *God and Empire: Jesus against Rome, Then and Now* (San Francisco: HarperOne, 2007).

22. Rosemary Radford Ruether, professor of theology, Claremont Graduate School; interview, August 21, 2007.

23. Ruether, interview, August 21, 2007.

24. Wallis, interview, September 11, 2007.

25. Ruether, interview, August 21, 2007.

26. Ruether, interview, August 21, 2007.

27. These themes of holding onto principle in the midst of insecurity and vulnerability were strong across all Christian subgroups. For example, Sr. Simone Campbell, director of Network, a national Catholic social justice lobby, talked about the need for Christians to embrace "a theology of insecurity." Simone Campbell, director, Network, a National Catholic Social Justice Lobby; interview, June 5, 2005. Rev. Susan Thistlethwaite, president of Chicago Theological Seminary (UCC), spoke passionately about losing our values to a utilitarian logic where the ends justify the means. Susan Thistlethwaite, president, Chicago Theological Seminary; visiting senior fellow in religion, Center for American Progress; interview, March 30, 2007.

28. Chittister, interview, November 30, 2007.

29. John Dear, SJ, author and peace activist; interview, December 7, 2007.

30. Brian McLaren, author, speaker, pastor; interview, July 18, 2007.

31. Jennifer Butler, director, Faith in Public Life; interview, May 18, 2007.

32. Timothy McDonald III, senior pastor, First Iconium Baptist Church, Atlanta, Georgia; chair, African American Ministers in Action, People for the American Way Foundation; interview, November 7, 2007.

33. Marcus J. Borg, *Jesus: Uncovering the Life, Teachings, and Relevance of a Religious Revolutionary* (New York: HarperCollins, 1996), 6.

34. Borg, *Jesus*, 5.

35. Ronald J. Sider, *Rich Christians in an Age of Hunger: Moving from Affluence to Generosity* (Nashville, TN: Word Publishing, 1997).

36. Ron Sider, president, Evangelicals for Social Action; interview, April 6, 2007.

37. Tony Campolo, professor of sociology, Eastern University; interview, July 18, 2007.

38. Dear, interview, December 7, 2007.

39. Dear, interview, December 7, 2007.

40. Alexia Salvatierra, director, Clergy and Laity United for Economic Justice; interview, August 20, 2007.

41. Salvatierra, interview, August 20, 2007.

42. Tracy Lind, dean, Trinity Episcopal Cathedral, Cleveland, Ohio; executive committee, We Believe Ohio; interview, May 25, 2007.

43. Weber famously concluded his own analysis rather dimly: "Under the technical and social conditions of rational culture, an imitation of the life of Buddha, Jesus, or Francis seems condemned to failure for purely external reasons." See Max Weber, "Religious Rejections of the World and Their Directions, " in *From Max Weber: Essays in Sociology*, ed. Hans Gerth and C. Wright Mills (London: Routledge, 1991), 357.

44. Karl Marx and Friedrich Engels, *The Communist Manifesto* (1848; New York: Oxford University Press, 1992).

45. Thistlethwaite, interview, March 30, 2007.

46. Butler, interview, May 18, 2007.

47. Thistlethwaite, interview, March 30, 2007.

48. This was Rev. Kottler's position at the time of the interview. At the time of publication, Rev. Kottler had taken the new position of executive director of the Let Justice Roll Living Wage Campaign in Chicago.

49. Jennifer Kottler, associate director, Protestants for the Common Good; interview, April 1, 2007.

50. Thistlethwaite, interview, March 30, 2007.

51. McLaren, interview, July 18, 2007.

52. McLaren, interview, July 18, 2007.

53. Thistlethwaite, interview, March 30, 2007.

54. Thistlethwaite, interview, March 30, 2007.

55. Kenneth L. Samuel, senior pastor, Victory Church, Stone Mountain, Georgia; interview, August 24, 2006. As prominent African American theologian Cornel West notes, in black theology, "black historical experience and the biblical texts form a symbiotic relationship, each illuminating the other." See Cornel West, *Prophesy Deliverance! An Afro-American Revolutionary Christianity* (Philadelphia: Westminster Press, 1982).

56. Harry Knox, director, Religion and Faith Program, Human Rights Campaign; interview, April 27, 2007.

57. Salvatierra, interview, August 20, 2007.

58. Salvatierra, interview, August 20, 2007.

59. Forbes, interview, March 17, 2007. In my interviews, many leaders mentioned the recent "God Is Still Speaking," a public media campaign by the United Church of Christ. The tag line always ends with a comma instead of a period, and on the official printed materials that are part of the campaign, there is a quote attributed to Gracie Allen, "Never place a period where God has placed a comma." The ads can be seen on the UCC website, "God Is Still Speaking," www.ucc.org/god-is-still-speaking/.

60. Thistlethwaite, interview, March 30, 2007.

61. The term "texts of terror" comes from Phyllis Trible's excellent but unsettling book, *Texts of Terror: Literary-Feminist Readings of Biblical Narratives* (Minneapolis: Fortress Press, 1984).

62. Knox, interview, April 27, 2007.

63. Rita Nakashima Brock, director, Faith Voices for the Common Good; interview, August 23, 2007.

64. Dear, interview, December 7, 2007.

65. Campolo, interview, July 18, 2007.

66. McLaren, interview, July 18, 2007.

67. Thistlethwaite, interview, March 30, 2007.

68. Steven Baines, director, Faith Action Network, People for the American Way Foundation; interview, February 16, 2007.

69. Tim Ahrens, senior minister, First Congregational Church, Columbus, Ohio; director, We Believe Ohio; interview, May 23, 2007.

70. Alexia Kelley, CEO, Catholics in Alliance for the Common Good; interview, March 27, 2007.

71. Laurie Goodstein, "Democrats Criticize Denial of Communion by Bishops," *New York Times*, May 20, 2004. The anguish caused to so many Catholics by this unprecedented decision to deny communion to a politician over his stance on a single issue was experienced firsthand by Kelley, who served as a religion advisor to Sen. John Kerry during his presidential campaign in 2004.

72. Lind, interview, May 25, 2007.

73. Ron Stief, director of the Office of Public Life and Social Policy, United Church of Christ; interview, October 28, 2005. This was Rev. Stief's position at the time of the interview. At the time of publication, Rev. Stief was director of field organizing for Faith in Public Life.

74. Baines, interview, February 16, 2007.

75. Dear, interview, December 7, 2007.

76. Sider, interview, April 6, 2007.

77. Wallis, interview, September 11, 2007.

78. Dear, interview, December 7, 2007.

79. Samuel, interview, August 24, 2006.

80. Rev. Robert Edgar, general secretary, National Council of Churches; interview, February 16, 2007. This was Rev. Edgar's position at the time of the interview. At the time of publication, Rev. Edgar had become president of Common Cause, a nonprofit, nonpartisan citizens' lobbying organization promoting open, honest, and accountable government.

81. Robert Edgar, *Middle Church: Reclaiming the Moral Values of the Faithful Majority from the Religious Right* (New York: Simon & Schuster, 2006).

82. Sider, *Rich Christians*.

83. Sider, *Rich Christians*. As issues that God "cares about," Sider specifically cited "the family and the poor, the sanctity of human life and racial justice, and creation care and peacemaking" and noted, "We've been arguing for decades that you just can't pick out one of those issues."

84. Campolo, interview, July 18, 2007.

85. Sider, interview, April 6, 2007.

86. Dear, interview, December 7, 2007.

87. Dear, interview, December 7, 2007.

88. Laurie Goodstein, "Evangelical Leaders Join Global Warming," *New York Times*, February 8, 2006. The issue of the environment has served as a line of demarcation between the old guard of the religious right, anchored primarily by James Dobson's Focus on the Family empire, on the one hand, and the growing number of centrist and progressive groups embracing a broader agenda on the other. David Gushee has recently written an excellent treatment of the emerging evangelical center: *The Future of Faith in American Politics: The Witness of the Evangelical Center* (Waco, TX: Baylor University Press, 2008).

89. Evangelical Environment Network, "Climate Change: An Evangelical Call to Action," Evangelical Climate Initiative, www.christiansandclimate.org/statement.

90. Dear, interview, December 7, 2007.

91. Kinnaman, *Unchristian*, 34.

92. Kinnaman, *Unchristian*, 16.

93. Kinnaman, *Unchristian*, 106.

94. Rev. Jennifer Kottler, borrowing from William Sloan Coffin, retorted that if Christians who objected to homosexuality based on Old Testament purity laws were consistent, they "should really be willing to say, 'Okay, I'm not going to sit around and eat ribs and watch football on Sunday afternoon.'" Kottler, interview, April 1, 2007.

95. Thistlethwaite, interview, March 30, 2007.

96. The theme of being a "whosoever church" has strong resonance in the black church. The only set of published interviews with African American ministers across the denominational spectrum on gay and lesbian issues took its title from this strong theme. See Gary David Comstock, *A Whosoever Church: Welcoming Lesbians and Gay Men into African American Congregations* (Louisville, KY: Westminster John Knox Press, 2001).

97. McDonald, interview, November 7, 2007.

98. McDonald, interview, November 7, 2007.

99. Rev. Dr. Kenneth L. Samuel, senior pastor, Victory Church, Stone Mountain, Georgia; interview, March 3, 2007.

100. Samuel, interview, March 3, 2007.

101. Samuel, interview, March 3, 2007.

102. Jim Wallis, *God's Politics: Why the Right Gets It Wrong and the Left Doesn't Get It* (San Francisco: HarperSanFrancisco, 2005).

103. Wallis, interview, September 11, 2007.

104. Sojourners, *Sojourners Annual Report 2006* (Washington, DC: Sojourners, 2006).

105. Sojourners extended an invitation, which was not accepted, to the leading Republican candidates for a September 2007 forum in Iowa. The forum was cosponsored by Catholics in Alliance for the Common Good, the ONE Campaign, Oxfam America, and Eastern University.

106. Disclosure: I served as the founding director and senior fellow at the Center for American Values in Public Life at PFAW from 2005–2006 and was an associated scholar in 2007 at the Center for American Progress. Both the program at PFAW and the program at CAP have been scaled down from their original scope. At CAP, the religion program continues to host a few scholars per year and convene large working groups on issues, but the energy for faith organizing has been directed toward the group Faith in Public Life, which CAP "incubated" as a separate nonprofit by providing support during its startup.

107. Catholics in Alliance for the Common Good, "Frequently Asked Questions," Catholics in Alliance for the Common Good, www.catholicsinalliance.org/faq.

108. Kelley, interview, March 27, 2007.

109. Catholics in Alliance for the Common Good, *End Year Progress Summary* (Washington, DC: Catholics in Alliance for the Common Good, 2007).

110. Chris Korzen and Alexia Kelley, *A Nation for All: How the Catholic Vision of the Common Good Can Save America from the Politics of Division* (San Francisco: Jossey-Bass, 2008).

111. Catholics United, "Ad Campaign Criticizes Pro-Life Members of Congress for Voting against Children's Health Insurance," Catholics United, www.catholics-united.org/schip-ads.

112. Faith in Public Life, "About Us: Mission," Faith in Public Life, www.faithinpubliclife.org/about/index.html.

113. I served as one of the coauthors (along with Rachel Laser, Randy Brinson, and Joe Battaglia) of the Third Way paper, *Come Let Us Reason Together: A Fresh Look at Shared Cultural Values between Evangelicals and Progressives*. See Laser et al., *Come Let Us Reason Together*.

114. Jennifer Butler, *All This in Just Two Years? Faith in Public Life's Second Year a Success* (Washington, DC: Faith in Public Life, 2007).

115. Jim Wallis, *The Great Awakening: Reviving Faith and Politics in a Post-Religious Right America* (San Francisco: HarperOne, 2008).

116. Wallis, interview, September 11, 2007.

117. Wallis, interview, September 11, 2007.

118. Diana Butler Bass, *Christianity for the Rest of Us: How the Neighborhood Church Is Transforming the Faith* (San Francisco: HarperSanFrancisco, 2006), 4.

119. "Lift Ev'ry Voice and Sing," which is commonly referred to as the "Black National Anthem," was originally written in 1901 by poet and civil rights leader James Weldon Johnson for a children's program in Jacksonville, Florida, celebrating

Abraham Lincoln's birthday. Kenneth Estell, ed., *The African-American Almanac* (Detroit, MI: Gale Research, 1994).

Chapter 3.
Knowing One Another:
How Progressive Muslims Are Fostering
Justice, Beauty, and Pluralism

1. Khaled Abou El Fadl, *Conference of the Books: The Search for Beauty in Islam* (Lanham, MD: University Press of America, 2001).

2. Public Broadcasting Service (PBS), *Interview with Khaled Abou El Fadl*, Public Broadcasting Service, http://www.pbs.org/wgbh/pages/frontline/shows/faith/interviews/elfadl.html.

3. PBS, *Interview with Khaled Abou El Fadl*.

4. Notably, Abou El Fadl went on to say, "The point is that I memorized the Qur'an by age 14, but I spent the rest of my life figuring out what it means." Abou El Fadl also conveyed one lesson, a lesson of humility, from this lifetime of learning: "I never say, 'God says' or 'God demands such-and-such.'" Khaled Abou El Fadl, Omar and Azmeralda Alfi Distinguished Fellow in Islamic Law, UCLA School of Law; interview, August 21, 2007.

5. Accurate estimates of the U.S. Muslim population present major methodological challenges. They have ranged from approximately two million to as many as six million, when using estimates based on reported affiliations by mosques. See Tom W. Smith, "The Polls—Review: The Muslim Population of the United States; The Methodology of Estimates," *Public Opinion Quarterly* 66, 2002. A major reason for the dearth of data on American Muslims is that obtaining a representative sample of a small, diverse population is resource intensive. For example, the Pew survey interviewed nearly 60,000 respondents in four languages (English, Arabic, Urdu, and Farsi) to obtain a final sample of 1,050 respondents. I use the Pew figures here as a conservative estimate. See Pew Research Center for the People and the Press, *Muslim Americans: Middle Class and Mostly Mainstream* (Washington, DC: Pew Research Center for the People and the Press, 2007).

6. Pew Research Center, *Muslim Americans*, 34.

7. Lisa Miller, "Islam USA: American Dreamers," *Newsweek*, July 30, 2007.

8. Pew Research Center, *Muslim Americans*. The relative affluence of Muslims in America contrasts sharply with European countries, where immigration patterns and interactions have been driven by the dynamic of colonialism. In Europe, Muslim populations often live in impoverished ethnic enclaves and the Muslim employment rate is 15 to 40 percent below the general population. See Miller, "Islam USA."

9. Pew Research Center, *Muslim Americans* 2.

10. Pew Research Center, *Muslim Americans*. While nearly half of Muslims in the United States (47 percent) say they think of themselves first as Muslim rather than as American, this rate of identity is far lower than in Great Britain, where 81 percent of Muslims think of themselves first as Muslim rather than as British.

11. Miller, "Islam USA."

12. Pew Research Center, *Muslim Americans*, 27.

13. The results on the frequency of prayer have come under some criticism because of the particular word used in the Arabic version of the Pew survey. Pew used the word *salat*, which describes the five daily ritual prayers. As Dr. Zareena Grewal pointed out in his critique of the findings, had Pew used the word *du'ah*, which means "supplications" and covers more informal forms of prayer, the numbers probably would have been higher and more directly comparable to the Christian numbers. See Zareena Grewal, "What's Wrong with This Picture?" *Islamic Horizons*, November–December 2007.

14. Pew Research Center, *Muslim Americans*, 8.

15. Patrick Condon, "Muslim Keith Ellison Seeks House Seat," Associated Press, June 29, 2006.

16. Pew Research Center, *Muslim Americans*, 41.

17. Pew Research Center, *Muslim Americans*, 2.

18. M. A. Muqtedar Khan, *American Muslims: Bridging Faith and Freedom* (Beltsville, MD: Amana Publications, 2002).

19. Miller, "Islam USA."

20. Pew Research Center, *Muslim Americans*. Certainly going to mosque every week, like going to church every week, does not automatically make anyone more conservative, but public opinion polls among both Muslims and Christians consistently show positive correlations between increased attendance and political conservatism.

21. As many noted in the wake of this report, the specific context for these feelings is the protracted Israeli-Palestinian conflict.

22. Islamic Society of North America (ISNA), Forty-Fourth Annual ISNA Convention, "Upholding Faith, Serving Humanity," Rosemont, IL, August 31–September 3, 2007.

23. Salam al-Maryati, "The Good and the Greater Good," paper presented at the Forty-Fourth Annual ISNA Convention, Rosemont, IL, August 31–September 3, 2007.

24. I classified these sessions strictly and only counted sessions that did not involve primarily Muslim interests. Out of seventy-five sessions, ten focused on broad social justice concerns, nine focused on broad civic engagement, and three

focused on moral issues related to war and terrorism. For example, sessions such as "Righting the Wrongs: Faith and Social Justice" and "Ending U.S.-Sponsored Torture: A Concern for All People of Faith" qualified, while sessions such as "The State of Human Rights of Indian Muslims" did not because it was primarily addressing concerns of a Muslim population.

25. As many pointed out at the time of her selection, Mattson also happens to be Caucasian and an academic, two attributes of privilege.

26. Omid Safi, *Progressive Muslims: On Justice, Gender, and Pluralism* (Oxford: Oneworld, 2003), 10.

27. Safi, *Progressive Muslims*, 10.

28. In this chapter, I rely on Omid Safi's perspective heavily on issues pertaining to the shape and general commitments of the progressive Muslim community. Omid Safi is the most widely recognized leader of the progressive Muslim movement; I was referred to him by many other interviewees to answer these general questions. In addition to his own role as a scholar-activist, he has edited the only existing volume on progressive Islam.

29. Safi, *Progressive Muslims*, 1–2.

30. Safi, *Progressive Muslims*, 1–2.

31. Safi, *Progressive Muslims*, 1–2.

32. As I note below, the much misunderstood term *jihad* actually means "to struggle." Both *jihad* and *ijtihad* come from the same Arabic root that means "to strive." See Safi, *Progressive Muslims*, 8.

33. M. A. Muqtedar Khan, "Common Ground: Two Theories of Ijtihad," United Press International, March 22, 2006.

34. Safi, *Progressive Muslims*.

35. Khan, "Common Ground."

36. Khan, "Common Ground."

37. Abdullahi Ahmed An-Na'im, professor of law, Emory University; interview, March 3, 2007.

38. George Packer, "The Moderate Martyr: A Radically Peaceful Vision of Islam," *The New Yorker*, September 11, 2006. In *The Second Message of Islam*, which An-Na'im translated into English, Taha notes two different periods of revelation. Whereas Muhammad propagated "verses of peaceful persuasion" during his earlier Meccan period, later in Medina "the verses of compulsion by the sword prevailed." Both Taha and An-Na'im take the more "tolerant and egalitarian" Meccan period— "where the Prophet preached equality and individual responsibility between all men and women without distinction on grounds of race, sex, or social origin"— to be the purest, ideal expression of Islam. See Mahmud Muhammad Taha, *The Second Message of Islam*, trans. Abdullahi Ahmed An-Na'im (Syracuse, NY: Syracuse University Press, 1987).

39. Saleemah Abdul-Ghafur, *Living Islam Out Loud: American Muslim Women Speak* (Boston: Beacon Press, 2005).

40. Saleemah Abdul-Ghafur, second-generation African American Muslim activist for women's equality in Islam; interview, March 2, 2007.

41. M. A. Muqtedar Khan, associate professor of political science, director of Islamic Studies Program, University of Delaware; interview, November 19, 2007.

42. Khan, interview, November 19, 2007.

43. Omid Safi, professor of religion, University of North Carolina; interview, September 14, 2007.

44. Rabia Terri Harris, founder and coordinator of Muslim Peace Fellowship and chaplain at Albert Einstein Medical Center in Philadelphia, summarized this progressive approach succinctly, saying, "Rather than starting with the tradition, progressives start with the presenting issues" in order to ask, "How as a Muslim can I authentically engage in a productive fashion with what really matters in our lives today?" Rabia Terri Harris, coordinator, Muslim Peace Fellowship; interview, August 3, 2007.

45. Abdullahi Ahmed An-Na'im, "The Future of Shari'a: Secularism from an Islamic Perspective," Annual Currie Lecture, The Center for the Study of Law and Religion, Emory School of Law, January 29, 2007. Emory University, www.sharia.law.emory.edu/; Abdullahi Ahmed An-Na'im, "A Celebration of Heresy," *Emory in the World*, Winter 2006.

46. An-Na'im, interview, March 3, 2007.

47. Safi, interview, September 14, 2007.

48. Safi, interview, September 14, 2007.

49. Khan, interview, November 19, 2007.

50. Abdul-Ghafur, interview, March 2, 2007.

51. Abdul-Ghafur, interview, March 2, 2007.

52. Pluralism Project at Harvard University, "Research Report: The Woman-Led Prayer That Catalyzed Controversy," Pluralism Project at Harvard University, www.pluralism.org/research/profiles/display.php?profile=73972.

53. Saleemah Abdul-Ghafur, "Preaching from the Ashes: Reclaiming the Legacy of Freedom," Progressive Muslim Union, www.pmuna.org/archives/2005/04/saleemah_abdul.php#more.

54. Abdul-Ghafur, interview, March 2, 2007.

55. Safi, interview, September 14, 2007.

56. The Sufi approach to Islam is gaining more attention in the United States. The year 2007 was the eight-hundredth anniversary of the Muslim mystic Jelaluddin Rumi, a prominent figure in Sufi literature. Rumi interestingly is the best-selling poet in the United States over the past decade. Moreover, Sufism is being identified by many as a "powerful antidote to Islamic extremism." See Jane

Lampman, "Sufism May Be Powerful Antidote to Islamic Extremism," *Christian Science Monitor*, December 5, 2007.

57. Dr. Khaled Abou El Fadl argued that there was a clear correlation between social situation and interpretive approaches. He noted, "During times when Islamic civilization thrived and was at its height of its achievement, you tended to find liberal, progressive, tolerant, humanistic thinking; and during times when the Islamic civilization was under siege—for instance, around the first Crusade or the Mongol invasions—then there would be conservatism." Abou El Fadl, interview, August 21, 2007.

58. Nazir Khaja, chairman, Islamic Information Service; interview, August 21, 2007.

59. Kecia Ali, *Sexual Ethics and Islam: Feminist Reflections on Qur'an, Hadith, and Jurisprudence* (Oxford: Oneworld, 2006).

60. Kecia Ali, assistant professor of religion, Boston University; interview, July 28, 2007.

61. Kecia Ali, "Acting on a Frontier of Religious Ceremony: With Questions and Quiet Resolve, a Woman Officiates at a Muslim Wedding," *Harvard Divinity Bulletin*, Fall/Winter 2004.

62. Umar Faruq Abd-Allah, chairman and scholar in residence, Nawawi Foundation; interview, November 14, 2007. This saying is listed at the thirteenth *hadith* in an-Nawawi's famous collection from the thirteenth century. See Nawawi, *An-Nawawi's Forty Hadith: An Anthology of the Sayings of the Prophet Muhammad* (Cambridge, UK: Islamic Texts Society, 1997).

63. Abou El Fadl, interview, August 21, 2007. Note that the pronoun rendered "we" in English in this verse does not reflect any plurality in the conception of God but rather is a "royal we," reflecting the divinity. There are similar plural pronouns in the creation account in the book of Genesis. The above quote is from Qur'an 49:13. This affirmation of human diversity as part of God's plan for creation is echoed in several places in the Qur'an. For example, Qur'an 5:48 says, "Unto every one of you We have appointed a [different] law and way of life. And if God had so willed, He could surely have made you all one single community: but [He willed it otherwise] in order to test you by means of what He has vouchsafed unto you. Vie, then, with one another in doing good works. Unto God you all must return; and then He will make you truly understand all that on which you were wont to differ."

64. Eboo Patel, founder and director, Interfaith Youth Core; interview, August 31, 2007.

65. Diana L. Eck, *A New Religious America: How a "Christian Country" Has Become the World's Most Religiously Diverse Nation* (San Francisco: HarperSanFrancisco, 2001).

66. An-Na'im, interview, March 3, 2007.

67. Patel, interview, August 31, 2007.

68. Reza Aslan, *No God but God: The Origins, Evolution, and Future of Islam* (New York: Random House, 2005).

69. Ali, interview, July 28, 2007.

70. Harris, interview, August 3, 2007.

71. This is perhaps more true of immigrant Muslims rather than African American Muslims, who, following the black church model where the church is the center of the community, tend to have a tighter relationship to a mosque. See C. Eric Lincoln and Lawrence H. Mamiya, *The Black Church in the African-American Experience* (Durham, NC: Duke University Press, 1990).

72. Khan, interview, November 19, 2007.

73. Abdul-Ghafur, interview, March 2, 2007.

74. An-Na'im, interview, March 3, 2007.

75. Abdul-Ghafur, interview, March 2, 2007.

76. Sarah Eltantawi, former communications director, Progressive Muslim Union; interview, July 24, 2007.

77. Harris, interview, August 3, 2007. Note that Muslims likely inherited fasting from Judaism's practice during Yom Kippur. Originally, in fact, the Muslim fast coincided with Yom Kippur and was later changed to the month of Ramadan, the month in which Muslims believe the Qur'an was first revealed to Muhammad. See Aslan, *No God but God*, 148.

78. Asra Nomani, "Daughters of Hajar," *The New People*, July–August 2004, Thomas Merton Center, www.thomasmertoncenter.org/The_New_People.

79. Historically, the rift in this ancient family—two sons of Abraham by different mothers—have manifested themselves in two different world religions, with Jews (and Christians somewhat figuratively) tracing their lineage back to Abraham through Sarah's son Isaac, and Muslims tracing their lineage back to Abraham through Hagar's son Ishmael.

80. Nomani, "Daughters of Hajar."

81. Teresa Wiltz, "The Woman Who Went to the Front of the Mosque," *Washington Post*, June 5, 2005.

82. Eltantawi, interview, July 24, 2007.

83. Abdul-Ghafur, interview, March 2, 2007.

84. Aslan, *No God but God*, 149.

85. For example, Safi noted, "There's a way in which justice in the Qur'an is linked together with everything that is lovely and beautiful, and both are described as the qualities of God. Everything that is fundamentally unjust and oppressive stands in opposition to God's will." Safi, interview, September 14, 2007.

86. Khan, interview, November 19, 2007.

87. The next three most frequently mentioned issues were civic engagement/education, poverty/inequality, and homosexuality.

88. Safi, *Progressive Muslims*, 10.

89. Safi, *Progressive Muslims*, 9.

90. Christopher Hitchens, *God Is Not Great: How Religion Poisons Everything* (New York: Twelve, 2007).

91. Patel, interview, August 31, 2007.

92. A'isha Samad, executive committee, We Believe Ohio, Cleveland, Ohio; interview, May 26, 2007.

93. Eltantawi, interview, July 24, 2007.

94. Khaja, interview, August 21, 2007.

95. Abdul-Ghafur, interview, March 2, 2007.

96. Harris, interview, August 3, 2007.

97. Harris, interview, August 3, 2007.

98. Muhammad ibn Ismail al-Bukhari, *The Translation of the Meanings of Sahih al-Bukhari*, 9 vols., trans. Muhammad Muhsin Khan (Alexandria, VA: Al-Saadawi Publications, 1996). This quotation is taken from the Hadith collection of Sahih al-Bukhari, taken by Sunni Muslims to be the most reliable Hadith collections.

99. Safi, *Progressive Muslims*.

100. Safi noted that his use of the term "God-forsaken" was careful and deliberate. He clarified, "For me, it is only appropriate to use that term for an activity which is so hideous that results in God forsaking his/her blessing toward a people." Safi, interview, September 14, 2007.

101. Feisal Abdul Rauf, *What's Right with Islam: A New Vision for Muslims and the West* (San Francisco: HarperSanFrancisco, 2004), xxi.

102. Feisal Abdul Rauf, imam of Masjid al-Farah, New York City; founder of American Society for Muslim Advancement (ASMA); interview, March 17, 2007.

103. Abdul Rauf, interview, March 17, 2007.

104. Abou El Fadl, interview, August 21, 2007.

105. Khan, interview, November 19, 2007.

106. Abdul Rauf, *What's Right with Islam*, 275.

107. Abdul Rauf, *What's Right with Islam*, 275.

108. An-Na'im, "Celebration of Heresy."

109. An-Na'im, "The Future of Shari'a."

110. An-Na'im, "Celebration of Heresy."

111. An-Na'im, interview, March 3, 2007.

112. Abdul Rauf, *What's Right with Islam*, 257.

113. John Courtney Murray, *We Hold These Truths: Catholic Reflections on the American Proposition* (New York: Sheed and Ward, 1960).

114. Abd-Allah, interview, November 14, 2007.

115. Abdul Rauf, *What's Right with Islam*, 283.

116. Safi, interview, September 14, 2007.

117. After several key board resignations, Progressive Muslim Union has become effectively dormant. While *Muslim WakeUp!* continues as a venue for liberal Muslims, Muqtedar Khan noted that its edgy, acerbic tone—reminiscent of the snarkiness of the blogosphere—has turned off many Muslims and prevented it from becoming a broader vehicle for progressive Muslims. M. A. Muqtedar Khan, "Is muslimwakeup.com Undermining the Progressive Muslim Movement?" Ijtihad, www.ijtihad.org/muslimwakeup.htm.

118. Eboo Patel, "About the Core," Interfaith Youth Core, www.ifyc.org/about_core.

119. Judy Valente, "Interview with Eboo Patel," *Religion & Ethics Newsweekly*, November 30, 2007.

120. Patel, interview, August 31, 2007.

121. Patel, interview, August 31, 2007.

122. Patel, interview, August 31, 2007.

123. Eboo Patel, "Days of Interfaith Youth Service (DIYS)," Interfaith Youth Core, ifyc.org/events/diys.

124. Valente, "Interview with Eboo Patel."

125. Patel, interview, August 31, 2007.

126. Patel, interview, August 31, 2007.

127. Rami Nashashibi, interview by Krista Tippet, *Speaking of Faith*, American Public Media, February 15, 2002. Speaking of Faith, speakingoffaith.publicradio.org/programs/2002/02/15_evil/index.shtml.

128. Rami Nashashibi, "Inner-City Muslim Action Network (IMAN)," IMAN, www.imancentral.org/.

129. Nashashibi, "Inner-City Muslim Action Network."

130. Margaret Ramirez, "Activist Muslim Profile: Rami Nashashibi," *Chicago Tribune*, May 3, 2006.

131. Safi, interview, September 14, 2007.

132. Safi, interview, September 14, 2007.

133. Safi, interview, September 14, 2007.

134. Patel, interview, August 31, 2007.

Chapter 4.
Just Sitting Down:
How Progressive Buddhists Are Being
Peace and Embodying Justice

1. There are two principal reasons this chapter is noticeably smaller than the other chapters. My interview methodology, which relied on a combination of popular press and recommendations by insiders, produced a smaller circle of potential engaged Buddhist leaders than it produced with other traditions. Moreover, even using surrogates to help broker introductions, I found these leaders much less accessible, with interview refusals running three times higher than rates of other traditions. This inaccessibility is partially the result of these leaders functioning both as monastics, which requires blocks of meditation time, and as gurus of sizable but somewhat insular communities of practitioners, which requires considerable travel and speaking engagements. This setup carries with it multiple layers of gatekeepers. Thus, in this chapter, I have supplemented the interview data with published written sources.

2. Pew Forum on Religion and Public Life, "The U.S. Religious Landscape Survey," Pew Forum on Religion and Public Life, religions.pewforum.org/reports.

3. Martin Bauman, "The Dharma Has Come West: A Survey of Recent Studies and Sources," Urban Dharma, www.urbandharma.org/udharma/survey.html; Diana L. Eck, "Statistics by Religious Tradition," The Pluralism Project at Harvard University, www.pluralism.org/resources/statistics/tradition.php#Buddhism.

4. Robert Thurman, professor of Buddhist studies, Columbia University; president, American Institute of Buddhist Studies; interview, December 18, 2007.

5. Diana Eck's *A New Religious America* contains a compelling and accessible introduction to Buddhism in America. See Diana L. Eck, *A New Religious America: How a "Christian Country" Has Become the World's Most Religiously Diverse Nation* (San Francisco: HarperSanFrancisco, 2001).

6. Lama Surya Das, founder, Dzogchen Foundation; interview, August 2, 2007.

7. David Ban Biema, "Buddhism in America," *Time*, October 13, 1997.

8. Das, interview, August 2, 2007.

9. Paul H. Ray, *The Cultural Creatives: How 50 Million People Are Changing the World* (New York: Three Rivers, 2001).

10. Dalai Lama, *Ethics for the New Millennium* (New York: Riverhead Books, 2001); Dalai Lama, Howard C. Cutler, and Ernest Abuba, *The Art of Happiness: A Handbook for Living*, sound recording (New York: Simon & Schuster Audio, 1998).

11. Because of his opposition to the war in Vietnam, Thich Nhat Hanh was not allowed to return home to Vietnam after his American visit. He currently lives in Plum Village, a Buddhist monastery in southern France, but he regularly teaches in the United States.

12. Thich Nhat Hanh, *Being Peace* (Berkeley, CA: Parallax Press, 1987).

13. Alan Senauke, head of practice, Berkeley Zen Center; director of programs and peacework coordinator, Buddhist Peace Fellowship; interview, August 23, 2007.

14. Senauke, interview, August 23, 2007.

15. Bill Aiken, director of public affairs, Soka Gakkai International; interview, July 23, 2007.

16. Das, interview, August 2, 2007.

17. Senauke, interview, August 23, 2007.

18. Susan Moon, ed., *Not Turning Away: The Practice of Engaged Buddhism* (Boston: Shambhala, 2004).

19. Susan Moon, "Editorial," *Turning Wheel Magazine*, January 1990.

20. Senauke, interview, August 23, 2007.

21. In an essay, "Vowing Peace in a Time of War," Senauke put it this way: "The injustice of poverty and wealth is itself a kind of violence. Really, we can't step outside of this system. But if each of us cultivates awareness of the links between consumption and violence, we can begin to make choices about what is of true value in our lives and how much we value the lives of others." See Alan Senauke, "Vowing Peace in a Time of War," in *Not Turning Away: The Practice of Engaged Buddhism*, ed. Susan Moon (Boston: Shambhala Press, 2004).

22. Senauke, interview, August 23, 2007.

23. Thich Nhat Hanh, "The Practice of Peace," in *Not Turning Away: The Practice of Engaged Buddhism*, ed. Susan Moon (Boston: Shambhala Press, 1991), 148.

24. Das, interview, August 2, 2007.

25. Thurman, interview, December 18, 2007.

26. Thurman, interview, December 18, 2007.

27. Das, interview, August 2, 2007.

28. George W. Bush, "Address to a Joint Session of Congress and the American People," The White House, www.whitehouse.gov/news/releases/2001/09/20010920-8.html.

29. Das, interview, August 2, 2007.

30. Das, interview, August 2, 2007.

31. Bernie Glassman, founder, Zen Peacemakers; interview, July 25, 2007.

32. The word *mandala* roughly translates to "the circle of life."

33. Glassman, interview, July 25, 2007.

34. Bernie Glassman, "Zen Peacemakers: General Information," Zen Peacemakers, www.zenpeacemakers.org/about/index.htm.

35. Glassman, interview, July 25, 2007.

36. Glassman, interview, July 25, 2007.

37. Joanna Macy, "Foreword," in *Not Turning Away: The Practice of Engaged Buddhism*, ed. Susan Moon (Boston: Shambhala, 2004).

38. Pew Forum on Religion and Public Life, "The U.S. Religious Landscape Survey, " Pew Forum on Religion and Public Life, religions.pewforum.org/reports.

39. The Unitarian Universalist Association (UUA) formed from two earlier traditions: the Universalists, who organized in 1793, and the Unitarians, who organized in 1825. They consolidated into the UUA in 1961.

40. William Sinkford, president, Unitarian Universalist Association; interview, September 27, 2007.

41. Sinkford, interview, September 27, 2007.

Conclusion:
Progressive & Religious:
The New Face of Religion in American Public Life

1. Mark G. Toulouse, "The Origins of the Christian Century," *The Christian Century*, January 26, 2000.

2. E. J. Dionne, *Souled Out: Reclaiming Faith and Politics after the Religious Right* (Princeton, NJ: Princeton University Press, 2008).

3. Tim Ahrens, "For Such a Time as This," presented at Faith Leadership Meeting, Faith in Public Life, Washington, DC, 2006.

4. We Believe Ohio, "About Us," We Believe Ohio, www.webelieveohio.org/index.php?option=com_content&task=view&id=13&Itemid=42.

5. Nate Anderson, "Meet the Patriot Pastors," *Christianity Today*, November 2006.

6. Ahrens, "For Such a Time as This."

7. Ahrens, "For Such a Time as This."

8. Tim Ahrens, senior minister, First Congregational Church, Columbus, Ohio; director, We Believe Ohio; interview, May 23, 2007.

9. Ahrens, "For Such a Time as This."

10. Ted Strickland, governor, State of Ohio; interview, June 15, 2007.

11. "National Election Pool Exit Poll," 2006.

12. Ahrens, interview, May 23, 2007.

13. Ahrens, "For Such a Time as This."

14. Ahrens, "For Such a Time as This."

15. Dionne, *Souled Out*.

16. Christopher Hitchens, *God Is Not Great: How Religion Poisons Everything* (New York: Twelve, 2007).

17. Ronald J. Sider, president, Evangelicals for Social Action; interview, April 6, 2007.

18. Hozan Alan Senauke, head of practice, Berkeley Zen Center; director of programs and peacework coordinator, Buddhist Peace Fellowship; interview, August 23, 2007.

19. Lama Surya Das, founder, Dzogchen Foundation; interview, August 2, 2007.

20. Eric Yoffie, president, Union for Reform Judaism; interview, March 14, 2007.

21. Omid Safi, ed., *Progressive Muslims: On Justice, Gender and Pluralism* (Oxford: Oneworld, 2003), 26.

22. Susan Thistlethwaite, president, Chicago Theological Seminary; visiting senior fellow in religion, Center for American Progress; interview, March 30, 2007.

23. Omid Safi, professor of religion, University of North Carolina; interview, September 14, 2007.

24. Jonah Pesner, director, Just Congregations, Union for Reform Judaism; interview, July 26, 2007.

25. Harry Knox, director, Religion and Faith Program, Human Rights Campaign; interview, April 27, 2007.

26. Robert Thurman, professor of Buddhist studies, Columbia University; president, American Institute of Buddhist Studies; interview, December 18, 2007. Even in the monotheistic traditions, where the emphasis on the human capabilities is less explicit in the texts, there is no escaping the fact that even if God is the revealer of truth in sacred texts, human beings must still interpret that truth in light of their own experiences. See James M. Gustafson, *Ethics from a Theocentric Perspective: Theology and Ethics*, vol. 1 (Chicago: University of Chicago Press, 1981).

27. M. A. Muqtedar Khan, associate professor of political science, director of Islamic Studies Program, University of Delaware; interview, November 19, 2007.

28. James A. Forbes, senior minister, The Riverside Church, New York; founder, The Healing of the Nations Foundation; interview, March 17, 2007.

29. Yoffie, interview, March 14, 2007.

30. Khaled Abou El Fadl, Omar and Azmeralda Alfi Distinguished Fellow in Islamic Law, UCLA School of Law; interview, August 21, 2007.

31. Thistlethwaite, interview, March 30, 2007.

32. Forbes, interview, March 17, 2007.

33. Rolando Matalon, rabbi, Congregation B'nai Jeshurun; interview, June 22, 2007.

34. Diana Butler Bass characterized a similar approach, encountered in her recent study of vibrant mainline Protestant congregations, as "moving into the future by reengaging their best past." Diana Butler Bass, *Christianity for the Rest of Us: How the Neighborhood Church Is Transforming the Faith* (San Francisco: Harper-SanFrancisco, 2006).

35. Or N. Rose, associate dean, The Rabbinical School of Hebrew College; interview, November 17, 2007.

36. Safi, *Progressive Muslims*, 16.

37. Saleemah Abdul-Ghafur, second-generation African American Muslim activist for women's equality in Islam; interview, March 2, 2007.

38. Senauke, interview, August 23, 2007.

39. Daniel Sokatch, director, Progressive Jewish Alliance; interview, September 20, 2007.

40. Sharon Brous, rabbi, IKAR Congregation, Los Angeles, California; interview, August 21, 2007; Tracy Lind, dean, Trinity Episcopal Cathedral, Cleveland, Ohio; executive committee, We Believe Ohio; interview, May 25, 2007.

41. Brous, interview, August 21, 2007.

42. Steven Baines, director, Faith Action Network, People for the American Way Foundation; interview, February 16, 2007.

43. Kecia Ali, assistant professor of religion, Boston University; interview, July 28, 2007. Dr. Ali noted that although English translations of the Qur'an regularly use the neutral pronoun "it" as a referent for the word "soul," the word "soul" is grammatically feminine in Arabic, as her rendering reflects.

44. Bill Aiken, director of public affairs, Soka Gakkai International; interview, July 23, 2007.

45. Bernard Glassman, founder, Zen Peacemakers; interview, July 25, 2007.

46. Susan Moon, "Editorial," *Turning Wheel Magazine*, January 1990.

47. Rosemary Radford Ruether, professor of theology, Claremont Graduate School; interview, August 21, 2007.

48. Kenneth L. Samuel, senior pastor, Victory Church, Stone Mountain, Georgia; interview, March 3, 2007.

49. Simon Greer, president, Jewish Funds for Justice; interview, March 16, 2007.

50. Robert Edgar, president, Jewish Funds for Justice; interview, February 16, 2007.

51. Matalon, interview, June 22, 2007.

52. Jim Wallis, president, Sojourners/Call to Renewal; interview, September 11, 2007.

53. Ruether, interview, August 21, 2007.

54. Wallis, interview, September 11, 2007.

55. Das, interview, August 2, 2007.

56. Michael Lerner, editor, *Tikkun* magazine; interview, August 23, 2007.

57. Lerner, interview, August 23, 2007.

58. Senauke, interview, August 23, 2007.

59. Umar Faruq Abd-Allah, chairman and scholar in residence, Nawawi Foundation; interview, November 14, 2007.

60. Simone Campbell, director, Network, a National Catholic Social Justice Lobby; interview, June 5, 2005, Ruether, interview, August 21, 2007.

61. There are hopeful signs that these lessons are being learned in the arena of partisan politics. See Amy Sullivan's detailed account of how Democrats have been closing the so-called "God gap." Amy Sullivan, *The Party Faithful: How and Why Democrats Are Closing the God Gap* (New York: Scribner, 2008).

62. In my previous book, I showed how religious views and groups can help political progressives stay true to their own principles. See Robert P. Jones, *Liberalism's Troubled Search for Equality: Religion and Cultural Bias in the Oregon Physician-Assisted Suicide Debate* (Notre Dame, IN: University of Notre Dame Press, 2007).

63. Madison argued, "Freedom arises from the multiplicity of sects, which pervades America and which is the best and only security for religious liberty in any society. For where there is such a variety of sects, there cannot be a majority of any one sect to oppress and persecute the rest." See James Madison, "James Madison, Virginia Ratifying Convention," University of Chicago Press, press-pubs.uchicago.edu/founders/documents/amendI_religions49.html.

64. David Saperstein, director, Religious Action Center for Reform Judaism; interview, July 10, 2007.

65. Sam Harris, *The End of Faith: Religion, Terror, and the Future of Reason* (New York: Norton, 2004), 21.

66. To be sure, many theistic progressive religious leaders would understand religion to be the product of human culture that reflects its ongoing relationship with God, but the theistic qualification does not change its status as a human product.

67. Forbes, interview, March 17, 2007.

68. National Association of Evangelicals, "For the Health of the Nation: An Evangelical Call to Civic Responsibility," in *Toward an Evangelical Public Policy*, ed. Ronald J. Sider and Diane Knippers (Grand Rapids, MI: Baker, 2004).

69. Richard Rorty, "Religion as a Conversation-Stopper," in *Philosophy and Social Hope*, ed. Richard Rorty (New York: Penguin, 1999).

70. Alexia Salvatierra, director, Clergy and Laity United for Economic Justice; interview, August 20, 2007.

71. Michael Walzer, *Politics and Passion: Toward a More Egalitarian Liberalism* (New Haven, Conn.: Yale University, 2005), 120.

72. Walzer, *Politics and Passion*, 110.

73. Walzer also argues that progressive fears of passion are rooted in a troubling old elitist Enlightenment ideology that artificially bifurcates reason and emotion and associates these attributes to "us" and "them": "The distinction between us and them is clear. We are educated, intelligent, liberal, and reasonable people, and . . . we constitute the center and hold all unruliness in check. Passion is associated with the others, the blood-dimmed tide surging in when the center collapses." Walzer creatively arrives at this analysis via an interpretive reading of William Butler Yeats's poem, "The Second Coming." Walzer, *Politics and Passion*, 112.

74. George Lakoff, *Don't Think of an Elephant! Know Your Values and Frame the Debate* (White River Junction, VT: Chelsea Green Publishing, 2004); Stephen Hart, *Cultural Dilemmas of Progressive Politics: Styles of Engagement among Grassroots Activists* (Chicago: University of Chicago Press, 2001).

75. Walzer, *Politics and Passion*, 119.

76. Walzer, *Politics and Passion*, 118.

77. Walzer, *Politics and Passion*, 130.

78. Dionne, *Souled Out*.

79. Jim Wallis, *The Great Awakening: Reviving Faith and Politics in a Post-Religious Right America* (San Francisco: HarperOne, 2008).

80. Thistlethwaite, interview, March 30, 2007.

81. King Jr., Martin Luther, "I've Been to the Mountaintop," American Rhetoric, www.americanrhetoric.com/speeches/mlkivebeentothemountaintop.htm.

Bibliography

Abd-Allah, Umar Faruq. Chairman and scholar in residence, Nawawi Foundation. Interview. November 14, 2007.

Abdul-Ghafur, Saleemah. Second-generation African American Muslim activist for women's equality in Islam. Interview. March 2, 2007.

———. *Living Islam Out Loud: American Muslim Women Speak.* Boston: Beacon, 2005.

———. "Preaching from the Ashes: Reclaiming the Legacy of Freedom; Reflections on the Wadud Prayer." Progressive Muslim Union. www.pmuna.org/archives/2005/04/saleemah_abdul.php#more.

Abdul Rauf, Feisal. Imam of Masjid al-Farah, New York City; founder of American Society for Muslim Advancement (ASMA). Interview. March 17, 2007.

———. *What's Right with Islam: A New Vision for Muslims and the West.* San Francisco: HarperSanFrancisco, 2004.

Abou El Fadl, Khaled. Omar and Azmeralda Alfi Distinguished Fellow in Islamic Law, UCLA School of Law. Interview. August 21, 2007.

———. *Conference of the Books: The Search for Beauty in Islam.* Lanham, MD: University Press of America, 2001.

Ahrens, Tim. Senior minister, First Congregational Church, Columbus, Ohio; director, We Believe Ohio. Interview. May 23, 2007.

———. "For Such a Time as This." Presented at Faith Leadership Meeting, Faith in Public Life, Washington, DC, 2006.

Aiken, Bill. Director of public affairs, Soka Gakkai International. Interview. July 23, 2007.

Ali, Kecia. Assistant professor of religion, Boston University. Interview. July 28, 2007.

————. "Acting on a Frontier of Religious Ceremony: With Questions and Quiet Resolve, a Woman Officiates at a Muslim Wedding." *Harvard Divinity Bulletin*, Fall/Winter 2004.

————. *Sexual Ethics and Islam: Feminist Reflections on Qur'an, Hadith, and Jurisprudence*. Oxford: Oneworld, 2006.

Ammerman, Nancy T., Mark Chaves, and Richard L. Wood. "Synagogues and Social Justice: Creating Sustainable Change within and beyond the Congregation." *S3K Report* no. 3, Fall 2007, 1–2.

An-Na'im, Abdullahi Ahmed. Professor of law, Emory University; human rights activist. Interview. March 3, 2007.

————. "A Celebration of Heresy." *Emory in the World*, Winter 2006, 2–6.

————. "The Future of Shari'a: Secularism from an Islamic Perspective." Annual Currie Lecture, The Center for the Study of Law and Religion, Emory School of Law, January 29, 2007. Emory University, www.sharia.law.emory.edu/.

Anderson, Nate. "Meet the Patriot Pastors." *Christianity Today*, November 2006, 47–50.

Aslan, Reza. *No God but God: The Origins, Evolution, and Future of Islam*. New York: Random House, 2005.

Baines, Steven. Director, Faith Action Network, People for the American Way Foundation. Interview. February 16, 2007.

Balmer, Randall Herbert. *Thy Kingdom Come: How the Religious Right Distorts the Faith and Threatens America; An Evangelical's Lament*. New York: Basic, 2006.

Banerjee, Neela. "Conservative Jewish Seminary Will Accept Gay Students." *New York Times*, March 27, 2007.

Bass, Diana Butler. *Christianity for the Rest of Us: How the Neighborhood Church Is Transforming the Faith*. San Francisco: HarperSanFrancisco, 2006.

Bauman, Martin. "The Dharma Has Come West: A Survey of Recent Studies and Sources." Urban Dharma, www.urbandharma.org/udharma/survey.html.

Biema, David Ban. "Buddhism in America." *Time*, October 13, 1997.

Black, Earl, and Merle Black. *The Rise of Southern Republicans*. Cambridge, Mass.: Harvard University Press, 2002.

Borg, Marcus J. *Jesus: Uncovering the Life, Teachings, and Relevance of a Religious Revolutionary*. New York: HarperCollins, 1996.

Brock, Rita Nakashima. Director, Faith Voices for the Common Good. Interview. August 23, 2007.

Bronner, Ethan. "Brandeis at 50 Is Still Searching, Still Jewish and Still Not Harvard." *New York Times*, October 17, 1998.

Brous, Sharon. Rabbi, IKAR Congregation, Los Angeles, California. Interview. August 21, 2007.

Buckley, Jorunn Jacobsen, William Scott Green, Jonathan Z. Smith, and American Academy of Religion. *The HarperCollins Dictionary of Religion*. San Francisco: HarperSanFrancisco, 1995.

al-Bukhari, Muhammad ibn Ismail, *The Translation of the Meanings of Sahih al-Bukhari*, 9 vols. Translated by Muhammad Muhsin Khan. Alexandria, VA: Al-Saadawi Publications, 1996.

Bush, George W. "Address to a Joint Session of Congress and the American People." The White House, www.whitehouse.gov/news/releases/2001/09/20010920-8.html.

Butler, Jennifer. Director, Faith in Public Life. Interview. May 18, 2007.

———. *All This in Just Two Years? Faith in Public Life's Second Year a Success*. Washington, DC: Faith in Public Life, 2007.

Campbell, Simone. Director, The Network. Interview. June 5, 2005.

Campolo, Tony. Professor of sociology, Eastern University. Interview. July 18, 2007.

Carwardine, Richard. *Lincoln: A Life of Purpose and Power*. New York: Knopf, 2006.

Catholics in Alliance for the Common Good. *End Year Progress Summary*. Washington, DC: Catholics in Alliance for the Common Good, 2007.

———. "Frequently Asked Questions." Catholics in Alliance for the Common Good, www.catholicsinalliance.org/faq.

Catholics United. "Ad Campaign Criticizes Pro-Life Members of Congress for Voting against Children's Health Insurance." Catholics United, www.catholics-united.org/schip-ads.

Chittister, Joan. Cochair, Global Peace Initiative for Women; Network of Spiritual Progressives. Interview. November 30, 2007.

Chomsky, Jack. Cantor, Congregation Tifereth Israel, Columbus, Ohio; executive committee, We Believe Ohio. Interview. June 15, 2007.

CNN. "Christian Right Leader Writes Off Giuliani." CNN, www.cnn.com/2007/POLITICS/05/17/giuliani.dobson/index.html.

Cobb, John B. *Progressive Christians Speak: A Different Voice on Faith and Politics*. Louisville, KY: Westminster John Knox Press, 2003.

Comstock, Gary David. *A Whosoever Church: Welcoming Lesbians and Gay Men into African American Congregations*. Louisville, KY: Westminster John Knox Press, 2001.

Condon, Patrick. "Muslim Keith Ellison Seeks House Seat." Associated Press, June 29, 2006.

Cooperman, Alan, and Thomas B. Edsall. "Evangelicals Say They Led Charge for the GOP." *Washington Post*, November 8, 2004.

Crossan, John Dominic. *God and Empire: Jesus against Rome, Then and Now*. San Francisco: HarperOne, 2007.

Dalai Lama. *Ethics for the New Millennium*. New York: Riverhead Books, 2001.

Dalai Lama, Howard C. Cutler, and Ernest Abuba. *The Art of Happiness: A Handbook for Living*. Sound recording. New York: Simon & Schuster Audio, 1998.

Das, Lama Surya. Founder, Dzogchen Foundation. Interview. August 2, 2007.

Dawkins, Richard. *The God Delusion*. Boston: Houghton Mifflin, 2006.

Dear, John. Author and peace activist. Interview. December 7, 2007.

Dionne, E. J. *Souled Out: Reclaiming Faith and Politics after the Religious Right*. Princeton, NJ: Princeton University Press, 2008.

Dreier, Peter, and Daniel May. "Progressive Jews Organize." *The Nation*, October 1, 2007.

Dumont, Louis. "A Modified View of Our Origins: The Christian Beginnings of Modern Individualism." *Religion* 12, 1982, 1–27.

Durkheim, Émile. *The Elementary Forms of Religious Life*. 1912; New York: Free Press, 1995.

Eck, Diana L. *A New Religious America: How a "Christian Country" Has Become the World's Most Religiously Diverse Nation*. San Francisco: HarperSanFrancisco, 2001.

———. "Statistics by Religious Tradition." The Pluralism Project at Harvard University, www.pluralism.org/resources/statistics/tradition.php#Buddhism.

Edgar, Robert. General secretary, National Council of Churches. Interview. February 16, 2007.

———. *Middle Church: Reclaiming the Moral Values of the Faithful Majority from the Religious Right*. New York: Simon & Schuster, 2006.

Eltantawi, Sarah. Former communications director, Progressive Muslim Union. Interview. July 24, 2007.

Estell, Kenneth, ed. *The African-American Almanac*. Detriot, MI: Gale Research, 1994.

Evangelical Environment Network. "Climate Change: An Evangelical Call to Action." Evangelical Climate Initiative, www.christiansandclimate.org/statement.

Faith in Public Life. "About Us: Mission." Faith in Public Life, www.faithinpubliclife.org/about/index.html.

Fein, Leonard. Founder, *Moment* magazine, MAZON: A Jewish Response to Hunger. Interview. July 24, 2007.

Feldman, Marla. Director, Commission on Social Action, Union for Reform Judaism. Interview. March 15, 2007.

Forbes, James A. Senior minister, The Riverside Church, New York; founder, The Healing of the Nations Foundation. Interview. March 17, 2007.

———. "The Healing of the Nations Foundation." Healing of the Nations Foundation, www.healingofthenations.com/index.shtml.

Gilgoff, Dan. *The Jesus Machine: How James Dobson, Focus on the Family, and Evangelical America Are Winning the Culture War*. New York: St. Martin's Press, 2007.

Girard, René. *Violence and the Sacred*. Baltimore: Johns Hopkins University Press, 1979.

Glassman, Bernie. Founder, Zen Peacemakers. Interview. July 25, 2007.

———. "Zen Peacemakers: General Information." Zen Peacemakers, www.zen-peacemakers.org/about/index.htm.

Goodstein, Laurie. "Democrats Criticize Denial of Communion by Bishops." *New York Times*, May 20, 2004.

———. "Evangelical Leaders Join Global Warming." *New York Times*, February 8, 2006.

Greeley, Andrew M. *The Catholic Imagination*. Berkeley: University of California Press, 2000.

Green, Arthur. *These Are the Words: A Vocabulary of Jewish Spiritual Life*. Woodstock, VT: Jewish Lights, 1999.

Green, John. *Fourth National Survey of Religion and Politics*. Akron, OH: Bliss Institute, University of Akron, 2004.

Green, John, and Steve Waldman. "The Twelve Tribes of American Politics." Beliefnet, www.beliefnet.com/story/167/story_16763_1.html.

Greenberg, Irving. *The Jewish Way: Living the Holidays*. New York: Summit Books, 1988.

Greer, Simon. President, Jewish Funds for Justice. Interview. March 16, 2007.

Grewal, Zareena. "What's Wrong with This Picture?" *Islamic Horizons*, November–December, 2007, 36–37.

Gushee, David P. *The Future of Faith in American Politics: The Witness of the Evangelical Center*. Waco, TX: Baylor University Press, 2008.

Gustafson, James M. *Ethics from a Theocentric Perspective: Theology and Ethics*. Vol. 1. Chicago: University of Chicago Press, 1981.

Gutow, Steve. President, Jewish Council for Public Affairs. Interview. June 21, 2007.

Harris, Rabia Terri. Coordinator, Muslim Peace Fellowship. Interview. August 3, 2007.

Harris, Sam. *The End of Faith: Religion, Terror, and the Future of Reason*. New York: Norton, 2004.

———. *Letter to a Christian Nation*. New York: Knopf, 2006.

Hart, Stephen. *Cultural Dilemmas of Progressive Politics: Styles of Engagement among Grassroots Activists*. Chicago: University of Chicago Press, 2001.

Harvard Hillel. "Harvard University and Radcliffe College Campus Information." Hillel, www.hillel.org/HillelApps/JLOC/Campus.aspx?AgencyId=17431.

Herberg, Will. *Protestant, Catholic, Jew: An Essay in American Religious Sociology.* Garden City, NY: Doubleday, 1955.

Heschel, Abraham Joshua. *Between God and Man: An Interpretation of Judaism.* New York: Free Press, 1997.

———. *The Sabbath: Its Meaning for Modern Man.* New York: Farrar, 1951.

Hitchens, Christopher. *God Is Not Great: How Religion Poisons Everything.* New York: Twelve, 2007.

Horowitz, Bethamie. "Finally, a Jewish Population Study Worth Studying." *Jewish Daily Forward*, March 9, 2007.

Hout, Michael, and Claude S. Fischer. "Why More Americans Have No Religious Preference: Politics and Generations." *American Sociological Review* 67, April 2002, 165–90.

Islamic Society of North America (ISNA). "Upholding Faith, Serving Humanity." Forty-Fourth Annual ISNA Convention, Rosemont, IL, August 31–September 3, 2007.

Jacobs, Jill. Director of education, Jewish Funds for Justice. Interview. June 20, 2007.

Johnston, Douglas, and Cynthia Sampson, eds. *Religion: The Missing Dimension of Statecraft.* New York: Oxford University Press, 1994.

Jones, David R. "Why Bush Won." CBS News, November 3, 2004.

Jones, Robert P. *The American Values Survey.* Washington, DC: Center for American Values in Public Life, People for the American Way Foundation, 2006.

———. *Liberalism's Troubled Search for Equality: Religion and Cultural Bias in the Oregon Physician-Assisted Suicide Debate.* Notre Dame, IN: University of Notre Dame Press, 2007.

Jones, Robert P., and Melissa C. Stewart. "The Unintended Consequences of Dixieland Postliberalism." *Cross Currents*, Winter 2006, 506–21.

Kafka, Franz. *Parables and Paradoxes: In German and English.* Bilingual ed. New York: Schocken Books, 1975.

Karabel, Jerome. *The Chosen: The Hidden History of Admission and Exclusion at Harvard, Yale, and Princeton.* Boston: Houghton Mifflin, 2005.

Keeter, Scott. "Will White Evangelicals Desert the GOP?" Pew Research Center for the People and the Press, May 2, 2006. Pew Research Center for the People and the Press, pewresearch.org/pubs/22/will-white—evangelicals—desert-the-gop.

Kelley, Alexia. CEO, Catholics in Alliance for the Common Good. Interview. March 27, 2007.

Khaja, Nazir. Chairman, Islamic Information Service. Interview. August 21, 2007.

Khan, M. A. Muqtedar. Associate professor of political science, director of Islamic Studies Program, University of Delaware. Interview. November 19, 2007.

————. *American Muslims: Bridging Faith and Freedom.* Beltsville, MD: Amana Publications, 2002.

————. "Common Ground: Two Theories of *Ijtihad.*" United Press International, March 22, 2006.

————. "Is muslimwakeup.com Undermining the Progressive Muslim Movement?" Ijtihad, www.ijtihad.org/muslimwakeup.htm.

King Jr., Martin Luther. "I've Been to the Mountaintop." American Rhetoric, www.americanrhetoric.com/speeches/mlkivebeentothemountaintop.htm.

Kinnaman, David. *Unchristian: What a New Generation Really Thinks about Christianity . . . and Why It Matters.* Grand Rapids, MI: Baker, 2007.

Kirkpatrick, David D. "Bush Allies Till Fertile Soil, among Baptists, for Votes." *New York Times,* June 18, 2004.

Knox, Harry. Director, Religion and Faith Program, Human Rights Campaign. Interview. April 27, 2007.

Kohut, Andrew, and Scott Keeter. "Religion and the Presidential Vote." Commentary, Pew Research Center for the People and the Press, December 6, 2004. Pew Research Center for the People and the Press, people-press.org/commentary/display.php3?AnalysisID=103.

Korzen, Chris, and Alexia Kelley. *A Nation for All: How the Catholic Vision of the Common Good Can Save America from the Politics of Division.* San Francisco: Jossey-Bass, 2008.

Kottler, Jennifer. Associate director, Protestants for the Common Good. Interview. April 1, 2007.

Lakoff, George. *Don't Think of an Elephant! Know Your Values and Frame the Debate.* White River Junction, VT: Chelsea Green Publishing, 2004.

Lampman, Jane. "Sufism May Be Powerful Antidote to Islamic Extremism." *Christian Science Monitor,* December 5, 2007, 13–15.

Langer, Gary. "A Question of Values." *New York Times,* November 6, 2004.

Laser, Rachel, Robert P. Jones, Randy Brinson, and Joe Battaglia. *Come Let Us Reason Together: A Fresh Look at Shared Cultural Values between Evangelicals and Progressives.* Washington, DC: Third Way, 2007.

Lerner, Michael. Editor, *Tikkun* magazine. Interview. August 23, 2007.

————. *The Left Hand of God: Taking Back Our Country from the Religious Right.* San Francisco: HarperSanFrancisco, 2006.

Lieberman, Joe. "Lieberman Renews Call for Larger, Lawful Space for Religion in American Public Life." Joe Lieberman, United States Senator, lieberman.senate.gov/newsroom/release.cfm?id=208625.

Lincoln, Abraham. "Second Inaugural Address." Yale University, www.yale.edu/lawweb/avalon/presiden/inaug/lincoln2.htm.

Lincoln, C. Eric, and Lawrence H. Mamiya. *The Black Church in the African-American Experience*. Durham, NC: Duke University Press, 1990.

Lind, Tracy. Dean, Trinity Episcopal Cathedral, Cleveland, Ohio; executive committee, We Believe Ohio. Interview. May 25, 2007.

Luchins, David. Vice president, The Orthodox Union. Interview. March 14, 2007.

Macy, Joanna. "Foreword." In *Not Turning Away: The Practice of Engaged Buddhism*, edited by Susan Moon, vii–viii. Boston: Shambhala, 2004.

Madison, James. "James Madison, Virginia Ratifying Convention." University of Chicago, press-pubs.uchicago.edu/founders/documents/amendI_religions49.html.

Marx, Karl, and Friedrich Engels. *The Communist Manifesto*. 1848; New York: Oxford University Press, 1992.

al-Maryati, Salam. "The Good and the Greater Good." Paper presented at the Forty-Fourth Annual ISNA Convention, Rosemont, IL, August 31–September 3, 2007.

Matalon, Rolando. Rabbi, Congregation B'nai Jeshurun. Interview. June 22, 2007.

McDonald III, Timothy. Senior pastor, First Iconium Baptist Church, Atlanta, Georgia; chair, African American Ministers in Action, People for the American Way Foundation. Interview. November 7, 2007.

McLaren, Brian. Author, speaker, pastor. Interview. July 18, 2007.

McLeod, Melvin. *Mindful Politics: A Buddhist Guide to Making the World a Better Place*. Boston: Wisdom, 2006.

Media Matters. *Left Behind: The Skewed Representation of Religion in Major News Media*. Washington, DC: Media Matters, 2007.

———. "*USA Today* Labeled Conservative Evangelical Huckabee Supporters as 'Value Voters.'" Media Matters, mediamatters.org/items/200801250016.

Messinger, Ruth. President, American Jewish World Service. Interview. June 22, 2007.

Meyer, David. "Moral Values Malarkey." CBS News, November 5, 2004. CBS News, www.cbsnews.com/stories/2004/11/05/opinion/meyer/main653931.shtml.

Miller, Lisa. "Islam USA: American Dreamers." *Newsweek*, July 30, 2007, 24–33.

Moon, Susan. "Editorial." *Turning Wheel Magazine*, January 1990.

———, ed. *Not Turning Away: The Practice of Engaged Buddhism*. Boston: Shambhala, 2004.

Murphy, Caryle, and Alan Cooperman. "Religious Liberals Gain New Visibility: A Different List of Moral Issues." *Washington Post*, May 20, 2006.

Murray, John Courtney. *We Hold These Truths: Catholic Reflections on the American Proposition*. New York: Sheed and Ward, 1960.

Nashashibi, Rami. "Inner-City Muslim Action Network (IMAN)." IMAN, www.imancentral.org/.

National Association of Evangelicals. "For the Health of the Nation: An Evangelical Call to Civic Responsibility." In *Toward an Evangelical Public Policy*, edited by Ronald J. Sider and Diane Knippers, 363–75. Grand Rapids, MI: Baker Books, 2004.

"National Election Pool Exit Poll." 2004.

———. 2006.

Nawawi. *An-Nawawi's Forty Hadith: An Anthology of the Sayings of the Prophet Muhammad*. Cambridge, UK: Islamic Texts Society, 1997.

Network of Spiritual Progressives. "Basic Tenets." Network of Spiritual Progressives, www.spiritualprogressives.org/.

———. "Join a Local Chapter." Network of Spiritual Progressives, www.spiritual progressives.org/article.php?story=localchapters.

———. "The Global Marshall Plan." Network of Spiritual Progressives, www .spiritualprogressives.org/article.php?story=20070228183252814.

———. "What Is an NSP Chapter?" Network of Spiritual Progressives, www .spiritualprogressives.org/article.php?story=20071031174507751.

Nhat Hanh, Thich. *Being Peace*. Berkeley, CA: Parallax Press, 1987.

———. "The Practice of Peace." In *Not Turning Away: The Practice of Engaged Buddhism*, edited by Susan Moon, 147–53. Boston: Shambhala Press, 1991.

Nomani, Asra. "Daughters of Hajar." *The New People*, July–August, 2004. Thomas Merton Center, www.thomasmertoncenter.org/The_New_People.

Packer, George. "The Moderate Martyr: A Radically Peaceful Vision of Islam." *The New Yorker*, September 11, 2006.

Patel, Eboo. Founder and director, Interfaith Youth Core. Interview. August 31, 2007.

———. "About the Core." Interfaith Youth Core, www.ifyc.org/about_core.

———. "Days of Interfaith Youth Service (DIYS)." Interfaith Youth Core, ifyc.org/events/diys.

Pesner, Jonah. Director, Just Congregations, Union for Reform Judaism. Interview. July 26, 2007.

Pew Forum on Religion and Public Life. "Public Expresses Mixed Views of Islam, Mormonism." September 25, 2007. Pew Forum on Religion and Public Life, pewforum.org/surveys/religionviews07.

———. "The U.S. Religious Landscape Survey." Pew Forum on Religion and Public Life, religions.pewforum.org/reports.

Pew Research Center for the People and the Press. *Moral Values: How Important?* Washington, DC: Pew Research Center for the People and the Press, 2004.

———. *Muslim Americans: Middle Class and Mostly Mainstream*. Washington, DC: Pew Research Center for the People and the Press, 2007.

Pluralism Project at Harvard University. "Research Report: The Woman-Led Prayer That Catalyzed Controversy." Pluralism Project at Harvard University, www.pluralism.org/research/profiles/display.php?profile=73972.

Public Broadcasting Service (PBS). "Interview with Khaled Abou El Fadl." Public Broadcasting Service, www.pbs.org/wgbh/pages/frontline/shows/faith/interviews/elfadl.html.

Ramirez, Margaret. "Activist Muslim Profile: Rami Nashashibi." *Chicago Tribune*, May 3, 2006.

Ray, Paul H. *The Cultural Creatives: How 50 Million People Are Changing the World*. New York: Three Rivers, 2001.

Rorty, Richard. "Religion as a Conversation-Stopper." In *Philosophy and Social Hope*, edited by Richard Rorty, 168–74. New York: Penguin, 1999.

Rose, Or N. Associate dean, The Rabbinical School of Hebrew College. Interview. November 17, 2007.

Rose, Or N., Jo Ellen Kaiser, and Margie Klein, eds. *Righteous Indignation: A Jewish Call for Justice*. Woodstock, VT: Jewish Lights Publishing, 2007.

Rosenn, David. Founding director, AVODAH, The Jewish Service Corps. Interview. March 15, 2007.

Rosenn, Jennie. Program director, Jewish Life and Values, Nathan Cummings Foundation. Interview. November 2, 2007.

Rosin, Hanna. "Redeem the Vote Spreads the Election-Year Gospel." *Washington Post*, October 29, 2004.

Rozell, Mark J., and Debasree Das Gupta. "'The Values Vote'? Moral Issues and the 2004 Elections." In *The Values Campaign? The Christian Right and the 2004 Elections*, edited by John Green, Mark J. Rozell and Clyde Wilcox, 11–21. Washington, DC: Georgetown University Press, 2007.

Ruether, Rosemary Radford. Professor of theology, Claremont Graduate School. Interview. August 21, 2007.

Rutenberg, Jim. "Emphasis on 'Moral Values' in Exit Poll Sparks Debate." *New York Times*, November 6, 2004.

Safi, Omid. Professor of religion, University of North Carolina. Interview. September 14, 2007.

———, ed. *Progressive Muslims: On Justice, Gender and Pluralism*. Oxford: Oneworld, 2003.

Salvatierra, Alexia. Director, Clergy and Laity United for Economic Justice. Interview. August 20, 2007.

Samad, A'isha. Executive committee, We Believe Ohio, Cleveland, Ohio. Interview. May 26, 2007.

Samuel, Kenneth L. Senior pastor, Victory Church, Stone Mountain, Georgia. Interview. March 3, 2007.

———. Interview. August 24, 2006.

Saperstein, David. Director, Religious Action Center for Reform Judaism. Interview. July 10, 2007.

Seelye, Katharine Q. "Moral Values Cited as a Defining Issue of the Election." *New York Times*, November 4, 2004.

Senauke, Alan. Head of practice, Berkeley Zen Center; director of programs and peacework coordinator, Buddhist Peace Fellowship. Interview. August 23, 2007.

———. "Vowing Peace in a Time of War." In *Not Turning Away: The Practice of Engaged Buddhism*, edited by Susan Moon, 220–27. Boston: Shambhala Press, 2004.

Sider, Ronald J. President, Evangelicals for Social Action. Interview. April 6, 2007.

———. *Rich Christians in an Age of Hunger: Moving from Affluence to Generosity*. Nashville, TN: Word Publishing, 1997.

Sinkford, William. President, Unitarian Universalist Association. Interview. September 27, 2007.

Slingshot Fund. "Slingshot: A Resource Guide for Jewish Innovation 07–08." Slingshot Fund, www.slingshotfund.org.

Smith, Tom W. "The Polls—Review: The Muslim Population of the United States; The Methodology of Estimates." *Public Opinion Quarterly* 66, 2002, 404–17.

Sojourners. *Sojourners Annual Report 2006*. Washington, DC: Sojourners, 2006.

Sokatch, Daniel. Director, Progressive Jewish Alliance. Interview. September 20, 2007.

Stief, Ron. Director of the Office of Public Life and Social Policy, United Church of Christ. Interview. October 28, 2005.

Strickland, Ted. Governor, State of Ohio. Interview. June 15, 2007.

Strode, Tom. "President Bush Wins Re-Election; Exit Polls Show Values Voters Made the Difference." *Baptist Press News*, November 3, 2004.

Sullivan, Amy. *The Party Faithful: How and Why Democrats Are Closing the God Gap*. New York: Scribner, 2008.

Taha, Mahmud Muhammad. *The Second Message of Islam*. Translated by Abdullahi Ahmed An-Na'im. Syracuse, NY: Syracuse University Press, 1987.

Thistlethwaite, Susan. President, Chicago Theological Seminary; visiting senior fellow in religion, Center for American Progress. Interview. March 30, 2007.

Thurman, Robert. Professor of Buddhist studies, Columbia University; president, American Institute of Buddhist Studies. Interview. December 18, 2007.

Tikkun Magazine. "2007 Rate Card." *Tikkun* Magazine, www.tikkun.org/magazine/2007ratecard.pdf.

Time Magazine. "The Time 100 Most Influential People of the Century," 1998–1999.

Tippet, Krista. Speaking of Faith: An Interview with Rami Nashashibi. 2002.

Toulouse, Mark G. "The Origins of the Christian Century." *The Christian Century*, January 26, 2000, 80–83.

Tracy, David. *The Analogical Imagination*. New York: Crossroad, 1981.

Trible, Phyllis. *Texts of Terror: Literary-Feminist Readings of Biblical Narratives*. Minneapolis: Fortress, 1984.

United Church of Christ. "God Is Still Speaking." United Church of Christ, www.ucc.org/god-is-still-speaking/.

Valente, Judy. "Interview with Eboo Patel." *Religion & Ethics Newsweekly*, November 30, 2007.

Vorspan, Al. Civil rights leader; director emeritus of the Commission on Social Action and vice president emeritus of the Union for Reform Judaism; founding director of Religious Action Center for Reform Judaism. Interview. March 15, 2007.

Wallis, Jim. President, Sojourners/Call to Renewal. Interview. September 11, 2007.

———. *God's Politics: Why the Right Gets It Wrong and the Left Doesn't Get It*. San Francisco: HarperSanFrancisco, 2005.

———. *The Great Awakening: Reviving Faith and Politics in a Post-Religious Right America*. San Francisco: HarperOne, 2008.

Walzer, Michael. *Politics and Passion: Toward a More Egalitarian Liberalism*. New Haven, Conn.: Yale University, 2005.

Waskow, Arthur. Director, The Shalom Center. Interview. May 16, 2007.

We Believe Ohio. "About Us." We Believe Ohio, www.webelieveohio.org/index.php?option=com_content&task=view&id=13&Itemid=42.

Weber, Max. "Religious Rejections of the World and Their Directions." In *From Max Weber: Essays in Sociology*, edited by Hans Gerth and C. Wright Mills. London: Routledge, 1991.

West, Cornel. *Prophesy Deliverance! An Afro-American Revolutionary Christianity*. Philadelphia: Westminster Press, 1982.

Williamson, Elizabeth. "Jewish Membership in Congress at All-Time High." *Washington Post*, January 12, 2007, 1.

Wiltz, Teresa. "The Woman Who Went to the Front of the Mosque." *Washington Post*, June 5, 2005.

Wood, Richard, and Mark R. Warren. "A Different Face of Faith-Based Politics: Social Capital and Community Organizing in the Public Arena." *International Journal of Sociology and Social Policy* 22, no. 11/12, 2002, 6–54.

Wuthnow, Robert. *The Restructuring of American Religion: Society and Faith since World War II*. Studies on Church and State. Princeton, NJ: Princeton University Press, 1988.

Wuthnow, Robert, and John Hyde Evans. *The Quiet Hand of God: Faith-Based Activism and the Public Role of Mainline Protestantism*. Berkeley: University of California Press, 2002.

Yoffie, Eric. President, Union for Reform Judaism. Interview. March 14, 2007.

Index

Note: *Italic* page numbers indicate tables.

Abd-Allah, Umar Faruq: on democracy, 148; on generosity, 183; on unity of humanity, 131–32

Abdul-Ghafur, Saleemah: on experience and truth, 127–28; on Hajar, 139, 140; on innovation in Islam, 123–24; on language, 16; on religious practice, 136–37; on tradition, 180; on war, 142–43

Abdul Rauf, Feisal, on democracy, 145–46, 148

abolitionist movement, 9, 83

abortion, 86, 108

Abou El Fadl, Khaled: on beauty, 114, 129, 154; on democracy, 146; on diversity of humanity, 132; on humility, 178; library of, 113–14; on Qur'an, 113–14, 222n4; on textual interpretation, 114, 124, 222n4, 226n57

Abraham (biblical figure), 138, 227n79

Abrahamic religions, prophetic tradition in, 163–64; engagement with tradition and, 180; in Muslim initiatives, 152–53; as religious practice in Christianity, 91, 95–96

Acts, book of, 87

Adam (biblical character), 131, 133

Advent, 81

advertisements, political, 108–9

African American Ministers Leadership Council, 88, 109

African American Muslims: in Congress, 116–17; mosques of, 227n71; September 11 attacks and, 141–42

African American Protestants. *See* black Protestants

agenda: Christian, 96–105; image of God, 55–59, 96–105; Jewish, 55–59; Muslim, 140–48

Ahrens, Tim: on media coverage, 23; on prayer, 92; in We Believe Ohio, 172–75

Aiken, Bill: on social engagement, 161–62; on unity of humanity, 181

Ali, Kecia: on equality of women, 131; on pillars of Islam, 134–35; on soul, 234n43; on unity of humanity, 181

Alinsky, Saul, 63, 214n110

almsgiving, 134, 137–38

American Jewish World Service, 35, 59

About the Author

Robert P. Jones, Ph.D., is the president of Public Religion Research, a consulting firm advising national advocacy groups, and a visiting fellow in religion at Third Way, a progressive think tank. His firm specializes in research on religion and values using national public opinion surveys and focus groups, as well as coalition building between progressive political groups and religious communities. Dr. Jones is a member of the national steering committee for the Religion and Politics Group at the American Academy of Religion and a member of the Society of Christian Ethics. He and his family attend the Interfaith Families Congregation in Silver Spring, Maryland.

Previously, Dr. Jones served as an affiliated scholar at the Center for American Progress and as the founding director and senior fellow at the Center for American Values in Public Life at People for the American Way Foundation (PFAW). At PFAW, he directed the American Values Survey, one of the largest public opinion surveys on religion and politics conducted in the last four years. Prior to his work in Washington, D.C., he was assistant professor of religious studies at Missouri State University and a teaching fellow in religion at Emory University. He holds a Ph.D. from Emory University and a M.Div. from Southwestern Baptist Theological Seminary.

Dr. Jones is also the author of *Liberalism's Troubled Search for Equality: Religion and Cultural Bias in the Oregon Physician-Assisted Suicide Debates* (University of Notre Dame Press).